HERBIE HANCOCK:
Blue Chip Keyboardist

Ken Trethewey

Jazz-Fusion Books

First published July 2010 by:

Jazz-Fusion Books
Gravesend Cottage
Torpoint
Cornwall PL11 2LX
United Kingdom

©*2010 Ken Trethewey*

ISBN: 978-0-9560083-3-6

All rights reserved. No part of this publication may be reproduced, stored in a retrieval system, or transmitted in any form, or by any means, electronic, mechanical, photocopying, recording or otherwise, without the prior permission of Jazz-Fusion Books.

*For Chris, Joe and Helen, my musical family,
who love music as much as I do.*

Publications by Ken Trethewey in the Jazz-Fusion Series:

John McLaughlin: The Emerald Beyond	(1 Sep 2008)	ISBN 978-0-9560083-0-5
Pat Metheny: The Way Up is White	(1 Dec 2008)	ISBN 978-0-9560083-1-2
Jazz-Fusion: Blue Notes and Purple Haze	(1 Dec 2009)	ISBN 978-0-9560083-2-9
Herbie Hancock: Blue Chip Keyboardist	(1 July 2010)	ISBN 978-0-9560083-3-6

Herbie Hancock at the Roundhouse, Camden Town, London, 11 November 2006 (photo: Ken Trethewey)

Contents

HERBIE HANCOCK:..1
Foreword 9
Early Career..12
Herbie Hancock: *Takin' Off* – 1962 (***) 18
Eric Dolphy: *Gaslight* – 1962 (*)...21
Freddie Hubbard: *Hub-Tones* – 1962 (***) 23
Herbie Hancock: *My Point of View* – 1963 (***) 24
Working with Miles Davis 25
Herbie Hancock: *Inventions and Dimensions* – 1964 (***) 28
Herbie Hancock: *Empyrean Isles* - 1964 (***) 29
Tony Williams: *Lifetime* – 1964 (*)..31
Herbie Hancock: *Maiden Voyage* – 1965 (*****)............................33
Herbie Hancock: *Blow-Up - The Original Soundtrack* – 1966 (****) 35
Herbie Hancock: *Speak Like a Child* - 1968 (***) 37
From Acoustic to Electric 38
Leaving Miles..39
Herbie Hancock: *The Prisoner* - 1969 (***)....................................41
Recording with Blue Note..44
Herbie Hancock: *Fat Albert Rotunda* – 1969 (***) 45
Herbie Hancock: *Baraka* – 1969 (**) 47
Herbie Hancock: *Mwandishi* – 1971 (*) 48
Herbie Hancock: *Crossings* – 1972 (*) 51
Herbie Hancock: *Sextant* – 1973 (*) 52
Herbie Hancock: *The Spook Who Sat By the Door* – 1973 (*).......54
Herbie Hancock: *Death Wish* – 1974 (*)...54
Herbie Hancock: *Head Hunters* – 1974 (*****) 55
Herbie Hancock: *Thrust* – 1974 (*****)..58
Herbie Hancock: *Dedication* – 1974 (***) 61
Herbie Hancock: *Man-Child* – 1975 (***) 62
Herbie Hancock: *Flood* – 1975 (****) 63
Herbie Hancock: *Secrets* – 1976 (***) 64
Herbie Hancock: *V.S.O.P.* – 1977 (***) 66
Ron Carter / Herbie Hancock / Tony Williams: *Third Plane* – 1978 (****) 68
Herbie Hancock: *The Herbie Hancock Trio* – 1977 (****)............69
V.S.O.P.: *The Quintet* – 1977 (***) 71
V.S.O.P.: *Tempest in the Colosseum* – 1977 (***) 72
Herbie Hancock: *Sunlight* – 1978 (***)...74
Herbie Hancock: *Feets Don't Fail Me Now* – 1979 (***)...............78
Herbie Hancock and Chick Corea: *An Evening With Herbie Hancock and Chick Corea In Concert* – 1978 (***)........................80

Herbie Hancock: *The Piano* – 1979 (***) 80
Herbie Hancock: *Direct Step* - 1979 (***) 82
V.S.O.P.: *Live Under the Sky* – 1979 (****) 82
Herbie Hancock: *Mr Hands* – 1980 (****) 84
Herbie Hancock: *Monster* – 1980 (***) 85
Herbie Hancock: *Magic Windows* – 1981 (**) 87
Herbie Hancock: *Herbie Hancock Trio with Ron Carter and Tony Williams* – 1981 (****) 89
Herbie Hancock: *Herbie Hancock Quartet* – 1982 (***) 90
Herbie Hancock: *Lite Me Up* - 1982 (***) 92
Herbie Hancock: *Future Shock* – 1983 (***) 93
Herbie Hancock: *Sound System* – 1984 (***) 96
Herbie Hancock: *The Herbie Hancock Trio In Concert* – 1984 (***) 99
Herbie Hancock and Foday Musa Suso: *Village Life* – 1985 (***) 99
Dexter Gordon: *Round Midnight* (CD and DVD) – 1986 (***) 100
Dexter Gordon: *The Other Side of Round Midnight* – 1986 (***) 102
Herbie Hancock and Foday Muso Susa: *Jazz Africa* – 1987 (***) 102
Herbie Hancock: *Perfect Machine* – 1988 (***) 103
Herbie Hancock: *A Tribute To Miles* – 1994 (****) 104
Herbie Hancock: *The Herbie Hancock Quartet Live* – 1994 (***) 105
Herbie Hancock Trio: *Live In New York* – 1994 (****) 107
Herbie Hancock: *Dis Is Da Drum* – 1994 (****) 108
Herbie Hancock: *The New Standard* – 1995 (****) 110
Herbie Hancock and Wayne Shorter: *1+1* – 1997 (***) 113
Herbie Hancock: *Gershwin's World* – 1998 (****) 115
Headhunters: *Return of the Headhunters* – 1998 (****) 119
Herbie Hancock: *Future 2 Future* – 2001 (****) 120
Herbie Hancock / Michael Brecker / Roy Hargrove: *Directions in Music* – 2002 (*****) 122
Herbie Hancock: Gig at the Lighthouse Centre, Poole, 3 May 2005 125
Herbie Hancock: *Possibilities* – 2005 (****) 128
Herbie Hancock: The Roundhouse Gig, Saturday 11 November 2006 129
Herbie Hancock: *River, The Joni Letters* – 2007 (*****) 132
Classical Herbie 135
Herbie Hancock's Headhunters: *Watermelon Man* (DVD)– 2008 (***) 136
Herbie Hancock: *The Imagine Project* – 2010 (*****) 137
Concluding Remarks 142
References 148
Discography 151
Index 179

Foreword

As far as I know, this is the first book that has been written about Herbie Hancock. Thus, in the year of his 70th birthday, I feel very privileged (and surprised) that I have been the first person to write a book about one of the world's greatest jazz musicians. Like many others, I first heard Herbie Hancock playing with Miles Davis during the 1960s and it was quite clear then that he was one of the leading jazz pianists. Even in the 1960s, everyone knew just how great a musician Miles was, and it was clear to us what a great privilege it must have been for Herbie.

When you are blessed with genius, the world is a different place than it is for the rest of us. What I could not have known then was just how far and wide Herbie's genius would penetrate into the world of music. His occupation of the jazz mainstream goes without saying, and he has been at the centre of that since he began playing professionally in New York City in the early 1960s. But his dazzling proficiency on the traditional acoustic piano has also led him to perform in European classical music contexts (albeit not extensively on record), as he did in 2008/9 with Chinese virtuoso Lang Lang. In my opinion, however, more important were his contributions and influence in the use of electronic keyboards. From the late 1960s, Herbie used his knowledge of electrical engineering and electronics to develop a sympathetic understanding of these very new instruments, to see how best they could be used in music, and thus to place himself at the very forefront of keyboard, synthesiser and computer music.

Observers could never have predicted Herbie's diversion into pop music. To many, it was entirely illogical. How could such a brilliant musical brain, capable of some of the highest level musical thinking, even consider the idea of playing what one Internet critic described as "disco schlock"? The answer to this frustrating question lies in Herbie's personality. Herbie is a kind, humorous, intelligent, courteous man with a very wide range of interests. He has never been heard to be adversely critical of anyone except his own critics, whom he has occasionally disparaged for their narrow-mindedness. I shall discuss his musical philosophy in more detail in the coming pages, but suffice to say here that Herbie has no musical boundaries. In such a context, it is not at all surprising that he made many recordings of disco music in the 1970s and 80s, laid the foundations for the 'techno' music genre years before it became popular, and then became a co-creator of the genre of hip-hop.

Despite playing such a big role in the advancement of jazz in terms of its absorption of technology, Herbie has also remained true to the tradition of acoustic jazz. He is as likely to be found playing George Gershwin or Cole Porter on an acoustic grand piano (albeit with an Apple computer positioned on the top) as he is to be rocking to a backbeat with a shoulder-slung instrument like the one on the cover of this book. From his position at the focus of the mainstream, and with the support of a panoply of similarly talented musicians, he has unquestionably moved the boundaries of that mainstream. For four decades – ever since the young 23-year-old pianist sat at the piano in Miles's band, Herbie Hancock has set the marker by which other jazz pianists have been measured (except perhaps for those players with a unique focus like Keith Jarrett and Cecil Taylor.)

Herbie's great span of musical participation creates problems for writers like me because, being human, I have my own preferences. This book is part of a large project on jazz-fusion, so I am naturally attracted to those parts of Herbie's career that fall into that category, and perhaps less so to freeform jazz or hip hop. In writing this book I have never tried to hide my own opinions, which, as part of my style, I have always tried to argue logically and consistently. As a serious listener to and a practitioner of jazz for over forty years, I feel entitled to take on the role of music critic in my senior years. I found the absence of any substantive publication about Herbie Hancock's career frustrating and took upon myself the job of filling that gap. It meant listening to (and purchasing) many albums that I might not otherwise have bothered with. The result is a book that presents a review of Herbie's career as evidenced by what is available on record. Because that represents such a small proportion of what Herbie has actually achieved, it is inevitably inadequate. I must point out that this is *not* a biography. I have concentrated here on Herbie's career as a solo artist, his own solo albums in particular. However, Herbie has made contributions to the recorded works of many other musicians; a list of some of these albums is at the end of this book. Some of his most important work was with Miles Davis, and to avoid repetition and to be sensible about allocation of space, a complete discussion of this material is not included here. I would re-direct interested readers to the other volumes of this series.

I hope that those of you who have little idea about Herbie or his music will gain some insight into the beautiful world encompassed by this extraordinary person. I hope that you will want to investigate his music more deeply and, in so doing, grow to love Herbie's work for yourselves. At a time of diminishing interest in jazz, that is an important motivation for me. I also hope that you will find my summary a useful guide to his recordings and styles. I should explain that my sub-title *Blue-Chip Keyboardist*, anchors this book in the series about jazz-fusion that I just referred to (see page 4), which I liken to a spectrum of colours. Each book has a different colour focus and I have chosen to emphasise Herbie's contributions to the use of electronic keyboards and synthesisers in jazz-fusion as being 'blue-chip'. In other words, he's simply the best!

Introduction

"Jazz is for the body because it is rhythmic, but it's also for the mind and for the soul, and it is very creative." So says Herbie Hancock, one of the most intelligent and gifted of modern jazz musicians. He may have recorded *Body and Soul* only once – on *Round Midnight* (1986) - but it clearly means a lot to him. And besides having a great sense of humour that is immediately obvious during his interviews, Hancock is one of the most eclectic musicians in jazz history, playing mainstream jazz, free jazz, jazz-rock fusion, bebop, funk, hip-hop, techno, dance and world-fusion, not to mention instrumental pop. In fact, at some point in his long career he must have tried just about every musical genre that has been invented - even if he didn't invent it himself! Some describe his musical journey as a zig-zag path, but he might prefer to use the term hip-hop. He has certainly moved unexpectedly sideways across genres on numerous occasions and has made big steps forward in some of them. Though he refuses to be categorised, some people descry a personal style described as a lyrical blend of gospel, bebop, and blues. However, this must be an oversimplification for someone as rounded as he is. I believe that Herbie Hancock's most important contribution has been to jazz-fusion, in the term's broadest sense, and I shall discuss this work in some detail.

Herbert Jeffrey Hancock was born in Chicago, Illinois on April 12, 1940. He began to play on a piano given to him by his parents for his seventh birthday and, like many jazz pianists, received an early education in classical music. By the time he was only eleven years old he was playing the first movement of Mozart Piano Concerto No 5 with the Chicago Symphony Orchestra at a young people's concert. At that time, he wasn't interested in jazz. "I knew of jazz, but I didn't like it. I always thought only older people liked jazz - you know, you had to be 19 or 20." [1]

It wasn't until he entered Hyde Park High School that he heard a classmate improvise *I'll Remember April* and *When Your Lover has Gone* – two pieces by George Shearing - on the piano. He was jealous that his friend "could do something on *my* instrument that I couldn't do." He began listening to George Shearing records at home and playing jazz in his own ensemble, attracted by other pianists such as Oscar Peterson, McCoy Tyner, Wynton Kelly and Bill Evans. Miles Davis's album *'Round About Midnight* (1956) was current at the time and featured Wynton Kelly on piano; Herbie must have been very impressed with what he heard. He also started listening to the blues of Muddy Waters and John Lee Hooker. "I was very much aware of blues, because it was on the radio all the time. I wasn't really aware that the blues was making the transition from acoustic to electric then, but that doesn't mean it didn't have any effect on what I was doing at the time."

As his interest grew he found himself trying to reproduce what he was hearing on record. He quickly realised there were easier ways to achieve his aims and began to learn musical theory. Again, he quips humorously, "I learned theory to find a shorter method to take things off a record." He believed strongly in the benefits of practice and developed the self-discipline of practice as a means of achieving his ambitions. There's a story about him having a day off during a series of recording sessions. Asked what he would like to do with his day off, he requested the hire of a room with a grand piano in it. [2]

Herbie also had a strong interest in science and technology. After High School, he went to Grinnell College in Iowa to study engineering, and finished with a double major in electrical engineering and music. What might then have seemed a strange combination to some was logical to him. Today, probably as a result of Herbie's influence on the music industry, many students follow such a course of study. Herbie's unusual education would prove to be of great assistance in the early 1970s when he began experimenting with electronic keyboards and synthesisers.

Herbie Hancock arrived on the jazz scene in the early 1960s, a time of explosive change in the world of music, which I have described in detail elsewhere. [3] He would use his incomparable creativity to ride the crest of not one but several waves of popular music revolutions and he has become one of the most successful jazz musicians of all time.

Early Career

If the 1930s and 40s had been the era of Big Band Jazz, the 1950s were the high point of small group jazz. In the big bands, although a few musicians were given the chance to stand out from the crowd, the larger numbers of musicians involved tended to obscure individual performances in favour of the musical compositions and the skills of the arranger. Of course, the bandleader himself was a star, but the music was what people were really looking for and, above all, the opportunity to dance. As one writer put it, "Music is often said to find a short cut to the heart, but the right sort of music takes a quick route to the legs." [4] The 1930s and 40s were all about discovering the Swing in jazz.

In the small group, however, the role of each musician was constantly refined. To sustain an audience's interest over the period of a gig, it was necessary to employ new strategies of both musical content and performance. Compositions were still important, but the themes became increasingly unimportant compared to the solos, which offered a musician the perfect opportunity to stand in the spotlight and wow the audience with his skills. For most of the 1950s, the great majority of small group jazz consisted of taking a 'standard' tune that people might be familiar with and 'jazzing it up' with rhythm and increasingly extravagant solos. Unlike today, it was a time when musicians got noticed because of their skills with an instrument. These remarkable levels of ability, demonstrated by the likes of King Oliver, Louis Armstrong and Jelly Roll Morton, caused many aspiring musicians to play better, and the material they chose to play was often taken from the great output of New York's Tin Pan Alley. Even as late as the mid-1960s, Miles Davis, the top jazz leader of all, could be heard leading his band in variations on such tunes as *Bye Bye Blackbird* and *If I Were A Bell*. Even the great John Coltrane made a big deal from playing Rodgers and Hammerstein's *My Favourite Things*. In the 1950s, in small group jazz there was far less emphasis on self-composition of new pieces than on the playing of popular pieces from the standard repertoire and self-promotion through soloing.

There was another, less overt, characteristic of small group jazz. Quartets and quintets represented polygamy on a grand scale, with musicians constantly hired and fired, guesting and jamming. Line-ups changed as rapidly as a burglar's address. Besides New Orleans, Chicago and Los Angeles, which had their own lively, but somewhat isolated jazz cultures, New York was the premier jazz club scene of the USA with all of the top musicians belonging to a vibrant and constantly changing community of creativity.

Any inspection of 1950s discographies reveals that this jazz was very much based around individuals, not bands. Sometimes, the very best bands such as the Jazz Messengers or the Modern Jazz Quartet would gain such a level of attention that their name was a must-have in any club's gig list. Because top pay was usually attached to playing in the band, the musicians therefore tended to stay longer, but in general, it was individuals – almost exclusively trumpet, saxophone or piano players - that were hired for gigs and recording dates. The contract holder decided which musicians were brought along. Depending upon the number of players, the event would result in the tentative and temporary creation of the John Smith Quartet or the Henry Higgins Trio for the duration of the booking, only for it to re-dissolve into the jazz ether once the gig was over. Sometimes, line-ups would vary by the day.

Throughout the 1950s, prior to the explosion of the pop/rock culture that would consume the later part of the decade in a shockwave of electric guitars and backbeats, jazz was unchallenged as the premier popular music form. Trumpeter Donald Byrd was at the top of his career, playing with all the best New York jazz musicians, including Art Blakey's Jazz Messengers, Jackie MacLean, Hank Mobley, Horace Silver, Art Farmer, and Sonny Rollins. Besides the constant gigging that was a musician's bread-and-butter, by 1959 Byrd was making regular recordings as a bandleader for Blue Note Records with musicians that included Hank Mobley (tenor sax) and Duke Pearson (piano). But he was also a member of the musician churn that included Pepper Adams (baritone sax).

Park "Pepper" Adams III (1930-86) was born in Highland Park, Detroit where he later met Donald Byrd and learned to become a first-class exponent of baritone saxophone. Along with the rather better known Gerry Mulligan, whose style was entirely different to Adams' big round tones, Pepper helped create the template for other baritone sax players to follow for years to come. The baritone saxophone is an impressive horn, although unusual as a lead instrument. Its presence is always very noticeable. Together, Byrd and Adams formed a quintet that made quite an impression on the jazz scene of the late 50s and early 60s. Don and Pepper began gigging together in the wider New York area sometime around 1956 and made their first recordings together in the Johnny Griffin Sextet early in 1958. During the course of the following years a front-line trumpet-sax partnership was formed that was almost as famous as Diz and Bird (Gillespie and Parker) or the leading pair from the West Coast, Gerry Mulligan and Chet Baker.

It was in this busy, fast learning environment that young Herbie soon found himself. By the time he had graduated, he was working in Chicago jazz clubs, one of his earliest professional gigs being a two-week stint with Coleman Hawkins in the latter half of 1960. But Herbie did not ignore his education and continued to take music courses at Roosevelt University. Other early gigs in Chicago were at the Birdhouse when, around December 1960, the Donald Byrd / Pepper Adams outfit rode into town. At some point the band needed a stand-in (or 'sub' in the jazz vernacular) for Duke Pearson who was unable to make the gig, and Herbie was selected. Herbie's relationship with Byrd was to prove a turning point in his life. Byrd spotted his ability at once and liked his style, which was fluent and inventive, fresher and rather more edgy than his contemporaries. They liked him so much that Byrd invited Herbie to deputise for Pearson in New York sometime around the end of 1960/ early 1961. Herbie formally took Pearson's place later, although Pearson was a friend to Byrd and Adams and they did not fire him. Pearson continued to work spasmodically with the band, but Herbie also gigged and recorded with the band on numerous occasions. Most of this material is readily available today, republished annually on a constantly churning roster of CDs.

Early in 1961, Herbie recorded some tracks with Byrd, Adams, Laymon Jackson (bass) and Jimmy Cobb (drums): *Jammin' With Herbie, Herbie's Blues, Rock Your Soul, Soul Power* and *Cat Call*. The disc, *Out of this World* (1961), released on the Warwick label was popular and originally listed with Byrd/Adams as leaders. Tracks covered were *Curro's, Day Dream* (also known as *Soul Power*), *Bird House*, *Out Of This World* and a piece called variously *Mr. Lucky Theme*, *Theme from Mr Lucky* or *Rock Your Soul*. Another track, *Beautiful Evening*, included Teddy Charles on vibraphone. Tracks from this and similar albums have appeared frequently on compilations that somewhat disingenuously spotlight Herbie as leader, rather than Don or Pepper. These albums include *Rock Your Soul*, *Day Dreams* and *Backtracks*, to name but three. The trumpet/ baritone sax pairing was a popular sound used also by Chet Baker and Gerry Mulligan and, when we hear the music today on Byrd/Adams/Hancock recordings such as *Curro's*, *Scoochie*, *I'm an Old Cowhand* and *Hot Piano*, it remains vibrant, light-hearted and very entertaining. Listeners should beware that these later-released albums have almost no information about the recordings, which are often given more than one name on different discs. Quite a number of Herbie's early recordings are in circulation today on albums that are, if not misrepresenting his work by excluding the details of the sessions, at the very least disguising the time period when they were made. Often recorded live and outside of the copyright protection of the major labels (such as Blue Note) for which Hancock was contracted, these recordings are turned over on a constant stream of new CDs. They use modern artwork to make them look like newer recordings when they actually come from the very early years of Herbie's career. In contrast, discs bearing the Blue Note label are always of the best quality with accurate information provided.

Sometime in the early part of 1961 Byrd invited Herbie to move to New York where, because of Hancock's young age (20), the two men shared accommodation in the Bronx for about two years. Byrd became almost like an elder brother to Hancock and gave him the benefit of a wealth of knowledge and experience in his early career.

Herbies's first appearance on a Blue Note album was *Chant* (1961), recorded under Byrd's leadership for the Blue Note label at Rudy van Gelder's New Jersey studio on 17th April just days after his 21st birthday. Along with Byrd, there was Pepper Adams (baritone sax), Doug Watkins (bass) and Eddy Robinson (drums). On May 2, Byrd and Adams were back in the Blue Note studio again to record the tracks for *The Cat Walk* (1961), although this time with Duke Pearson instead of Herbie on piano.

Adams and Byrd went with Herbie to a club called the *White Whale* in New York where they rehearsed with Butch Warren, a bass player from Washington, and Billy Higgins, a drummer from LA. They liked what they heard and the new rhythm section was hired. [5] In September this group recorded the album *Royal Flush* (1961), which went out under Byrd's leadership. Warren and Higgins were also to form a famous partnership that played on many other Blue Note albums over the two years that followed, supporting numerous top musicians like Jackie McLean, Sonny Clark, Don Wilkerson and Dexter Gordon. Later, Warren faded from prominence, but Higgins' career waxed ever brighter. *Royal Flush* was also the last time that Adams and Byrd would appear together on record.

Herbie contributed one of his own compositions, *Requiem*, to the *Royal Flush* album. It was the first time that one of his compositions had been recorded for an album. As the title might suggest, the formal part of his composition is taken from the gospel music environment, although it never turns into a dirge. Opening with a section of eight bars that represents the preacher's call on piano followed by horn responses, the bluesy theme oscillates between D minor and C minor. Then, it's into a sixteen bar section of solos that adopts a familiar minor blues structure using Dm, Gm and Am7 in a medium swing tempo and walking bass line. The piece is made more interesting by the occasional insertion of a D major instead of D minor. It is certainly a notable start for the young Hancock.

Three months later, in a December recording session for Blue Note, Herbie was contributing more material to Byrd's album *Free Form* (1962). His composition *Night Flower* was one of the five selected tracks, the other four written by Byrd himself. With Warren and Higgins again in support, we now hear Hancock lined up alongside the formidable 28-year-old Wayne Shorter on tenor saxophone. As far as we know, this is the earliest recording of the two men together. Both busy men on the New York circuit, they had probably already met and (who knows?) maybe even blown together, but not until now on record. Wayne was at the height of his career with Art Blakey's Jazz Messengers, a band that was constantly in demand for both live gigs and recordings, so Herbie would certainly have known about him. Shorter was a frequent visitor to the Hackensack studios, although he had only just completed his own second album as leader, *Second Genesis* (1961). This was one of the earliest times that Herbie would play with Wayne; the two men would become closest of friends in the near future.

The structure of *Night Flower*, a slow, sensual ballad, shows an increased level of chordal sophistication that Byrd had clearly identified as worthy of a place on the album. All three solos are notable for their luscious sounds, but Herbie's is especially fluid. For many ears, this track stands out as the best on the album, and that's no mean feat when compared with the work of the very experienced Byrd. Later, for the CD edition of the album, a sixth track, *Three Wishes*, also written by Herbie and recorded at the same time, was added. Although this track is not in the same league as *Night Flower*, its very inclusion on the list for recording shows that Byrd's confidence in Herbie was high and his enthusiasm for his young sideman's abilities was solidifying.

Byrd's album *Free Form* is important for another reason too. As the title implies, it is an example of an experiment in what was being called 'The New Thing' or 'The Free Thing'. With the jazz world still shocked at the impact of Ornette Coleman's *The Shape of Jazz To Come* (1959), and more recently *Free Jazz* (1961) recorded almost exactly 12 months earlier, Byrd was one of those jazz musicians who was keen to understand the potential of Coleman's new ideas. And there, sitting alongside him in Byrd's own band was one of the very participants in those experiments – Billy Higgins had been drummer at both the sessions that led to Coleman's revolutionary recordings. Byrd was already the holder of two music degrees and had been offered positions as a Professor of jazz (which he later took up). As a jazz scholar he was ideally suited to carry out his own investigations into the possibilities of free jazz. Thus it was within the eleven minutes of the track *Free Form* that Byrd, Shorter, Higgins, Warren and Hancock explored the dark caverns of group improvisation. In complete contrast to the traditional (yet still forward-looking) content of the rest of the album, the piece *Free Form* adopted some very strange practices. Byrd's own explanation of his design follows.

"The theme is based on a tone row. The first statement and the second are symmetrical in that the intervals are the same; but in each the row begins on a different note. When the two parts are put together they make a scale. The notes in this row are used throughout the piece in several different forms and patterns. We move in and out of that basic framework. The tune has no direct relation to the tempo. I mean that nobody played in the tempo Billy maintains and we didn't even use it to bring in the melody. Billy's work is just there as a percussive factor, but it's not present as a mark of the time. There is no time in the usual sense as far as these soloists are concerned." [6]

Byrd's words alone are enough to tell me that I will not like this music. I have never enjoyed this kind of unstructured cacophony with its mechanical, robotic algorithm. To Herbie, this was an exciting new experiment. The 21-year-old was at an early stage in his career and feeding eagerly off the many and varied jazz interactions to which he was being exposed. He was immersed in the deepest part of the pool of experimentalist jazzers at the time of greatest change in the music world. It was inevitable that much of what he heard and tried would impact permanently upon his style. For the moment it is enough for us to note that he was now indulging in the kind of music that put him right at the very cutting edge of jazz. For the rest of his career he was never afraid to court controversy if it was compatible with making what was, for him, the most exciting music. Meanwhile, he was now ready to make records of his own.

Herbie Hancock: *Takin' Off* – 1962 (***)

By 1962, Herbie was reportedly studying for a master's degree at the Manhattan School of Music under the tutorship of Vittorio Giannini. [7]. Nevertheless, his career was about to take off in a big way with the interest shown in him by the most important record label in jazz. Blue Note was a recording company well known to lovers of jazz because of its mission to record the very best music in that genre. Even today, the Blue Note label continues to appear on CDs where it remains prestigious. The company was established in 1939 by Alfred Lion and Francis Wolff, two friends who emigrated to the USA from Germany at the end of the 1930s. Lion was the main driving force behind the music. He produced many of the albums his company recorded at a time when the job title 'record producer' was embryonic. Wolff was a professional photographer whose work appeared on the album covers. Many of the uncredited photos on the album covers and sleeve notes were taken by Wolff and have been reproduced in countless books and magazines. Amongst the early stars that Lion and Wolff recorded were Thelonius Monk, Art Blakey, J.J. Johnson, Bud Powell and Miles Davis.

It was almost impossible for a young piano player to get even an audition for Blue Note, but Donald Byrd told Herbie to go to meet Lion and tell him he was being drafted into the army. Lion and Wolff agreed to hear Herbie but said they needed some material with obvious commercial potential if they were to sign him. Herbie went away to try to come up with something. He thought of Horace Silver's funky-blues jazz tunes and tried to write a piece along those lines. The result was *Watermelon Man* and a recording contract. Expecting to play a collection of standards to complete the selections for his first record, Herbie was very surprised when Lion then told him to write three more original tunes. Herbie said that Lion simply *never* did that, and that he believed it was Lion's recognition of the potential *of Watermelon Man* that had led him to make that decision. [8]

Herbie recorded *Takin' Off* on 28 May 1962, a time (so different from today) when an album was recorded in a single day! Though he was twenty-two, Wolff's photographs make him look like a teenager, too young to be capable of producing such wonderful sounds. The youthful images were repeated on later albums, giving a false sense of Herbie's real age. The musicians he chose to play alongside him were Dexter Gordon (saxophone), Freddie Hubbard (trumpet), Billy Higgins (drums) and Butch Warren (bass), all of whom are today recognised as premier league mainstream jazz musicians.

Dexter Gordon (1923-90) was already an established star – reputedly the first tenor sax star of bebop. He was born in Los Angeles, son of a doctor amongst whose patients were Duke Ellington and Lionel Hampton. Not surprisingly, Gordon got off to a flying start in jazz. Early in his career, Dexter was hired by Lionel Hampton, but by 1947 found himself hanging out with Miles Davis during the time when Parker and Gillespie visited California. His early career was frequently blighted by hard drugs, which resulted in him serving several prison terms. Nevertheless, he was a good enough tenor saxophone player to become well known for duet duels with Wardell Gray. The most famous of these duels became known as 'The Chase', in which the two saxophones traded, first, 32-bar choruses, then 16, 8 and 4 bars. This alternating style of play inevitably set one player against another in the musical equivalent of a western-style shoot-out and the generated tension caused a level of excitement in the audiences that is probably missing from records. After a lean period during the 1950s, Gordon made a strong comeback with a record called *The Resurgence of Dexter Gordon* (1960). This led to a new contract with Blue Note and the albums *Doin' Alright* (1961), *Dexter Calling* (1961), *Go!* (1962) and *A Swinging Affair* (1962). The first two of these albums were recorded shortly before he went into the studio with Herbie Hancock on 28 May. By the end of 1962, Gordon was still not accredited to play in cabaret in New York so he went on an extended visit to Europe that lasted for 15 years. During this time he became a close family friend and godfather to the future Metallica drummer, Lars Ulrich.

The rhythm section Hancock chose for his band was formidable. Dexter Gordon had already worked frequently with drummer Billy Higgins and bassist Butch Warren, whilst Herbie had also worked with the two rhythm kings during his time with Donald Byrd. Instead of Byrd, a young up-and-coming trumpeter Freddie Hubbard (b1938) was present this time. His own recording career had started in 1960 and he would be a regular collaborator with Herbie and Wayne Shorter for many years to come.

The album kicks right off with *Watermelon Man*, a piece that older listeners will probably be familiar with, even if they don't like jazz. This was an exceptionally visionary way to begin a musical career, for it was without doubt an early fusion piece created some years before musicians really considered such a thing. *Watermelon Man* was a title that had already been used by Duke Ellington. However, Herbie remembered the character well from his boyhood in Chicago and he could hear the rumble of the man's cart over the cobble stones. This was translated into the tune's haunting rhythm, which Leonard Feather points out, is also typically used in gospel music. [7] The combination of the gospel riff with Higgins' drum patterns, removed from the usual swing time, makes this sound immediately different. The first 8-bar lines are played in unison with a short break into harmony by the horns. Bars 9-14 are comprised of pairs of supercool piano chords that lead to a climax that ends in a rim shot and silence through which the soloists play.

Three Bags Full was a title that came to Herbie's mind when he thought the melody he had created sounded rather middle Eastern – "like a shepherd maybe way off in Baghdad or somewhere". [9] The Arabic tones are taken up by Dexter Gordon at the start of his solo at 2.00, but are soon dissipated as he gets stuck in. Herbie plays a classic jazz improvisation with his quick-fire right handed single note technique, supported by chords in the left hand. Later at 3.45 he takes up the double-handed chord style. It's impressive stuff, for his playing is always perfectly executed and imaginative and his jazz chords are sophisticated and rich. Billy Higgins is similarly innovative during the theme, which rises to a crescendo as the pitch and the tension build over the sixteen bars.

Empty Pockets is an exciting piece, written in standard 12-bar form but with Herbie's theme exploiting some colourful pairs of chords played over a swinging, funky rhythm and a walking bass.

The Maze was given its title because of the angles that Herbie perceived in the theme. Again, Higgins is especially creative: when it would be easy to lay down straight fours of rhythm, he is constantly searching every nook and cranny of the tempo. The format is unusual, for there are three piano solos with sax and trumpet sandwiched between them. In the first two piano solos, the trio breaks into a much freer improvisation, departing from the tempo of the piece in a kind of reference to the randomness of the maze. With the repeated return to the piano it's as if the listener, lost in the maze, is repeatedly returning to the place he last visited.

Driftin' has a 32 bar theme in the AABA format. Although the piece has echoes of *Watermelon Man*, the lolloping feel to the rhythm renders it sexily cool and once again Dexter Gordon's saxophone gives the piece real credibility, enhanced by the mellower tones of Hubbard's flügelhorn.

Alone and I is a sophisticated jazz ballad, whose first four notes are strongly reminiscent of the Gershwin/Weill composition *My Ship* from Miles Davis's album *Miles Ahead* (1957) that Herbie would have been familiar with. Structurally, the piece is something of an exercise in chordal progression. Although the melodic path seems clear at first, there are a number of points where the theme steps off track, but the soloists, Herbie especially, demonstrate their supreme skills by holding firm to the harmonic structure. Gordon's plaintive playing of the melody leads into Herbie's rich accompaniment and the result is very smooth and sexy.

The inclusion of alternate takes on the re-mastered CD edition leads to some interesting comparisons, for each master take was chosen for its supposed stronger appeal to the popular audience, its trumpet and saxophone solos both containing rasping tones instead of the more thoughtful jazz performances of the alternate take. Even Herbie is trying to appeal to the populace with an almost honky-tonk style in his solo. The jazz fan will almost always prefer the alternate take for its slicker, more technical playing than its reliance on snazzy performance devices. The alternate take is affected by some curious, out-of-place tapping at the end, which may have been the reason for its relegation from the original LP.

Throughout the album, Gordon is making plenty of errors, more so than perhaps might be expected. This is representative of the method of making these records where a couple of days was usually allocated to rehearsal and one final day for recording. When a musician was not playing regularly in the company of others, mistakes were a sign of unfamiliarity with the music and the musicians. All this does not, however, prevent Gordon from going for it in all the up-tempo pieces. Even on *Watermelon Man*, where we should remember its strangeness to the players of the day, Dexter is clearly up for it – what Miles would have fondly described as "playing his ass off." [10]

Hancock's unique mixture of gospel, blues, and bebop on the opening track *Watermelon Man* caught people's attention. Mongo Santamaria recorded the tune, which became a top-ten hit at a time when there was only one record chart. What a start for Hancock! It was his first composition on the first track of his first album. He was one of only a few jazzers to know what it was like to sell records in numbers comparable with those of pop stars. *Watermelon Man* was a remarkable piece of music, for we need to remember how unusual this composition was in 1962 on any kind of album, especially on a jazz album. *Watermelon Man* contained elements of blues, soul, gospel and jazz and could easily be considered as a jazz-fusion track well ahead of its time, except that it was played on acoustic (i.e. *not* electric) piano and bass. Later, it was reformulated for the *Head Hunters* album and, as jazz-fusion became established, *Watermelon Man* in its electric format became the most popular item at Herbie's live gigs. However, back in 1962, on the back of the generous royalties, Hancock went out and bought an AC Cobra sports car – one of the fastest on the road at that time.

Eric Dolphy: *Gaslight* – 1962 (*)

Apart from his own debut album, there is little music recorded in 1962 that features Herbie Hancock, although he was surely extremely busy playing six or seven nights a week in the New York City jazz venues. Birdland, situated on Broadway and close to the famous 52nd Street, was one venue where he spent a lot of time sitting in (usually with Donald Byrd) with bands led by a variety of musicians such as Hank Mobley, Jackie McLean and Al Grey. One very poor recording (I must presume this is an early example of what we would today call an 'unofficial' or 'bootleg' album) exists of the Eric Dolphy Quintet playing at the Gaslight Café, a coffee house in New York's second music focus, Greenwich Village, on 10 July 1962. Recorded with what sounds like a single poor quality microphone, it features Dolphy with Herbie Hancock on piano, Eddie Armour (trumpet), Richard Davis (bass) and Edgar Bateman (drums). (The same music has been published on other Dolphy albums, for example, *Left Alone* (2003) on the Stash label.)

Eric Dolphy (1928-64) was another of the leading jazzmen of the time, extremely proficient on flute, alto saxophone and (unusually for jazz) bass clarinet. The early part of his career in the 1950s seems to be dominated by experiments with the 'Third Stream' genre in which jazz was blended with European classical music. However, historians place Dolphy in the category of avant-garde musicians. Dolphy made many recordings during the period 1959-64, many of them of considerable interest to students of jazz history, for this was a very fertile time when all kinds of experimentation were taking place. Dolphy had been closely involved with much of this activity, not least by taking part in Ornette Coleman's radical album *Free Jazz* (1960). However, Dolphy was never quite a subscriber to the society of formless music composers, preferring to investigate music-making with unconventional harmony. We are told that he adopted a harmonic structure based upon the 12-note scale (a technique he would have experienced in his studies of Schoenberg and other 20th century European classical music composers). This makes his music sound unorthodox and, to many ears, tuneless with little apparent relationship to what was going on in his band.

To ears anticipating conventional harmonies, *Gaslight* is a disappointing, if nevertheless historic snapshot of jazz in these very unusual times. Herbie is playing in an environment that he must have found very exciting. The first of three lengthy tracks is *Miss Ann*, a kind of Charlie Parker extrapolation in which Dolphy, having delivered some kind of theme, breaks loose on alto sax to a fast 4/4 accompaniment. Herbie comps with chords liberally selected from the thousands on offer, and takes a substantial solo in which he clearly adopts the same keyless style that the composition appears to require. *Left Alone* focuses on Dolphy's competent flute playing in a more traditionally composed Billie Holiday ballad, which Herbie plays fairly straight, including another solid solo. Track 3 is *G.W.* that continues the tradition of meaningless titles and revisits the bebop formula for a further twelve minutes of directed, but ultimately misguided, energy and spaghetti-like melodic strands. Once again, Herbie's accompaniment appears to be a sequence of chords that are entirely unrelated to the soloist's contributions, whilst Richard Davis and Edgar Bateman are having their own kind of party by laying down a solid four-in-a-bar rhythm. Herbie's lively solo makes you feel that there is music in there somewhere if only you could find it. The final track is *245*, a Dolphy composition that once more exhibits his tuneless melodic style on alto sax, and is edited to just four minutes with no other solos. I find such music depressing, but the recording, bad though it is, does at least reveal that it sounded better to those present who were (presumably) in various degrees of anaesthetised consciousness. Of only passing interest for Herbie's career, the record is undoubtedly significant for students of Dolphy, whose career was cut short by his death in 1964 at the age of 36.

Freddie Hubbard: *Hub-Tones* – 1962 (***)

In 1962, Freddie Hubbard was probably the most exciting young trumpet player in jazz. Hubbard (1938-2008) was born in Indianapolis where, in his teens, he worked with Wes and Monk Montgomery, and his lifetime friend, saxophonist James Spaulding. In 1958 he moved to New York and almost immediately played with many of the top jazz musicians. It wasn't long before he was contracted to Blue Note, for whom he made his first album as leader, *Open Sesame* (1960). Late in the same year, after Ornette Coleman watched him play alongside Don Cherry, Coleman invited 'Hub' to play on his revolutionary album, *Free Jazz* (1960). He was clearly making all the right moves and displaying prodigious amounts of talent. In 1961, after appearing with John Coltrane and making his fourth album for Blue Note, *Ready for Freddie* (1961) alongside Wayne Shorter, Hubbard joined Art Blakey's Jazz Messengers, then the second biggest band in jazz after Miles's outfit. (Naturally, the top job in trumpet-playing was already taken!) Despite his participation in the free jazz experiments, Hubbard was recognised for his solidly held place in the jazz mainstream. Of course, 'mainstream' was a fluid term used as an indicator of a kind of central point in the spectrum of jazz, but that didn't mean that the marker was immovable. Indeed, bands led by the likes of Blakey, Miles and Horace Silver were constantly pushing the boundaries, whilst deliberately not stepping over the boundary into free jazz. So Hubbard, even by the age of 24, was regarded as one of the leading mainstream players, working at the edges of the known jazz Universe.

Hub-Tones was Hubbard's sixth album in barely three years. For the first time, he hired Herbie Hancock for the piano seat in his 'pick-up' band. James Spaulding, who was now in New York was invited to join Freddie, along with Reggie Workman (bass) and Clifford Jarvis (drums). The album is an entertaining mix of fast and slow numbers, greatly enriched by Hubbard's own compositions (four out of the five tracks are his) and Spaulding's delicious alto sax and flute sounds. For Herbie, it's very much a supporting gig, although he is given plenty of opportunity to show his chops. In particular, the title track is a stunner, played at a speedy tempo such that its jagged opening theme is made extraordinarily difficult to play. Once that is out of the way, the sequences of machine-gun quavers from trumpet, sax and piano are as good as you'll hear anywhere. Spaulding's rich flute sounds are the highlights of the tracks *Prophet Jennings* and *Lament for Booker*, whilst his alto is in top form on *You're My Everything* and a tune dedicated to him by his composer friend, *For Spee's Sake*.

Herbie Hancock: *My Point of View* – 1963 (***)

Herbie was so impressed with his AC Cobra sports car, bought with the spoils of an unexpected hit record, that he named a track after it, *King Cobra*, on his second album *My Point of View* (1963), recorded in March 1963. Sadly, the music was unable to match the performance of the car and the album sold poorly.

Hancock had tried to repeat the magic formula that had worked with *Watermelon Man* on *Takin' Off* with the track *Blind Man, Blind Man* but the title was apt. Hancock seemed to have lost all sense of colour and his musicians, unused to the shackles of playing to a single chord seemed as short-sighted as a short-sighted man in a myopia contest. *Watermelon Man* had been different for them too, but at least they could take on the challenges of its chord changes. This was a tedious and unimaginative construction based on a single chord that left them floundering – wondering how to fill the bar space allocated to them. The painfully repetitive track was not in the same league as its eminent predecessor. As before, Herbie resorted to gospel music for his inspiration, hoping to capture more of the novelty that had clearly appealed to so many *Watermelon Man* listeners. He planned to add colour with an enhanced frontline that consisted of Donald Byrd, Grachan Moncur III (trombone) and Hank Mobley (tenor sax). On top of that, he had hired Grant Green to provide the comparatively unusual presence of the electric guitar, but despite all this, it is the mind-numbing monotony of the A minor chord that is so disappointing. Hank Mobley sounds completely lost as he tries to improvise over the chord. You can almost hear him wondering where on earth he can go with it. There's nothing wrong with what he plays, but he has used up his ideas by the second or third bar and is clearly glad when he can hand over to Hancock.

The second track, *A Tribute to Someone*, like each of the other four tracks, is a Hancock composition. It was most unusual that all the tracks on Hancock's albums continued to be his own compositions. This later proved to be a great asset for it is said that, thanks to Donald Byrd, Herbie had retained the rights to his own compositions, enabling him to re-use his hits in later years to considerable financial advantage. The reversion to conventional structures and harmonies is like a breath of fresh air after the dispiriting opening track. The seriously swinging back-room of Herbie with Chuck Israels (bass) and Tony Williams (drums) is delightful as Byrd delivers the kind of melody that any of the top jazzers would have been proud to write. Williams was teaming up with Herbie for the first time on record here, and the 17-year-old plays like a seasoned pro. Herbie's lively solo is delivered mostly with single right-handed notes, whilst Mobley is solid and sweetly melodic. Green and Moncur are absent, Green appearing only on tracks 1 and 5.

The main theme to *King Cobra* is a colourful piece of ensemble playing that is both novel in harmonic style and richly orchestrated to make full use of the available horns. Unfamiliar with the number, and presumably lacking practice, the soloists cope manfully with the complex chord structure as each takes his turn in the spotlight. The piece ends with a fade on a drum solo that is comparatively restrained by Williams' later standards. The unusual sound of *King Cobra* has a refreshing presence on the album, hinting at other future jewels.

The Pleasure is Mine sounds like a caricature of a Broadway show tune in which a popular Tin Pan Alley ditty is folded using some clever harmonic origami. An otherwise thoughtful ballad, it takes on a rather larger-than-life character thanks to Herbie's vision.

The album ends with *And What If I Don't*, a cool, gently swinging 16-bar blues in which Grant Green returns to add some new textures. It's a very acceptable, if predictable, way to end what was, at the time, a good album. Despite the presence of *Blind Man, Blind Man*, all of the tracks except the last would have sounded exciting and fresh in 1963. The rhythm section, led by the perceptive Tony Williams, is especially good throughout. Herbie's playing is mature and harmonically rich, full to the brim with deep-seated swing. His compositions (no doubt under the watchful eye of the ever-present Donald Byrd) show very good measures of innovation and skills of orchestration.

Working with Miles Davis

In early May 1963, soon after they had recorded *My Point of View*, Herbie had the biggest opportunity of his life – an invitation to join the No.1 band in the world. Davis had recently been in Los Angeles recording tracks for what would become the album *Seven Steps to Heaven* (1963), but was unhappy with some aspects of the music he had laid down. Back in New York, Davis decided to re-record three of the tracks, but his pianist, the west-coast-based Victor Feldman, had commitments in Los Angeles and was unable to join Miles in New York. Miles needed a new pianist. Davis: "I had met Herbie Hancock about a year or so earlier when the trumpet player, Donald Byrd brought him by my house in

West 77th Street. He had just joined Donald's band. I asked him to play something for me on my piano and I saw right away that he could play. When I needed a new piano player I thought of Herbie first and called him to come over. I was having Tony Williams and Ron Carter over so I wanted to know how he would sound with them. They all came over and played every day for the next couple of days...On around the third or fourth day I came downstairs and joined them and played a few things. Ron and Tony were already in the band. I told Herbie to meet us at the recording studio the next day." [11] The story makes the date May 13th. Hancock accepted the invitation, and stayed with Davis for the next five years. Davis's band became known as his 'Second Great Quintet' and is today regarded by many as one of the finest of all jazz ensembles.

Herbie has been much influenced by his time in Davis's employment. Herbie: "Once Miles would start to play on top of these things we were doing, all of a sudden, it was as though he would go to the core of it. I would be all over the piano, but Miles would play a few notes that would just wipe out all that fancy stuff I was playing...You could never tell what was going on with Miles. You'd always leave the session not knowing if they got anything of any value because it was always so different."

A notable change in style occurred when Davis suggested that Herbie should play long sections with only his right hand. Strangely, it was a technique largely untried until then. If you listen to *So Near, So Far* on *Seven Steps to Heaven* (1963), for example, Herbie's solo consists very much of block chords. It's a wonderful improvisation in the style that was prevalent at the time. However, Miles encouraged Herbie to drop it in favour of the single note right hand method. Later on the same album, in *Joshua*, he plays more with the right hand, but develops this still further on later albums by playing even less with his left hand. It's a good example of Miles's philosophy that 'less is more'.

Miles: "Tony would lead the tempo and Herbie was like a sponge. Anything you played was cool with him; he just soaked up everything. One time I told him that his chords were too thick, and he said, 'Man, I don't know what to play some of the time.' I said, 'Then Herbie, don't play nothing if you don't know what to play. You know, just let it go. You don't have to be playing all the time!' ...Herbie was like that at first; he would just play and play and play because he could and because he never did run out of ideas and because he loved to play....When he first came with us I told Herbie, 'You're putting too many notes in the chord. The chord is already established and so is the sound. So you don't have to play all the notes that are in the bottom. Ron's got the bottom.'" [12]

Listening to Miles and taking his advice, Herbie found that the whole sound of the band was changed. Another colour had been added to the sound of jazz.

For a long period of time during 1964-1966 Miles had a lot of problems with his hip that stopped him from playing. Rather than allow the band to disintegrate through lack of work, Miles allowed the boys to play alongside Freddie Hubbard. Thus Hancock, Williams and Carter, frequently with Hubbard too, spent much time playing together and were able to develop a deep knowledge of each other's style. As all good teams do, their music together became greater than the sum of their individual contributions and the type of music they chose to work in was the music of the moment – an avant-garde style of free improvisation. They became so familiar with each other's playing that it crept into their work with Miles.

Remarkably, for someone who was never backward in coming forward, Davis said that it was *he* who learned the art of playing free from his young sidemen. "If I was the inspiration and wisdom and the link for this band, Tony was the fire, the creative spark; Wayne was the idea person, the conceptualizer of a whole lot of musical ideas we did; and Ron and Herbie were the anchors. I was just the leader who put us all together. Those were all young guys, and although they were learning from me, I was learning from them too, about the new thing, the free thing...I knew that I was playing with some great young musicians that had their fingers on a different pulse."

The new band set a precedent for Miles in which he hired young musicians, instead of mature, experienced ones. This was an approach he would use from now on. It worked. Herbie's playing alongside the extraordinary Ron Carter (b1937) and the uniquely talented Tony Williams (1945-97) proved to be a coup for Miles. In his book about Miles, Carr wrote: "So far as straight 4/4 time-playing was concerned, it was to prove itself to be possibly the greatest rhythm section of all time, and Hancock, Carter and Williams seemed to have an inexhaustible variety of ways of creating and releasing tension, expanding and contracting space." [13] Miles was so pleased with his new band he asked his agents to set up as many gigs as possible.

There are many fine solos from Herbie, recorded live during his time with Miles – too many to describe here – but one of my favourites is his solo for *Joshua* on *Miles Davis in Europe* (1963). However, it is his contributions to the seven great studio albums of the Second Great Quintet that stand amongst the very finest and most influential of recorded jazz. The studio albums that Herbie recorded for Miles are as follows: *Seven Steps to Heaven* (1963), *E.S.P.* (1965), *Miles Smiles* (1967), *Sorcerer* (1967), *Nefertiti* (1968*), Miles in the Sky* (1968), *Filles de Kilimanjaro* (1969). Herbie did appear on *In a Silent Way* (1969), *A Tribute to Jack Johnson* (1971) and *On the Corner* (1972), but very much as a guest at the recordings, rather than as a member of the band. All of these have been discussed in detail in my book on Miles Davis so I won't reproduce that here.

Herbie Hancock: *Inventions and Dimensions* – 1964 (***)

In his liner notes for Herbie Hancock's third album, *Inventions and Dimensions* (1964) Net Hentoff wrote: "This session is one of the most spontaneous jazz dates ever recorded." [14] Well, hyperbole is, to some extent, expected from someone tasked to write liner notes, but this record probably *is* the most spontaneous so far recorded *by Herbie*. We recall that, as well as Ornette Coleman's more well-known explorations of 1959/60, by this time, avant-garde free jazz had already been taken a great distance into the unknown by the chaotic percussive pianist, Cecil Taylor. Indeed, Block has written that Taylor was one of the creators of free jazz in 1957, pre-dating Coleman's work. [15] By the early 1960s, saxophonist Albert Ayler was also performing very long, entirely freeform pieces that were described by some as the introduction of "naked aggression" into jazz. These two men did as much as any other musicians to introduce audiences to the abandonment of rules in jazz performance. In a 1960 interview with Ira Gitler for *Down Beat* magazine, Charles Mingus, recognising that it was time for a change, made his own observations about the state of jazz. "I'm not saying everybody's going to have to play like Coleman, but they're going to have to stop playing like Bird (Charlie Parker)." [16] In a sense, this set down the marker for what is now known as the 'post bop' period of jazz, i.e. *after* Parker.

For *Inventions and Dimensions*, Herbie was intent on moving in a more *avant-garde* direction, whilst not dispensing with *all* rules. Hentoff remarks that Herbie does not place himself in any 'school' by adopting this approach, for the music on this album is formulated to his own designs. Herbie told Hentoff, "On this date, I told the musicians not to assume anything except for a few rules I set for each piece, and every time those rules were different." [17] Herbie goes to some lengths to explain that the musicians *could play what they wanted*. In the event, the musicians *chose* to play somewhat conventionally: there *is* conventional rhythm and there *is* conventional harmony and the bass line *does* mostly walk. Herbie says that he *does* actually count off tempos at the start of each piece, even if there is no pre-planned melody to embark upon. Herbie attributes his new approach to the experiences he had playing alongside Eric Dolphy. "It was my first exposure – as a participant – to 'free' music." [17] Some of this is now available for us to hear on Dolphy's album *Gaslight* (1962).

The musicians that Herbie chose for this recording were, it seems, also not inclined to dispense with too many rules, despite apparently being given the chance. Herbie: "Paul Chambers did often play a walking or a recurring rhythm, but that was because he *wanted* to play that way. I didn't suggest it and he could have done whatever he wanted." [17] They could have (presumably) dispensed with all harmony and gone for totally chromatic notes and random chords; they could also have broken free from the pre-selected rhythms, but they were not ready to do either of those yet. However, by his very choice of musicians - suggested in part from discussions with Miles Davis - Herbie had gone for two percussionists with Brazilian roots, Willie Bobo and Osvaldo 'Chihuahua' Martinez. This undoubtedly played a large part in the final, conservative result. For bass, Miles had also recommended Paul Chambers who was working with Herbie here for the first time.

Succotash, we are told, was a title chosen because it is an onomatopoeic word that sounds like what Willie Bobo was playing on drums. Only the time signature was pre-determined. The chords were supposedly free, yet we notice that Chambers chooses to follow Herbie. *Triangle* is apparently three-sided, with a section of 12/8 sandwiched between two sections of 4/4. Again, no pre-set chords, yet a kind of blues results. Not so adventurous, then? The fast tempo piece, *Jack Rabbit*, was held down by a repeated bass motif from Chambers, but was still restrained compared to what *might* have happened. Hanock said, "I and the others played whatever we wanted." Well, it could have sounded a lot worse had the musicians chosen not to follow each other. Perhaps *A Jump Ahead* is the most interesting from the point of view of experiment. Paul Chambers was given the opportunity of choosing a root (or pedal) note at random, after which Herbie drove forward sixteen bars of improvisation based on the selected note. The problem of how to end the piece was resolved here with a fade-out. The result is certainly interesting. *Mimosa* is, at least, a more 'conventionally' composed jazz piece, based around a chord pattern that Herbie had worked on with Miles. There is a melodic line also, although this was improvised at the session.

Hentoff commented that Herbie had joined the ranks of musicians who had decided that the search for more freedom did not necessarily involve a descent into the chaos of Ayler and Taylor. Bob Blumenthal, a seasoned commentator on Miles Davis, is at pains to point out that, in many ways, the music presented here is more 'open' even than the music of Coleman and Taylor, whilst not descending into cataclysmic kinetics. [18] Indeed, for an indication of just how advanced the trio work of Herbie, Ron Carter and Tony Williams had become, we are pointed towards the recording of Miles's band at the Juan-Les-Pins Festival in Antibes, France, recorded just over a month earlier and preserved on the record *Miles in Europe* (1964). Clearly, for some musicians, there was plenty still to be achieved in the post bop jazz world without resorting to harmonic and temporal anarchy. At least in this point in time, the album does place Herbie Hancock firmly in the camp of *avant-garde* jazz musicians.

Herbie Hancock: *Empyrean Isles* - 1964 (***)

By June 1964 Herbie was in a much better command of his career, such that for his next visit to the Blue Note studio, he was able to take along Miles's band, with Freddie Hubbard taking Miles's spot. In almost any analysis, it was a bold thing to do. Indeed, it is remarkable that Davis *allowed* Hancock to do this at all. (Later, Weather Report had clauses in their contracts that disallowed any three members from playing together outside of the band.) Nevertheless, there were some significant differences between his proposed content for his album and what was happening in Miles's band.

Herbie's use of the title *Empyrean Isles* to describe this collection of music is the start of a kind of strategy for applying a theme to his albums. Some writers see the music as a collection of tone poems based on a kind of ancient mariner theme – the idea of embarking on some fantastic voyage of discovery in the days when the explorers really didn't quite know what was over the horizon. Herbie's vision of a group of mythical islands created by volcanoes and populated by new species of creatures was most attractive. The idea that somewhat abstract pieces of instrumental music, unpolluted by lyrics, could be represented by imaginative titles and grouped into a theme was unusual. It ran counter to Miles's normal practice: he didn't really care less about titles and had no interest in attaching meanings to his music. This strategy was useful in cases where the music was avant-garde enough to cause people to turn away without listening. Herbie included a minimum-form, abstract piece called *The Egg*, supposedly named after a volcano on Cantaloupe Island. Perhaps it helps to have a mental image in mind when you listen to this music. *The Egg* is 14 minutes of almost spontaneous improvisation, except for the merest of motifs played at the start to act as a jumping-off platform. Clearly, this was cutting-edge stuff in 1964. Most people will not play this more than once and many will not get past the first few minutes. Purists would, of course argue, that there should be no need for any kind of meaningful title and that for the music to be any value it is no longer fresh (i.e. spontaneous) if you listen to it for a second time. The obvious allusion is that an egg discovered on a mythical island in an unknown land could give birth to absolutely anything. However, since I simply do not like to listen to this kind of music, I can only conclude that the mother of this egg was a turkey.

Often, on Blue Note CD reissues, two versions of the opening tune *One Finger Snap* are available. The snap takes the form of a rapid snatch of gunfire played twice in unison on trumpet and piano. This is a lively piece played in the modal style. Unlike the catchy and popular modal pieces on Miles's *Kind of Blue* album, say, where the improvisations take place over conventional chord sequences, this style, whilst still using the standard major / minor diatonic scales that most ears are familiar with, nevertheless bases the harmonies on rather less conventional chord sequences. It has the effect of making the piece seem farther from our grasp. It's clever stuff for most musicians, but made to sound easy by those who eat, drink and sleep scales and arpeggios.

Oliloqui Valley is similar in construction to *One Finger Snap* except that, in accordance with its title, which refers to another site of wonder and delight on the fabled island group, this is sweeter and more welcoming. The chord sequence is similarly unexpected, but has the effect of winding up the sense of anticipation as the would-be explorer moves deeper into unknown territory and farther away from his comfort zone. Again, there are two quite different versions of this composition on the CD.

Empyrean Isles is dominated by Herbie's wonderful discovery of a three-chord sequence that has intrigued and thrilled listeners ever since. The three chords are at the core of the third track, *Cantaloupe Island*. In their simplest form they could be expressed as the sequence Fm, Db7, Dm, but Herbie plays them in such a way as to render them even more exotic. Included in the Fm is the fifth note, C, so that the ear also hears the transition progress chromatically from C to Db and D. He also includes the F in each chord, locking the three chords to the same root. I think this single chord progression is the highlight of the entire album, and there is plenty of evidence in support. For example, *Cantaloupe Island* was selected shortly afterwards by Blue Note boss and producer Albert Lion as the title and headline track on an early compilation of Herbie's 'Best'. Much later, in 1993, the music was heavily sampled by American rap band Us3 and released as *Cantaloop (Flip Fantasia)*. The record was included on the band's album *Hand on the Torch* (1993) and as a single became a big hit, reaching #9 in the Billboard Top 100. Herbie's composition presents the opening Fm in a Gospel riff style similar to the one he uses with the same Fm root on *Watermelon Man*. His formula for success had been proven twice over.

Tony Williams: *Lifetime* – 1964 (*)

George Coleman played saxophone in Miles Davis's quintet during the period from the time of Herbie's joining until after the famous concert at the Philharmonic Hall, Lincoln Center, NYC in February 1964. This concert led to two of the most loved and best known albums in the Miles Davis repertoire, *Four and More* (1964) and *My Funny Valentine* (1964), also later released on one two-disc album called *The Complete Concert* (1964). Coleman was on wonderful form for this concert and his playing on these recordings is quite sublime, due in no small part to his habit of practising for hours in his hotel room. However, this disciplined approach to playing jazz is reported to have annoyed Miles. When he found out that Coleman was practising in private, he told Coleman that he (Miles) paid him to experiment on the bandstand, not in his hotel room. Tony Williams, influenced by the current fashion of improvisation without reference to previous practices, did not like Coleman's style of play. Young gun Tony was still only 18 years old and very enthusiastic about 'playing free'. Already he had gained a position of influence over Miles because Miles saw Tony as the focus for the way his band was playing.

Miles: "Tony Williams never liked the way George played, and the direction the band was moving in revolved around Tony. George knew that Tony didn't like the way he played...George played everything almost perfectly and Tony didn't like saxophone players like that. He liked musicians who made mistakes, like being out of key. But George just played the chords. He was a hell of a musician, but Tony didn't like him. Tony wanted somebody who was reaching for different kinds of things, like Ornette Coleman. Ornette's group was his favourite band...I think Tony was the one who brought Archie Shepp to the Vanguard one night to sit in and he was so awful that I just walked off the bandstand. He couldn't play and I wasn't going to stand up there with this no-playing motherfucker." [19]

It was at this time that Miles began suffering badly with his hip. There was a hiatus for the band during which Herbie, Ron and Tony worked on their free style of playing (often with Freddie Hubbard deputising for Miles). Coleman simply did not like their freer, less conventionally harmonic approach and, knowing he was unpopular and likely to lose any argument within the band, handed in his resignation. Tony wanted Miles to hire Eric Dolphy, but Miles didn't go for it. Miles: "Eric was a beautiful guy as far as his personality went, but I never liked his playing. He could play, I just didn't like the *way* he played. A lot of people loved it, I know Trane did, and Herbie, Ron and Tony did too." [20] Miles really wanted to get Wayne Shorter, but he wasn't available at first. Miles hired Sam Rivers, who played on just one album, *Miles in Tokyo* (1964), recorded on 14th July. By September, Miles had succeeded in prising Shorter away from his long-held position with Art Blakey. Wayne Shorter appears on the album *Miles in Berlin* (1964), recorded on 25th September. Of Wayne, Miles said: "At first, Wayne had been known as a free form player, but playing with Art Blakey for those years and being the band's musical director had brought him back in somewhat. He wanted to play freer than he could in Art's band, but he didn't want to be all the way out either. Wayne had always been someone who experimented *with* form instead of someone who did it *without* form. That's why I thought he was perfect for where I wanted to see the music I played go." [21]

That August, Tony Williams was given the opportunity to record an album of his own for Blue Note. It was called *Lifetime* (1964) and many people confuse it with Williams' later electric jazz-fusion band of 1969: there is no relationship. According to Blumenthal [18], it was the first complete album of avant-garde jazz released by Blue Note and must have represented a commercial gamble. All of the compositions were by Williams, a young man who, as a drummer had had almost no formal musical education. That didn't seem to matter in these times. We can guess from the above discussions about Tony's leanings towards free jazz that there wasn't a lot of compositional skill on display. Let's remember too, that Herbie was also a subscriber to the free jazz movement, although he didn't feel the necessity to let go completely of his roots in the jazz mainstream. We are told that Herbie helped with the arrangements. [22] Herbie did not play on the first three tracks, but he did play on *Memory* which is led off by Bobby Hutcherson on vibraphone who moves on to a free improvisation between the two men and Tony. With its fade-out ending, the track sounds like a shortened version (because of lack of spcae on a vinyl disc) of a long improvisation. Herbie also played (curiously, without Williams!) alongside Ron Carter for the final track, *Barb's Song to the Wizard*. This is another piece of free improvisation based on a melodic fragment in 3/4 tempo. The title was, reportedly, a reference to a mutual friend paying tribute to Miles. [18] This album gives listeners a very good impression of the state of thinking of the members of Miles's rhythm section in the middle 1960s as the Second Great Quintet was climbing its lofty peak behind a leader who did not subscribe to the 'free thing'. Many analysts would claim that it was *because* the rhythm section had experimented so much that Davis's band became such great mountaineers.

Herbie Hancock: *Maiden Voyage* – 1965 (*****)

1965 was a bad year for Miles. His hip was having such an effect on his health that he found it hard to perform at any live gigs. We can assume that it was with his blessing that his own band, with Hubbard taking Miles's place went into the studio on 17th May to record one of Herbie's greatest albums and certainly one of his unequalled tracks, *Maiden Voyage*. All of the tracks on this album have had wide coverage ever since they were put down on this record. Herbie has recorded them on numerous occasions and they have occupied slots on the programmes of countless live performances.

Almost a continuation of the mood of *Empyrean Isles*, this album has a similar consistency of feeling, encapsulated by the track titles, that constitutes what we might today call a theme, yet recorded in a time when 'themed' albums in jazz were unknown. The ocean takes up a large part of the imagery, so there is plenty of the feeling of excitement and anticipation as, for example, a vessel sets out on its first voyage into the unknown. Listeners can easily put themselves in the place of Captain Cook, say, who could easily have discovered the Empyrean Isles, or of Charles Darwin on his voyage to the Galapagos Islands. This is pre-fusion 'mainstream' jazz at its very best – entirely novel for its time, not revolutionary, but, like Darwin, probing the very nature of evolution.

A modal piece in the style of *So What* from Miles's *Kind of Blue*, the simple chord changes and stunning melody of *Maiden Voyage* form a perfect combination that has remained timeless over the four decades since its release. The novel sound and feeling created by the changes allows the soloists to reach out as freely as the harmony allows – something they were all good at. In a sense this is the antidote to free jazz. One of the reasons for the success was the presence of George Coleman whose superb lyricism was perfect for this piece of music. After flawlessly matching him with Hubbard as they play the spine-tingling opening melody, the point at which the saxophone opens up from 1.22 is chillingly superb. His solo is complemented with a perfect parallel performance from Hubbard from 2.30. Finally comes Herbie's delicious improvisation from 4.36, this time moving further away from his own theme, aided and abetted by Carter and Williams as, like those early brave mariners, they dispense with the maps. This recording of *Maiden Voyage* is as good as anything from *Kind of Blue*.

Eye of the Hurricane is another modal piece with a short memorable melody and some fascinating breaks in the rhythm that quickly extend into prolonged solos that stick to the simple chord sequences. Hubbard takes the opportunity to play in the kind of free style he had now become used to. His solo is littered with grunts and growls and other devices that would never have been heard from a trumpet as few as seven or eight years earlier. In contrast, the predictable Coleman plays with fluidity and grace over a backing that other players might have used to trip out. Herbie's solo is mostly right hand only with long polished runs that now are part of his trademark sound.

Herbie clearly loved the track *Little One* by including it here on his own album so soon after he had recorded it (in January 1965) with Miles for his album *E.S.P.* (1965) where the piece would take on a life of its own. The two versions are structurally quite similar, but sound significantly different. Both have a theme played *rubato* at the beginning and end, between which, from 1.24, there is a sequence of solos based around the root note of F but which diverge unpredictably from the focus in small steps, creating a feeling of restless, anxious searching. Rather than a typical cameo of a musician's newborn child, which usually inspires warm, positive feelings, this is perhaps better attributed to the discovery of a new species of mammal in the long grass of Oliloqui Valley.

Survival of the Fittest is a well-chosen name for a piece that seems to describe the apparently chaotic, yet ultimately beautiful forces of nature that underpin evolutionary theory. Here, another exploration into free jazz is balanced with sections of carefully composed and expertly played ensemble music. With Coleman not just on board but bosun's mate, Herbie clearly did not intend to play anything too abstract, for we remember that Coleman had left Miles's band three months earlier on the basis that he didn't want to play as freely as perhaps his colleagues might have liked. The last section of the piece is a free improvisation shared between Tony, Herbie and Ron. First Tony plays a free solo, then from 9.00 Herbie embarks upon an energetic cadenza that has crashing chords. The piece comes to an end with a final burst from Tony. It's a great example of how the juxtaposition of avant-garde modernist music with music written in structured, harmonic forms generates the yin and yang that completes a holistic album, rather than one that is unidirectional into the abstract. When *Dolphin Dance* starts out, the tensions that remain from the previous piece are washed away entirely amid the beautiful spectacle of imaginary dolphins caressing the turquoise blue ocean waves. It's enough to send me right out to the travel agent.

In summary, *Maiden Voyage* was a true milestone album for Herbie, encapsulating a remarkable blend of loose, free jazz, whilst retaining a grip on conventional forms and harmonies. Unsurprisingly, the album was inducted into the Grammy Hall of Fame in 1999.

Herbie Hancock: *Blow-Up - The Original Soundtrack* – 1966 (****)

In 1966 Herbie accepted a commission to compose the music for a film called *Blow-Up*, directed by Michaelangelo Antonioni. Very much inspired by the Beatles' social revolution that became the Swinging 60s and momentarily turned London into the hippest city in the world, the plot centres on Thomas, a photographer making the most of the excesses of those times. As one reviewer put it, this is the "... story of a mindless, beauty obsessed, celebrity idolizing, drug addicted, and violence obsessed culture." [23] Sounds rather like 2010 to me!

Herbie was an inspired choice for music needed to encapsulate such a wide range of moods and activities. Clearly, at 26, he was young enough to be entirely at one with the popular culture, but he was also skilled enough to be able to write music across the genres of blues, rock 'n' roll, Latin and abstract jazz, as well as music for larger groups. This would seem the perfect opportunity to create some jazz-fusion... Of course, no-one was explicitly engaged in anything so formal. As I have discussed elsewhere [24], by 1966 there was a growing conscious momentum to blend jazz with rock and blues, although efforts were mostly intuitive rather than explicit. Herbie had already been experimenting thus in his own albums, on tracks such as *Watermelon Man, Blind Man, Blind Man* and *Cantaloupe Island*. Here we find further examples.

The opening track *Main Title Blow Up* is a kind of jazz-rock fusion because it is presented in two halves – the first a rock piece, the second, spliced directly onto it at 0.38, is jazz. The contrast is very satisfying to jazz fans as the cool sounds of jazz take over from the crude rock 'n' roll sounds. The intriguing question is, "Who performs the first 37 seconds of rock music?" Since there is no indication to the contrary, we must assume that it is the Hall/Smith/Carter/de Johnette configuration. If so, then this recording is even more curious than it appears at first. Next come two versions of a piece called *Verushka*, both very good blues performances. Part I is focussed on Jim Hall and Jimmy Smith playing a standard 12-bar blues in a 'call and answer' format. Part II features Phil Woods playing a great solo to the same chords on alto sax. *The Naked Camera* brings Joe Henderson (tenor) and Joe Newman (trumpet) to the foreground with Herbie's piano trio behind and Ron Carter's bass motif prominent. Beginning calmly and coolly, the players soon work themselves up into a free-jazz lather. It's about now that we become aware of the faded endings, used throughout this soundtrack. It's curious how the medium of the silver screen reduces the value of the music to the point where it isn't worth finishing the pieces. *Bring Down the Birds* is a pretty good attempt to blend a jazz pastiche onto a basic rock 'n' roll backdrop and is a real example of early jazz-fusion. In contrast, *Jane's Theme* is a slow, sexy jazz ballad, led by Jim Hall with Jimmy Smith's organ and Carter and de Johnette gently in the background.

Inserted somewhat carelessly into the middle of the running order is a rare performance by the Yardbirds – rare because it contains both Jeff Beck and Jimmy Page performing a number called *Stroll On*. It is said that the film's director Antonioni wanted to feature a band called The In-Crowd (later called Tomorrow) but when they were unavailable, he used the Yardbirds instead. [25]

The Thief has Jimmy Smith now leading with Jim Hall in support. The piece includes a nice solo from Ron Carter playing acoustic bass in this electric environment. As you might expect, *The Kiss* is a delicate jazz ballad that tries to seduce listeners from the world of pop music. The playing is led by Jim Hall, and followed by a most restrained solo from Joe Henderson. *Curiosity* is a short, medium tempo jazz piece led by tenor sax, and is followed with another short piece of horny Latin jazz called *Thomas Studies Photos*. Herbie himself leads the band for *The Bed*, another ballad that depicts exactly the images the film requires. Herbie's contributions end with a flourish of horns and energy that is a superb foretaste of what is to come decades later. This all-too-brief fifty-two seconds starts in the jazz vein and then breaks into what can only be described as backbeat-grounded big band jazz. It's great, but frustratingly short.

The CD edition ends with two tracks by Tomorrow, presumably as a consolation prize for not making it into the movie.

In summary, this record is a significant milestone in the history of jazz-fusion, appearing to encapsulate features of later 1970s music in a quite advanced way. Many other famous fusioneers were only just starting to think about how it might be done. Here, with the help of an electronic organ and a jazz electric guitarist, Herbie is clearly demonstrating what later turned out to be the most popular formula for jazz-fusion.

Herbie Hancock: *Speak Like a Child* - 1968 (***)

Apart from Ron Carter, Herbie employed an entirely new group of musicians for his next album - not a team of first division heavyweights, but players seemingly chosen only to play the written parts that Herbie presented them with. The album notes show that Thad Jones was playing flügelhorn, Peter Phillips bass trombone and Jerry Dodgion alto flute, three instruments designed to offer tones in the lower, mellower ranges. It was also an album with a bright spotlight on Herbie himself, for none of these musicians would play a solo on the album. Whilst the horn section adds new colours that were untypical of most other albums, each of the songs was very much about the development of Herbie's ideas for the piano trio format.

The first track is *Riot*, a lively though not chaotic piece in which the horns are used to colour the bookends of Herbie's piano studies. After a tricky opening theme that dodges between recognisable tempos and stretches the abilities of the players, Herbie launches himself into two stretches of trio improvisation based upon the modal style. At 2.38 the horns come in for a section of written ensemble playing during which they sound like a swarm of bees before Herbie returns at 3.12 for another bite of the honeycomb. At 3.41, Herbie does his own impression of winged creatures before a brief drum interlude from journeyman drummer Mickey Roker brings the players back to a repeat of the intro.

The title track is a gentle Latin swing that is entirely unchallenging for Roker. There are nice brassy colours painted over the rather mysterious theme that twists through the scales whilst still managing to sound attractive. Once again, the horns are used entirely for background colour. Ron's beautifully recorded bass is constantly probing the harmonies yet solidly supporting Herbie's explorations. The written content of the piece is significant here and the result is a very classy piece of music that is tight and harmonically exciting. As a result of this track being digitally remastered in 2004, Herbie was awarded a Grammy for "Best Jazz Instrumental Solo".

Next is *First Trip*, the only one of the six selections written by Ron Carter. It's a real swinger that comes as a welcome change after so many of Herbie's increasingly deep constructions of late. Carter is a very clever writer too, as evidenced by his contributions to Miles's band in the face of very strong competition from Wayne and Herbie. The rest of the band sits this one out as the very likeable tune moves energetically towards its faded ending.

The horns are back for *Toys*, a pensive, moderately paced piece that seems to depict that well-known scene from the film Toy Story, set in a darkened bedroom at midnight as the lid to the toy box mysteriously rises and all the toys come out to play. This is fun, but slightly unsettling.

Herbie's eulogy *Goodbye to Childhood* is an altogether sadder tale. Once again, the horns are used around the outer wrappings, but the core of the piece is a complex melodic pattern that most listeners will find either entrancing or depressing because of its constantly churning harmonies and untouchable melody. It's as if Herbie too is sad to report the end of those days of innocence when the world is limited only by one's imagination.

Fortunately, the magic returns for *The Sorcerer*, a fast, swinging piece with a fine melody that, like the magician's secrets, is difficult to discover unless you know the piece well. It's a composition that Herbie returns to many times over the coming years for his live gigs.

From Acoustic to Electric

On 4 December 1967 there was a most unusual event in the Columbia recording studios in New York's 30th Street. On return from his autumn tour of Europe, Miles had assembled his band for some recording sessions, as usual, looking ahead to the next year. But he knew that change was on the horizon and the studio work at this point was more about experiment than the recording of tracks for a specific album release. His usual band was present, but so was a 22-year-old electric guitarist from Philadelphia, Joe Beck, whom Miles knew from his work with the Gil Evans Orchestra. Miles had not recorded with an electric guitarist in a small group setting since the early 1950s, and this was an entirely new direction that was a direct result of the impact that the electric guitar was having on the wider world of music. Miles was already listening to the music of James Brown, Muddy Waters and even Jimi Hendrix, with whom he would soon become friends. With the passing of Miles's close friend John Coltrane in July 1967, another era in jazz seemed to have ended. Tingen believes that Coltrane's death had been another factor in making Miles rethink his approach. [26]

So, with a band that now included the electric guitar as a foreground instrument for the first time, Miles made a couple of takes of a piece called *Circle in the Round*. For the first time on record Herbie played a celeste. The celeste (or celesta) is a piano-like instrument having a keyboard but with fewer octaves. Its sound is, however, not at all like a piano, but rather like a glockenspiel, with a softer, subtler timbre. The instrument is not electric and it is most unusual in a jazz environment, clearly part of the experiment. According to Cook, Herbie's use of the celeste "shifts him to a halfway-house between the acoustic instrument and the tinkling shimmer of the electric keyboard, which Davis would oblige him to use next." [27]

On 28 December 1967 the same band was in the studio again. This time they recorded *Water on the Pond*. This was Herbie's debut on the Fender Rhodes electric piano that Miles had bought for him. Cook: "The leader had had the idea after hearing Joe Zawinul play an electric piano with Cannonball Adderley's band, a device that had seemed to make Adderley's music funkier as well as more obviously electric in feel." [27] Herbie: "...I came into the studio and there was no acoustic piano to be seen, but in the corner was a Fender Rhodes, an instrument I'd never played before. So I asked Miles what he wanted me to play and he said, 'Play that!' I was thinking, 'That toy? Oh, Okay then...' I turned it on and played a chord and it sounded beautiful with a really warm bell-like sound. I learned that night not to form an opinion about things you have no experience of." [28]

Herbie's next outing for Miles was on 12 January 1968 in Columbia Studio B where he recorded *Fun*, again playing Fender Rhodes, but this time with another electric guitarist, Bucky Pizzarelli. The music had a fast 3/4 metre with Williams doubling the tempo on hi-hat. It showed no signs of leaning towards the fusion of rock rhythms, although the choice of instrumentation is clearly designed to create a different sound. None of these three tracks were released until years later. Today, of course, the recordings are precious statements of an important time of transition in the history of jazz.

Leaving Miles

The experiments continued throughout the early part of 1968. More sessions took place with guitarists Joe Beck and George Benson. On 16th February, Miles's entire band became absorbed into the Gil Evans Orchestra for some tapings of a piece called *Falling Water*. Then it was back to the bread-winning club gigs until May when Miles's band – without an electric guitarist present - recorded the rest of the music for the album *Miles in the Sky* (1968). One track from the January recordings, *Paraphernalia*, with George Benson on guitar, made it onto the album.

But there was greater change afoot and that summer the end of Herbie's time as a member of one of the most highly regarded bands of all time came unexpectedly during the recordings for the album *Filles de Kilimanjaro* (1968).

The tracks *Tout de Suite, Petits Machins* and *Filles de Kilimanjaro* had been recorded on 19, 20 and 21 June 1968. Miles was by now aware that Herbie and Tony Williams were thinking of leaving his band to form their own groups. Ron Carter was purportedly growing tired of touring and wanted to spend more time in New York. Miles thought he had other motivations too. In his autobiography, he wrote: "for all intents and purposes the group broke up when Ron decided to leave for good because he didn't want to play electric bass." [29] In July he replaced Ron temporarily with Miroslav Vitous, who would later become a co-founder of jazz-fusion megaband Weather Report.

After several occasions when Miles was forced to hire deputies for the bass position, Miles decided the time had come for a permanent change. During August, Miles recruited a new bass player from England, Dave Holland. Herbie accepted the job of welcoming Holland to the USA one Thursday in August, ready to play a series of gigs at Count Basie's Club the following night. The detailed story is well recounted by Carr. [30] It was a typical case of a new face turning up on the night with almost no preparation and no rehearsal and being expected to play straight off.

As with everything Miles did, there was a curious twist, especially in view of the fact that he believed Ron Carter would not play the *electric* bass. Presumably he had broached the idea of using electric bass with Ron and received a cool response. So, despite all that we are supposed to believe about Miles 'going electric' at this point, it comes as a surprise that Holland believed that Davis had hired him because of his work on the acoustic bass. "Miles had seen me play acoustic bass in a very conventional jazz context. As far as Miles knew, I only played acoustic bass. There was no electric bass at all in the music and he never asked me to play electric bass. I was playing only acoustic for the first year. I still played acoustic on *Bitches Brew*, and I volunteered to play electric bass after that because I felt the music needed it." [31] Miles's autobiography backs it up to some extent: "Dave Holland played the stand-up bass and I could groove behind that in a way that I couldn't when Harvey Brooks brought in his electric bass sound. [32] ... My interest was in finding an electronic bass player because of the sound it added to my band. I was still on the lookout for someone who would eventually play that instrument all the time in my band, because I didn't know then if Dave would want to switch to playing that instrument." [33]

With the Basie's Club gigs over, Herbie went off to get married and left right away for his honeymoon in Brazil. On the first night he got food poisoning and a doctor told him to stay in bed as he had a swollen liver. Then came a call from Miles's agent that the band had a gig and could Herbie get back for it? Clearly the answer was no, so at the last minute Miles hired Chick Corea. It turned out to be more than a casual job for Corea: once Miles had seen him perform, he could see the shape of a new band forming. Corea was immediately hired for the final recording sessions of *Filles de Kilimanjaro* at which the tracks *Mademoiselle Mabry (Miss Mabry)* and *Frelon Brun (Brown Hornet)* were laid down. Miles's new album stands as a marker of a great change in jazz history, straddling two of the most significant phases in the history of jazz. Meanwhile, Herbie had been fired – well, sort of.

Though he was no longer a member of what Miles called his 'working band', he had not fallen out with Miles. There was an open invitation for Herbie to turn up at recording sessions, which he continued to do until July 1972 at the end of the sessions for *On the Corner* (1972). Herbie went back into the studio during September and November 1968 for what are now known as the sessions that formed part of the project *In A Silent Way* (1969). Herbie and Chick *both* played electric pianos in what was now a sextet, alongside Miles, Wayne and Tony, with Holland on bass. Not all of the tracks recorded (including the earlier experiments with electric guitar at the end of 1967) were released on the original album *In A Silent Way*. Some were held over in the vaults for release on *Water Babies* (1976), *Circle in the Round* (1979) and *Directions* (1981). Others were not released until the publication of the *Complete In A Silent Way Sessions* (2001). Again, there was no electric guitar present. Miles seemed to be hedging his bets because the inclusion of an electric guitar in jazz music at this point was a statement of serious musical intent that he seemed not yet ready for.

In February 1969, the experiments continued, again with Herbie and Chick on keyboards, but now the band was an octet with a *third* keyboardist, Joe Zawinul. Once again, an electric guitar was included. This time Miles seemed to have made up his mind by employing a brilliant young electric guitarist from England called John McLaughlin. It wasn't until November, after Miles had once more returned from his European tour, that Herbie recorded with the band again.

Herbie Hancock: *The Prisoner* - 1969 (***)

Herbie Hancock was heavily involved in what are now regarded as the seminal sessions at which Miles Davis converted his band from acoustic into electric. He therefore played a significant early role in the establishment of a new genre of music later called jazz-rock fusion – the assimilation of elements of rock music into jazz. Oddly, as far as his own recordings were concerned, Herbie seems to have remained on the sidelines of jazz-fusion. Miles had left the acoustic piano behind to concentrate on electric sounds. For the time being, at least, Herbie wanted to continue to use acoustic sounds in hios own projects. In the spring of 1969, he brought together his largest band yet for a new album that would once again embrace a theme. This time the mood shifted from the fantastic voyages of discovery and the magic of childhood to the real world and the oppressed state of black people in the USA. These issues had come to a head in the mid-1960s and climaxed with two terrible murders. In 1968, the Civil Rights Act came into force in the United States, but two of its leading supporters, Martin Luther King and Robert Kennedy had both been shot dead. It is hardly surprising that political matters were at the top of the agenda, and black musicians were as keen to express their views as any other group of citizens.

The cover of *The Prisoner* (1969) shows a caged Herbie Hancock. This music was recorded on 18, 21 and 23 April 1969 barely one year after Dr King's assassination on 4 April 1968 and only nine months after Robert Kennedy's death on 6 June 1968. We might have expected a bucketful of anger - an opportunity for Herbie to indulge in the kind of free jazz that enraged members of the audience at Cecil Taylor concerts. However, that's not what we get with this album. The titles clearly refer to current political topics, but the music is almost defiant in its refusal to shout in protest.

Uniquely, Herbie uses two groups, each of nine musicians to purvey his latest ideas epitomised by the opening track, *I Have A Dream*. The band is essentially a sextet comprised of Herbie with Johnny Coles, Garnett Brown, Joe Henderson, Buster Williams and Albert Heath. However, supplementary musicians were employed in permutations that made it a nine-piece band for the ensemble work. As on *Speak Like a Child* (1968), Herbie goes for a mix of instruments that emphasise the mellower tones: flügelhorn (Johnny Coles) rather than trumpet, alto flute (Joe Henderson) as well as flute (Hubert Laws or Jerome Richardson), bass clarinet (Romeo Penque or Jerome Richardson) instead of clarinet and bass trombone (Tony Studd or Jack Jeffers) as well as trombone (Garnett Brown). Buster Williams was now the favoured bass player, a musician who had been making a name for himself with the Jazz Crusaders in California, and Albert 'Tootie' Heath played drums.

I Have A Dream opens in a style we associate more with Gil Evans than Herbie's style to date. Clearly influenced by his closeness to Gil Evans and by his own recent experiences of composing film scores, the rich orchestration of this track is intriguing as it flexes across the chord changes Herbie has devised. There's lots of horn colour, but the composition has essentially abandoned playing in a given key with its related chords and changes – what Herb Wong called a "pervasive tonal center". [34] This music is freed from those kinds of boundaries that, whilst lending modernity to the sound, make it less accessible to untrained ears. Herbie takes the lead solo, followed by flügel and sax. The choice of Johnny Coles is interesting for his looseness of pitch. It won't go down well with some listeners but is a clear characteristic of this kind of jazz that Herbie considers to be at the cutting edge in 1969. Joe Henderson on tenor saxophone demonstrates his propensity to play freely, whilst respecting the composer's pre-defined boundaries. At times, it's as if his choices of scale are running parallel to the ones being played by the rest, a technique much explored by Michael Brecker. Overall, the impression left by this track is always positive rather than negative as Herbie's natural optimism takes charge.

The polarity reverses, however, for *The Prisoner*, as the title might suggest. It's a much freer vehicle for the main players to explore and the result is a negative tension as the main characters work out just how tortuous the escape route is from the harmonic prison of modern jazz. This is a complex and very advanced musical painting. An opening Gil Evans-type theme is soon set aside by Cole's frothy line to the accompaniment of some jagged flute tones. With an early drum break from 0.52 that sets the scene for the energetic development of the core improvisation, Tootie Heath shows he is a good substitute for Tony Williams. Then Joe Henderson begins a long and fascinating tenor sax journey that exhorts us to find the key to his cuffs. Chaotic though this all may sound at first, the team is working to some careful orchestration and listeners can have a lot of fun working it out, especially as many of the features that might sound pre-planned are actually spontaneous interactions. (The solution, of course, is to be found in a comparison with the alternate takes available on the RVG edition.) Herbie plays a similarly searching solo with some orchestrated motifs until the piece runs out of steam at 6.32. But it's a false ending and the piece ends as it started with a final flügelhorn flourish and a run on the electric piano that is almost an afterthought.

Firewater is a conventional 'swing' jazz number, written by Buster Williams and so it is clearly different from the other pieces. It is by far the most accessible of the tracks. There is little that is memorable about *He Who Lives in Fear* except the strong correlation between the mood of the piece and its title. Almost exclusively a piano trio played in a robust, brisk style, the entire mood is depressing and it feels like it would be well placed as part of Herbie's *Death Wish* movie score. The original recording ends with *Promise of the Sun*, which does have a hook in the form of a recurring four-note motif and swings with rather more optimism. Once again, the orchestral colour is restricted to the top and tail of the piece, as the bulky filling is taken up with the piano trio.

As a musician now working for himself outside the protective envelope of a leader like Miles, on this album Herbie seems keen to make his statement even more meaningful and appealing. For the sleeve notes he told his interviewer that he was aiming to appeal to and communicate with people [35] but I would have to disagree with the idea that there are singable, memorable tunes on this album. I do not believe that 'ordinary people' can hum or remember tunes such as these with no "pervasive tonal center." Indeed, it's left to Buster Williams to provide the most user-friendly music on the album. That's not to say that the album is not a success: the title track at least is quite superb. Apart from the obvious connotations of the titles and the artwork, the theme does not actually permeate the music in an impressionistic sense, at least. The album is not so much a protest about the suppression of civil rights of African-American people as it is an invitation to those in his band to demonstrate how free they are in the environment he has created for them. In that respect, it is partly successful even though the opportunities to solo are few for the band members. The music goes about its business successfully, even if, in retrospect, it was at serious risk of being swept aside by the jazz-rock maelstrom. Blumenthal sensed this at the time as he wrote about his disappointment with the album, not just for its lack of electric sounds, but also for its lack of solos. [36] but then described how in April 1970 the same sextet had blown him away at a live gig with extended solos, even greater freedom of performance and with Herbie exclusively playing electric piano. It should not therefore surprise us that this recording would mark the end of this particular phase of Herbie's career.

Recording with Blue Note

Liberty Records acquired Blue Note in 1965, and Albert Lion, Hancock's producer, sponsor and early mentor, retired in 1967. At this point, Wolff or pianist Duke Pearson produced most Blue Note albums. (Wolff died in 1971.) The music business was in the midst of a serious metamorphosis brought about by the enormous impact of rock. Despite a few commercially successful albums, the shock waves from the rock music explosion had seriously affected the viability of jazz, yet jazz was not helping itself by continuing to indulge in forms of musical expression that the public did not wish to buy. Blue Note had specialised in jazz from the bop and avant-garde genres – all played with traditional acoustic instruments – and the company did not see its future with artists from the 'modern' tradition in which electric instruments were the norm. In 1969 United Artists purchased Liberty Records and the associated Blue Note brand. (When EMI purchased United Artists in 1979 it phased out the Blue Note label until 1985 when it was re-launched as part of EMI Manhattan Records.)

Throughout the 1960s, Herbie came to know the Van Gelder studios in Englewood Cliffs, New Jersey as a second home. Recording engineer Rudy Van Gelder had opened the studios in 1959 and they quickly became established as one of the foremost venues to record jazz in the USA. Just as the many virtuoso musicians who walked through his doors, Van Gelder was a virtuoso in his own business. He got the famous architect Frank Lloyd Wright to build him a cutting-edge recording studio that would become world-renowned. Girtler wrote: "In the high-domed, wooden-beamed, brick-tiled, spare modernity of Rudy Van Gelder's studio, one can get a feeling akin to religion". [37] Herbie had recorded all of his own albums there, and as one of the nation's leading pianists, had been hired to play as a sideman on a large number of albums by other leading musicians such as Blue Mitchell, Hank Mobley, Lee Morgan, Jackie McLean, Stanley Turrentine, Kenny Burrell, Tony Williams, Freddie Hubbard, Donald Byrd and, of course, Miles. Herbie had also become close friends with the saxophonist from Miles's band, Wayne Shorter, and Wayne used Herbie on a number of his own albums from December 1964 to August 1969. The two men would work together consistently afterwards.

Herbie Hancock: *Fat Albert Rotunda* – 1969 (***)

The story goes that in 1968 Herbie Hancock decided to get married and chose to take his bride to Brazil for their honeymoon. Unfortunately Herbie contracted food poisoning and his return to the USA was delayed. However, Miles Davis was a man on a mission and, by the time that Hancock returned, Chick Corea had taken his seat. Herbie found himself unemployed, despite having been Davis's premier keyboardist over the years since 1963. To make matters worse, Hancock's own contract with Blue Note had run out too.

Though he had lost his job and his record contract with Blue Note, Hancock was not one to let the grass grow under his feet. He immediately obtained a contract for a series of albums with Warner Brothers, Columbia's main competitor at that time. He accepted a commission to compose music for a TV show that featured Bill Cosby. An album that resulted from this work was *Fat Albert Rotunda* (1969), and, even though it was now for the Warners label, not Blue Note, he recorded it at Van Gelder's studio in New Jersey.

It's easy to suggest that an album of music written for a movie or TV show must be, by definition, inferior. After all, the composer is required to fulfil a particular commercial specification, rather than enjoy complete artistic freedom. Nevertheless, in this case, it's hard to argue the case for or against without additional knowledge that I do not possess. What I can say is that this album is notable for several reasons. It is the first of Hancock's records exclusively using the electric piano. *Albert* is also an especially funky album, which for its time was innovative. Hancock's career as a premier league musician recording mainstream jazz was over for the time being. Many jazz fans hated the change of genre and accused him of selling out. No-one could have guessed that this would be only a flash in the pan and that Hancock's career would take another twist on the next album.

I want to give Herbie full credit for this progression into funk, but this record suffers from its dependence on the mind-numbing boredom of the single chord vamp. Music formats don't get much simpler than this, and, adapted from black funk music, it became the template for much early fusion music. On paper, the band looks pretty impressive with a line-up of Joe Henderson (sax, flute), Johnny Coles (trumpet), Garnett Brown (trombone), Buster Williams (electric and acoustic bass), and Tootie Heath (drums). After a very strange intro with lots of tinny musings, the band gets off to a promising start with *Wiggle-Waggle*, a kind of 12-bar blues chopped down to eight. It's the kind of thing we've all heard a lot now, but this was a trailblazer and even today is a real foot-tapper. Intrinsically it's a simple piece in what is now regarded a classic format; many a school band would make a great attempt at playing this today. Henderson gets away with a good solo and we need to remind ourselves that this kind of solo was still quite underdeveloped and explains why parts sound rather immature. Once again, Johnny Coles's loose harmonic style sounds simply erratic and unprofessional to the uneducated ear, but rest assured, it's meant to sound like this! Hancock is up next and, of course, sounds like he's been playing electric piano for a century – his playing is by far the most mature of the band.

Albums that start off with a rip-roaring track can go in one of two ways. Sadly, this one takes the wrong direction. *Fat Mama* is the first of the dreadful vamps. The first minute gives the theme, which is pleasant enough, if rather facile, and if it were followed up with some new ideas it could have been a good follow-on to *Wiggle-Waggle*. Instead, it drones on like an old vinyl with a stuck needle. There's very little attempt even to develop an improvisation, and I suspect that this is a result of the prescription for TV.

Tell Me A Bedtime Story redresses the balance on the positive side and for the first time we get some really nice splashes of the colour of jazz-fusion. The band is tight, and Heath's drums are both creative and impeccably timed to Hancock. The wind instruments, led by Henderson on flute, are well blended and the piece is structurally and harmonically interesting. The formula is balanced more to orchestration than improvisation, but that's not such a bad thing when the music is good and this formula will be well used in the future in many of the pieces I shall describe later.

With *Oh! Oh! Here He Comes* it's back to the boring vamps. The groove is fine – better than on *Fat Mama* – but if only Hancock could have seen fit to introduce some variety! Williams seems unsure about how to play electric bass in this style and the sound of it is ridiculous when viewed from 2006. We won't hold that against him: Jaco Pastorius is still only an unknown teenager.

Jessica is an interesting slow ballad with some edgy harmonies and a melody much more in the style of his compositions for Blue Note. Herbie is back on acoustic piano and the new jazz-fusion style is on the back burner. This is a very good piece that is out of context on this album. *Fat Albert Rotunda* is yet another vamp cloned from the two previous ones. Henderson does his best to liven up the proceedings with a tenor sax solo that's desperate to break out of the harmonic shackles, but there's nothing more to say about these six and a half extremely monotonous, monochrome minutes.

Lil' Brother is a better attempt to create some lively funk, but this time Henderson is well out of his depth with some rather poor improvisations. A guitarist, unmentioned in the sleeve notes and who is also clearly heard on the previous track, displays his own immature ideas of working with the new genre. I think this last track sums up the whole album. Apart from *Jessica*, which is a composition from a different box entirely, we have been presented with a collection of primitive ideas that, in the words of teacher, "shows promise, but could do better". We're going to have to wait until 1974 before Hancock is ready to move in the direction that jazz-fusion demands, by which time his competitors will already be there. In the meantime, Hancock, still convinced that he should work in free-jazz, was heading into the abstract.

Herbie Hancock: *Baraka* – 1969 (**)

An album released more recently is of a collection of tracks led by the Heath Brothers (Tootie and Jimmy), but now marketed, for obvious commercial reasons, under Herbie's name. Albert 'Tootie' Heath had already become friends with Herbie and recorded on both *The Prisoner* (1969) and *Fat Albert Rotunda* (1969). His brother was saxophonist Jimmy Heath and a third brother Percy (not present here) played bass. The brothers had been much influenced by Ornette Coleman and the free jazz movement, and had been making their own contributions throughout the 1960s. On 11 December 1969, at an unknown location, Albert and Jimmy convened with Herbie and others to record some exploratory music. It does not appear to have been released contemporarily, but is available today with the title *Baraka* (2005) and (misleadingly) *The Very Best of Herbie Hancock* (2006). The cover picture of Baraka gives the impression that this is a live album, which it is not – at least, not in the sense that it was recorded in front of a live audience.

For their one-off adventure, they had successfully recruited Coleman's trumpeter colleague, Don Cherry, and his percussionist Ed Blackwell. The line-up was completed by Buster Williams and Billy Bonner (flute). The music is clearly a jazz-fusion, but not one of jazz-rock. Hogeland writes: "The sound these artists achieve is classic for the period: the adventurous soloing ... is held within groove-oriented, funk influenced rhythms representing the best of what was called jazz-rock fusion – whose antecedents here, as in much of Hancock's ... work in particular, are more in soul, salsa and African traditional and pop music than in rock." [38]

A young man, born James Forman of Philadelphia, also played a big part in the proceedings. He was Jimmy's son. Now calling himself James Mtume, he had adopted an African name and was establishing himself as a percussionist and composer of free-form jazz. He would later become a percussionist with Miles's band for no less than five years from 1971-76. The recordings were entitled *Baraka*, *Maulana*, *Kawaida*, *Dunia* and *Kamili*. All were composed by Mtume, except for *Dunia*, which had been created by Tootie.

Kamili is a beautiful piece that is conventionally placed in jazz and has echoes of Herbie's *Maiden Voyage* in the way is oscillates about two key centres. Even allowing for the liberated excesses of free-form jazz, of which there is a range here from the 'mild' (*Baraka*) to the 'quite extreme' (*Dunia*), the depths are truly plumbed in *Kawaida*, a mixture of spoken and wholly improvised sounds. The words are a kind of moral prospectus for the African people that I could never criticise. As an 'entertainment' this is a non-starter, but Herbie's participation is perhaps an indication of the development of his personal philosophy as an African-American. We shall see, for example, how (with Buster Williams) he shortly forms an entirely new kind of band in which the musicians, like Mtume, adopt African names.

Herbie Hancock: *Mwandishi* – 1971 (*)

After poor sales of *Fat Albert Rotunda* (1969), the first Warner album, Hancock was adjudged not to be producing material that was satisfactorily commercial so Warner Brothers brought in a new producer, David Rubinson to give Hancock some direction. They formed a strong professional relationship that lasted well over a decade. Rubinson was born in 1942 in Brooklyn, New York. In 1963 he graduated in English from Columbia University and worked as an Associate Producer at Capitol Records during 1963-4. He was with Columbia Records as a staff producer from 1964-69, after which he went into partnership with Bill Graham in the Fillmore Corporation in San Francisco. There, from inside the management team of Fillmore West, Rubinson was involved with recording the fledgling rock band Santana when they debuted in 1968; amazingly, the music was not released until 1997. Rubinson formed David Rubinson and Friends Inc. in 1971, a production company responsible for many albums in Herbie's mid-career. Five years later, Rubinson built the Automatt, the first automated recording studios in San Francisco. He retired from record production in 1983 to concentrate on management and film production.

Warner Brothers wanted Hancock to create music that had more potential for profit, but the outcome was not what they had intended. A series of three albums was released under the banner of a band called Mwandishi. Hancock added the synthesizer of Patrick Gleason to his echoplexed, fuzz-wah-pedaled electric piano and clavinet, and the recordings became spacier and more complex rhythmically and structurally, creating their own corner of the avant-garde that the record-buying public continued to ignore. He became deeply immersed in electronics and soon was able to create entirely new music using large arrays of keyboards. The 'group improvisation' approach was essentially the same that Weather Report had decided to use. With Anthony Braxton, Chick Corea was adopting a similar, though more outrageous, approach in their band, Circle. Hancock: "We decided it would be interesting to approach the music as a group solo. We wanted to share creativity and didn't want to be bound by traditional jazz conventions."

In this incarnation, Hancock, now 31, was interested in promoting his African heritage, so, along with the other members of his sextet, he adopted an alternative name from Swahili. Hancock used *Mwandishi* meaning writer/composer, whilst trumpeter Eddie Henderson, a qualified psychiatrist, used *Mganga* (Doctor of Advice). Saxophonist Bennie Maupin called himself *Mwile* (Body of Good Health), trombonist Julian Priester used *Pep Mtoto* (Spirit Child), Buster Williams chose *Mchezaji* (Player) which was appropriate for playing bass, whilst Billy Hart thought *Jabali* (Strength) most suitable for a drummer.

It's notable that, even now, the albums are attributed to Herbie Hancock himself (under an African pseudonym) rather than under the name of a band. Throughout his career, Hancock has rarely allowed himself to become absorbed into a band, preferring to retain his musical independence. Each of the three Mwandishi albums has only three tracks, which is always disconcerting when you decide to buy an album 'cold'. At record store prices, there is a strong risk of feeling seen off. It's much more of a fair gamble buying an album that has more tracks because of the increased chance of there being at least a couple that you like. This is almost never compensated by the music contained in the long tracks themselves, even when they contain different sections.

The first track, *Ostinato (Suite For Angela)*, is a good example of a whole style of playing that Hancock and Co. purposefully designed. Thus, it is worth analysing in a little detail because it helps to explain a lot of the rest of the music on the three Mwandishi albums.

As well as introducing an ever-increasing number of electronic sounds, Hancock's plan throughout the Mwandishi project was to experiment with unusual time signatures, in this case, 15/4. Now, it's all very well writing music with fifteen beats to a bar, but it is most unnatural and everyone – including the musicians – will split the music into an eight followed by a seven. The style is that of a vamp. There are effectively just two chords throughout the entire piece

– one on the first eight beats and the other on the seven. There is no melody, little harmony to speak of, which means that there is nothing here that most people would describe as beautiful. In fact, the bass has a line that is repeated continuously in the foreground and it is this that becomes the *de facto* melody or theme that the musicians use as a focus for what they play. Then it's a matter of how far they wish to deviate from the theme. By the end of this piece the bass phrase is so firmly planted in your head that you carry it around in your head all day long. It's like some kind of Chinese water torture with the constant drip, drip, drip hammering at the door of your brain – you *will* learn this line, you *will* learn this line...

It's worth pointing out that this sad devaluation of the bass is a feature of the leading edge of jazz, as was being defined by Miles Davis at this time. Completely constrained and with little or no scope to contribute anything of significance to a piece, the bass is sacrificed in favour of other instruments. (Remember, Dave Holland played just two or three notes in *Bitches Brew*.) It left the field wide open for other electric bass players to clean up and it's hardly surprising that people such as Jaco Pastorius and Stanley Clarke would soon emerge to re-invent bass playing.

Tempo can be accelerated and decelerated at will when the musicians understand each other, and tensions can be created or relaxed by varying the intensity of their improvisations. The band is playing tightly together so this is done carefully and with success. The rhythm is solid and, together with the repetitive bass almost hypnotic. It may be that this type of idea is the forerunner of trance music. I do not intend to imply that Hancock was involved in drugs at this point but we have to admit that most jazz musicians were drug users at certain times in their careers and this kind of music is strongly associated with the abuse of drugs, having grown out of the psychedelic period of the mid- to late-1960s. The music passes through a series of sections, pretty much as we might expect with bass and drums sustaining the theme whilst keyboards and horns take turns to lead. The use of bass clarinet adds a certain additional texture and colour to what would otherwise be a drab pastiche. Altogether, the track is a mixed bag with some interest, excitement and clear evidence of good musicianship, but leaves me feeling that my time is wasted listening to this.

You'll Know When You Get There is a rather different offering. The music is calm and constructive with some pleasant harmonies, and there is structure that is all too difficult to discover. But the lead instruments never present us with anything we might recognise as a theme or melody. Occasional sections of ensemble playing offer us some firmer ground, but the rest is quite aimless and there is too much uncertainty for us to feel any association with what is going on.

Wandering Spirit Song is a track of more than twenty minutes that surely does its fair share of wandering and, clearly lost, ends up in no-man's-land. Once again, we are presented with extended sections of music with nothing to welcome us inside. Like the second track, the music is, for the first ten minutes or so, quite soothing and does not make me feel alienated, but neither does it stir any sign of emotion or excitement. From about eleven minutes into the recording Bennie Maupin takes the music head on with his awful bass clarinet, making an already miserable instrument sound utterly guttural. No doubt, that was intended. This is followed by almost total degeneration into noise, at which point I am certain I have wasted my money. Sadly, the story does not end here.

Herbie Hancock: *Crossings* – 1972 (*)

With the album *Crossings*, Hancock was clearly aiming to continue with the kind of project begun a year earlier. The band is the same and the music is similar in many ways: interesting at times, lively at others and with some atmospherics, but there is never any opportunity for the listener to own this music. It's just something that goes on in my house. I always feel that it's like I have a Japanese guest in my house and we don't speak each other's language. What a waste! There's so much we could find out about each other but there is no strand of commonality between us; you can't hold a deep conversation with sign language. Given that there are so many other far better albums from the same period it is hard to understand why I would waste my money buying it, or my time playing it. I get far more pleasure from having guests I can talk to.

Sleeping Giant is a complex construction that lasts for almost twenty-five minutes. It begins with a section of improvisation on African drums and percussion, whilst some background electronic sounds make the music sound like the accompaniment to another of James Bond's semi-night-time forays into the jungle of the current bad guy's remote uninhabited island. At 2.30 we emerge into the daylight of a structured piece set in fast 3/8 time or an up-tempo 4/4 time played in triplets – whatever you prefer. Herbie plays an extended theme on electric piano whilst the percussion holds up the original fast pace. Buster Williams is improvising alongside him on bass mostly throughout. At 7.15 the pace stops and becomes *a tempo*. The rest of the band now begins to play some atmospheric lines that are written and have some good harmonies over some intriguing chord sequences. At 9.17 we hear a really funky bass line from Buster Williams that is too prematurely conceived to take us where we would like to go, but is very good for the time in which it is being played. It's a cue for some group improvisations from the others, with trombone leading. However, by 11.10 the piece becomes funky again with bass lines on guitar and synthesiser working in unison. By 12.45 the music has faded into another freely timed link section to what becomes at 13.35 another funky incarnation with Hancock leading on another electric piano solo that completes at 16.20 with a cool coda and chord. The next section is a free improvisation with Williams and Maupin into which the others gradually intrude, picking up on another up tempo 4/4 section of vamp with Maupin leading. At 22.10 the section is abruptly ended and another timeless link introduces the final flourish of improvised wind sounds. This composition is a lively and interesting piece that represented a promising start for the album.

Quasar, on the other hand, is a most uninteresting assembly of bits and pieces in which nothing comes to the fore except continuing ad libs from lead instruments recorded with lots of reverb. Furthermore, *Water Torture* displays most of the characteristics that Miles Davis was using on *Bitches Brew* and *Live Evil*. Thus, the album that promised much with its good opening track ends in disappointment. Some listeners will feel that this track is aptly titled. The sleeve notes to the album contend that Hancock was influenced by Sun Ra at this point but he had certainly been influenced by Miles too!

Herbie Hancock: *Sextant* – 1973 (*)

Having given Herbie three albums to produce something they could sell, Warner could be forgiven for feeling that he had failed them. Nevertheless, his stock was still very good. In 1973, Herbie signed a worldwide recording contract for Columbia Records, joining the same house that was publishing Miles's music. As we shall see later, Herbie also signed a separate deal that allowed him to record special projects for Sony (Japan). Curiously, although these projects would be ideal to accompany his Japanese tours, at the time, they were not considered commercial enough for Columbia's worldwide record distributions. The result would be the creation of a small treasure trove of material that even today has not had its rightful degree of exposure.

Hancock's band Mwandishi was still intact and Columbia accepted the same format for a third Mwandishi album. *Sextant* is probably the most experimental of the three Mwandishi albums. Again, the format was the one being promoted by Miles Davis that extended the practice of free improvisation over minimum compositional structures. As Davis was also finding out, this music did not go down well with the record-buying public, and although Hancock had been told this at the start of the Mwandishi project, he was only just beginning to realise it.

The album consisted of three tracks: *Rain Dance*, *Hidden Shadows* and *Hornets*. Some extremely advanced improvisation is found on the tracks *Hornets* and *Hidden Shadows* (which has a time signature of 19/4). The band was clearly fulfilling its aim of establishing the sound of the synthesiser as the way forward that others should follow! The trouble is that, like kids let loose in a toyshop, they just seemed to try at random every possible sound that was available to them. Among the many instruments Hancock used were Fender Rhodes piano, ARP Odyssey, ARP Pro-Soloist Synthesizer and the Minimoog. Yes, it's true that free jazz had no rules governing such things, but it seemed to take musicians a long time to appreciate that, to the ears of those not actually making the sounds, the result was really rather awful. Hancock must have thought he was progressing, but from my point of view this album is the worst of the three. Electronics were making a huge impact upon the range of musical instruments that were available and, with his synthesiser representative Patrick Gleason, Herbie pulled in everything that was available for use on this record. Possibly foremost amongst them were the 2600 and soloist ARP synthesisers, but they used the Mellotron as well as the electric piano fitted with echoplex and a clavinet with both echoplex and fuzz-wah-wah! Somewhere amongst them a device called a phase shifter was also used.

One aspect of all three tracks is that they possess rhythm and are not entirely devoid of form. *Rain Dance* consists of a rhythmic sequence liberally punctuated by electronic noises that bear no relation to the title. The album's artwork misleads us into thinking that there is a link here to Africa and its people, whilst also proposing some extraterrestrial content, which is more accurate – it might as well have been played by Martians. On a superficial level, there is no structure, no theme, no melody, no harmony, no tension, no climax and no ending. As if that were not enough, at a deeper level there is no beauty, no humanity and no soul. The technology used in this way results in music that relates more to androids working on Ripley's alien space station than our planet or the humans who live on it. Is it surprising that so few copies of these discs are sold? Being devoid of all of the positive qualities I have listed does not invalidate the piece as a musical statement. In a world of free expression, artists are at liberty to create whatever they want, even if there are very few other humans who can relate to it. In further defence, it was created at a time when jazz-fusion and the electronic instrumentation was still novel. It was also a time when notions of the relationships between mankind and planet Earth were extremely immature. None of this, however, makes it more pleasurable listening.

Hidden Shadows is a kind of Martian slow funk, which is, I suppose, an advance on the previous piece and, once you overcome the initial reaction against the electronics you can discover elements of interest within. The main structure remains a Davis-style vamp over a single chord with some soloing. There's a theme and some traditional ensemble playing. It's the best of the three tracks; it's not horrible – just monotonous.

On an album lasting just thirty-nine minutes, more than nineteen of them are taken up with a tedious piece entitled *Hornets*. Bob Belden [39] describes the piece as a 'hardcore groove', and though I have to agree with that description, I believe that grooves are something to be eagerly anticipated – something that might get you going. Not this one. It is simply a long and very boring repetition of the same chord over which bass player Buster Williams plays mostly the same notes. Everything else is a frantic mess. There are recognisable sections during which band members take turns to make the lead noise, but noise is all it is, and even though it might bear some passing resemblance to flying insects, it hardly merits a waste of nineteen minutes of my listening time. An interesting footnote is that in 2001, this piece reappears on the album *Future 2 Future* where it is transformed into something really worth listening to.

The Mwandishi records received mixed reviews and sold poorly. After this album, even Herbie realised that a change of direction was urgently called for. It would lead him on to one of his greatest successes with his album *Head Hunters* (1974).

Herbie Hancock: *The Spook Who Sat By the Door* – 1973 (*)

Following his success with *Blow Up* (1966), Herbie continued his association with film scores by writing and producing the music for *The Spook Who Sat by the Door* (1973), a film directed by Ivan Dixon. The film is about the unsuccessful recruitment of a black agent into the CIA and his subsequent criminal activity. This soundtrack album is now very rare and, in any case, has very little interest to most music fans, except as an audio representation of the movie, which is very good, especially as there are significant clips of the dialog included. The music is very representative of the nature of the storyline, but it makes little sense without the visual images that they were designed to support. Of purely academic interest is the fact that the title track, *The Spook Who Sat By The Door*, was used on the album *Thrust* (1974), but renamed *Actual Proof* (see below). As such, it is an interesting early version of a great funk-jazz piece of the mid-1970s. Most of the other tracks are little more than short acoustic sketches, usually funk grooves continuously repeated. It may well have become a sampler's treasure trove years later.

Herbie Hancock: *Death Wish* – 1974 (*)

Herbie's next movie soundtrack was *Death Wish* (1974), directed by Michael Winner. The film starred Charles Bronson who played a vigilante avenging the death of his wife at the hands of a group of punks. Herbie's skills in composition and orchestration were now more important than his small group jazz chops. Nevertheless, his experience with free jazz was used to the full for the kind of music that sounds great when it accompanies images of violence and intrigue, but is much less appealing as stand-alone music. Whilst the title track is a lively piece of electric jazz that fusion fans will appreciate, the remainder of the tracks are too abstract to appeal to most palettes. Herbie sounds as if he is playing electric keyboards on the first track at least, but it is very difficult to discover the names of the musicians on the various tracks, a fact that further diminishes its value to present-day ears. Both of these movie soundtrack albums show how Herbie was developing his mastery of, what was then, an exponentially increasing number of synthetic keyboard sounds. As with much of the synthesiser-based music of this period, it sounds very dated today.

Herbie Hancock: *Head Hunters* – 1974 (*****)

Writing a short piece in 1996 for the sleeve notes of a reissue of *Head Hunters* Herbie was honest enough to admit that by 1972 his experiments in the kind of ethereal jazz he had been making with the Mwandishi sextet had run their course. Sales were poor and it was expensive to keep a sextet on full heat. Despite being an early exponent of jazz-fusion in his compositions *Watermelon Man* (1962) and *Cantaloupe Island* (1964), his soundtrack music for *Blow-Up* (1966) and a popular form of funk used on *Fat Albert Rotunda* (1969), he had not yet found his niche in the new world of jazz-fusion. His use of electrified keyboards had commenced in December 1967 at the behest of Miles, but he had continued to prefer the principles of mainstream and free jazz rather than backbeat-driven popular formats. Now, instead of further exploration of the "far-out, spacey stuff", Hancock decided it was time to reconnect with life on Earth [40] (That didn't seem to stop him using space and sci-fi themes on future albums, however!) He had been listening to Sly Stone and James Brown, and their music and rhythms had permeated his skin. He had also taken up Buddhism, and through his regular chanting, had found ideas about a funkier sound bubbling up inside. He decided he wanted to combine jazz and funk elements and struck it rich immediately. His next album was *Head Hunters* (1974), a monster album that became the first jazz album in history to go platinum – more than a million albums sold in the USA alone. The success he had enjoyed with the single track *Watermelon Man* was now repeated with an album.

Some would say that this album, recorded in 1973, placed him firmly at the forefront of jazz history. At the time of writing, my impression is that Herbie is the current grand master of jazz – the patriarch, for in a business that relies upon fame and sales, musical talent alone is not enough. Herbie probably made enough money from *Head Hunters* to have retired in the style of a rock superstar, but he is without doubt the most famous jazz musician alive today. It is also a well-known fact that for all his presence in the world of pop music, which was extensive throughout the 1970s and 80s, Herbie never felt limited to it and has consistently refused to be pigeon-holed in any given style of music. This creates problems for the average jazz listener who will almost certainly find a proportion of Hancock's albums unpalatable.

Some listeners may feel that *Chameleon* is too dated for them. Generally speaking, the best music stands the test of time by not becoming dated. Herbie retained the form of a vamp or groove for this composition. The six-note bass motif that opens the number is used pretty much throughout the piece. It is no consolation to be told that this music was "truly innovative" or "groundbreaking" – which, of course, it was. And the fact that it was such a chart-topping album counts for nothing with those who can see no further than the Afro hairstyles, the psychedelic outfits and flared trousers. The track is almost sixteen minutes in length and contains so much music that is not affected by fashion that we must try to overcome our natural inclination to turn our noses up at it.

The funk-filled intro is entirely unhurried, slowly developed and establishes a true groove. When the theme starts at 1.30, it is as a distillation of all the seventies cops and robbers movie themes. So there you have it! This music was the pattern on which so much later music was based, so much so that, if you were a teenager or in your early twenties during this period, it is now an integral part of your culture. The very act of taking a groove and repeating it 'endlessly' was a characteristic of the discotheque culture, fuelled, as it undoubtedly was for some, by marijuana, LSD or heroin.

Harvey Mason's drumming alone is a good reason for getting this album, not only on this track. From 4.00 Herbie takes an extended solo on synthesiser that pushes back some boundaries. Then at 7.38, after a review of the main theme, there is a new section with exceptional drum rhythms. Herbie moves from synthesiser to electric piano and the sound suddenly takes on a timeless character, a fact that identifies the contemporary synthesiser sounds as the source of old-fashioned-ness. Bill Summers adds a strongly sympathetic contribution on percussion and Paul Jackson is starting to make his electric bass sound more like the instrument we know today. A final interesting point about the track is the noticeable increase in tempo that takes place from beginning to end. Almost certainly this was not deliberate, although there is an increase in the drive and intensity of the playing. It is merely an indication of the lack of control in the recordings of the time. The blame would normally rest fare and square on the shoulders of the drummer, whose job it is to hold the tempo constant, but I hesitate to criticise Mason, who contributes so much other brilliance to this record.

Another interesting point is the small part played by Bennie Maupin. Though he does get a solo towards the end, he plays just a few bars with the main theme. The rest is a pure funk groove built upon the rock, rather than the jazz feel. Perhaps this is why it went down so well with the public at large, rather than jazz fans who were not sufficiently numerous to make this such a commercial success. So, overall, is this record now old-fashioned? Well, honestly yes, but it's still a fantastic sound.

I have already mentioned the next track *Watermelon Man*, the opening track of his first album and more than ten years ahead of its time when it was written. Back in 1962 Herbie had found the inner prescience to create a jazz-fusion hit of the future, long before anyone else had even considered blending the two genres. Herbie's other important composition, *Cantaloupe Island* (1964), bears the same hallmark, though it was nowhere near as big a hit at the time. In any case, the result was astonishing. *Watermelon Man* was covered the world over by bands of all persuasions, and Hancock found himself in constant demand to play it. It was even used in one of the last gigs that Miles Davis played, a star-studded reunion event in Paris in July 1991, recorded about ten weeks before his death. So here it is in glorious Technicolor on the *Head Hunters* album, but re-coloured by the *Chameleon* in the best tradition of jazz-fusion. The opening bars were the inspiration of Bill Summers wanting to create an African groove, but Harvey Mason drove the concept as a whole. The result is stunning. Here you can leave behind all your prejudices about old-fashioned music for this is truly timeless. This cool jazz groove is so delicious that you can easily miss the theme entirely, even though it must be known to a large percentage of the population of the developed world. Apparently, the opening bars were an appropriation of the sound of Central African pygmies.

The track *Sly* pays tribute to Sly Stone for it was Hancock's love of his funky style that provided the inspiration for this entire period of his career. [40] The tune begins in a minor key that sets up a subdued groove with lots of open space and no apparent reference to the highly-strung funk music associated with Sly Stone. Then, after about a minute and a half, there is a short burst of funk, followed by a move to an up-tempo improvisation on saxophone. The background adopts the same style that we find on so many recordings of this time – the single chord vamp. Here, Maupin's work lasts for three minutes. Then, after a short interlude Hancock replaces him on electric piano, driving at high speed across a similarly flat landscape. Once again, the drumming is exceptional for its time, and makes us wonder why Mason was not more famous. (Mason appears on Stanley Clarke albums in the late 1970s.) Overall, this is a highly rated track, though it does appear that the two long middle sections are entirely unrelated to the theme.

The final track is *Vein Melter* another groove-based slow piece laden with undisguised connotations to the drug use that was taking an ever-increasing hold on members of the new 'progressive' society. Again, there is no fashion baggage, just a sound picture that would have made Joe Zawinul proud. The theme is like an ice-cold coke (pun intended), the dark tones formulated as much from Maupin's bass clarinet – now sounding rather more appropriate – as from Hancock's rich keyboard musings. The rhythm is a pulse as much as a beat and the overall impression is perhaps more of the pleasure than the pain of drugs.

As well as being a pivotal, five-star jazz-fusion album, *Head Hunters* is an example of what would become known as crossover music, and is remarkable for a number of reasons. One of the strangest is that, in helping to define the new fusion music of jazz-rock, it did so without recourse to an electric guitar at a time when rock music was heavily dominated by electric guitars. Herbie knew all about the Mahavishnu Orchestra, and had been to their gigs, but, being a non-guitarist, he couldn't begin to compete with that sound and was not interested in following that band's path. Now his own significant commercial success in a more obviously jazzy environment than the apparently rock-infused Mahavishnu sound encouraged many people to experiment with jazz who would not otherwise have listened to it. Overall, *Head Hunters* should be on every jazz lover's shelf where it should not be allowed to gather dust.

Herbie Hancock: *Thrust* – 1974 (*****)

The introduction to *Palm Grease* is important for it immediately tells us what jazz-fusion rhythm is all about. It's worth remembering that, whilst Charlie Parker was reinventing saxophone playing in the 1940s, the techniques used on the other instruments advanced incrementally. Over a period of several decades, the playing of each instrument in turn was revolutionised, for example, guitar, by the likes of Hendrix, Page and Clapton, and piano by people such as Bud Powell and Bill Evans. Acoustic bass was inadequate for the demands of jazz-fusion until Jaco Pastorius and Stanley Clarke emerged to kick electric ass. Viewed from 2010, drumming in the 1960s had also become an embarrassment. Drummers raised on swing rhythm were most uncomfortable with the feel of jazz-fusion. Drummers like Philly Joe Jones (who Miles Davis really liked) began to sound almost primitive in the context of how music was evolving. For a time, Buddy Rich billed himself as the world's greatest, but on the basis of having the most highly developed technique in the 'traditional' style of mainstream jazz. Those 'in the know', however, voted Tony Williams as the best in the business during the years of the Second Great Quintet (1964-68). I argue that it was the influence of the jazz-fusion process that provided the momentum to *revolutionise* jazz drumming. Billy Cobham led the way for drumming on Mahavishnu Orchestra albums, and then on his own records from 1970, but the present new generation of jazz drummers began with Dave Weckl, who, for a time, was unquestionably the world's best with Vinnie Colaiuta and Dennis Chambers close behind. The change process from the fifties and early sixties drummers had been initiated by a number of people, of which Tony Williams, Harvey Mason and Mike Clark were but three. There are many others I could list, but we should also not forget the contributions made by the exceptional British drummers Jon Hiseman and Bill Bruford.

Hence, if *Head Hunters* had not already done so, this album is a fine example of the transition to the new style of jazz-fusion drumming. Drummer Mike Clark had been hired to replace Mason and with his playing on this track he proved immediately that the decision to hire him was the right one. The fantastic groove that he sets up with Hancock's funky synthesiser and Jackson's excellent bass line is absolutely humming. He's actually playing a common time 4/4 rhythm, but you wouldn't believe it until you count it yourself because it is so syncopated. It's not possible for us to imagine today just how amazing contemporary audiences found this innovative sound.

The overall sound of the band here was so good that it was copied many times during coming years, and reached many diverse locations. For example, from 1975 onwards, it influenced the music to TV cops-and-robbers series *Starsky and Hutch* (written by Tom Scott). At 2.24 there's a change of key and Maupin's tenor sax comes in at 2.40 for an improvisation that moves through several key changes – again Hancock employs modulations rather than a sequence of chords. Unlike the kind of modulations we shall hear about with Pat Metheny, these are quite unsubtle, but do at least relieve some of the monotony that starts to develop when a groove goes on too long. And you couldn't really describe the theme as a melody – it's more like a jingle and that's why it's so reminiscent of 70s TV music. The track ends with sixty seconds of electronica to remind us of the irrelevant sci-fi theme shown on the cover. But despite my criticism, made from the comfort of 2010, there's a great deal going on here and in the context of 1975 it is wonderfully inventive. On the sleeve notes of the re-issued CD, Clark tells us that this track was canned first time. That alone is remarkable.

For *Actual Proof*, Clark reports that he was under a lot of pressure. Producer David Rubinson asked Clark to lay down a rhythm that Clark felt insulted his abilities. When he objected, Rubinson got angry and said that if Clark didn't nail it first time then he must do it his (Rubinson's) way. Clark went away and did some Buddhist-style meditation and it worked first time, just the way he wanted. Herbie, a convert to the religion, changed the name of the track from *The Spook Who Sat by the Door* to *Actual Proof* as a demonstration that Buddhism really works!

The start of the track isn't much indication of what is to come because it sounds like a fast funk at first. There's an interesting sequence of chords to outline the funk/rock theme and then a difficult melody line outlined on Maupin's flute. Then by 1.38, the music has accelerated and is flying along with a strong straight-ahead feel. Hancock is in the driving seat for a long electric piano solo that makes everyone puff to keep up with his pace, but Clark really works out on drums and generates a superbly imaginative accompaniment. Periodically the funk/rock motif is thrown at us but it's very much an aside to the intensive work going on with Hancock that continues to around 8.00. This is serious keyboard playing by anyone's standards. At 8.35, late in the piece, Maupin comes in for a flute lead, but the piece is now winding up to a clean ending.

At last, with *Butterfly* we get a very good melody from Hancock. Right from the start, there is a very sexy mood and a melody played on two very contrasting instruments – the high pitch of the saxello and the low pitch of the bass clarinet. The first two minutes are an absolute joy as the superb melody twists and turns unexpectedly; all kinds of musical sounds emerge from the background as Maupin tells the story. From 2.08, Maupin begins an improvisation on his high-pitched instrument, retaining the sexuality at first, but soon winding it up. It's now that the disappointment begins for the improvisations are played over what is essentially a single chord. Hancock begins his improvisation at 4.30 on electric piano and the same thing happens. How much better the music would have been with some new angles. There is variety in terms of what is played – different keyboards come in, different percussion sounds are used and the combinations of instruments are varied, but the chord focus is constant and it soon becomes quite boring. Even the lovely cool eroticism is lost as the soloists are inclined to develop the tension in their improvisations. At 9.10, the theme returns to our considerable relief and we can sit back and enjoy the real musical highlights of this track again. Herbie must have thought it was a good piece, for it reappears several times later on in his recorded career.

The funk is back with a vengeance for *Spank-A-Lee* – everything seems to be multiplied by two for this spanking track that is extravagantly rhythmic. For much of the time it is the exact opposite of the sparse atmospherics on offer on some of the Mwandishi tracks. This is crammed full of activity – perhaps even too full at times, but as an example of a funky groove it's hard to beat. You could say this is all groove and not much else, but there is a theme and at 2.21, the music takes an unexpected but welcome turn to add a little variety to the single chord playing. Maupin takes a good solo on tenor sax whilst the others thrash away behind him. By 4.50, he's thrashing away too and at 5.02 he starts the wind-down process. The band tones down its funk a little as he starts a new phase of improvisation that eventually brings the track to a somewhat uncertain ending that is a slight anticlimax considering what has preceded it.

Thrust is a very good album, even by today's standards, and we shouldn't take anything away from it just because, in places, it sounds like a 70s TV soundtrack. We need to remember that it was this music that led to so many other familiar pieces – *"Thrust" itself is the very reason it sounds old-fashioned*! Some of you may even prefer it to *Head Hunters* because of the sheer funkiness and grooves that abound, but I don't want to make that distinction.

It's one of those little idiosyncrasies of jazz that occurs because jazz bands are constantly changing their line-ups that the band responsible for the *Head Hunters* album became informally known by that name. However, it is clear that Hancock (or perhaps his lawyers) did not consider himself to be part of a band of that name. Without their leader, the remaining musicians adopted the Headhunters name (joining the two words together in the process) to make two further successful albums, *Straight from the Gate* (1977) and *Return of the Headhunters* (1998) on which Hancock appeared as a guest! Herbie had given his blessing to their enterprise, but retained the right to protect his musical independence by not officially joining the band.

Herbie Hancock: *Dedication* – 1974 (***)

Over the course of his career, Herbie recorded a number of albums in Japan under a clause in his 1973 contract that allowed for 'special projects' for Sony to be released only in Japan. The first was *Dedication* (1974), a solo album recorded in the Koseinenkin Hall in Tokyo on 29 July 1974. As Belden and Rubinson later put it: "*Dedication* was to be an electro-acoustic solo performance. The first side was all just Herbie and the solo acoustic piano, no effects. On the second side, Herbie performed live as he created electronic sounds and effects in real time, captured as a complete performance. So, both performances were in fact recorded live, but were very different musically." [41]

The album is still very scarce. The first two tracks are *Maiden Voyage* and *Dolphin Dance*, both played on acoustic piano. Suffice to say here that Herbie uses the freedom of the solo environment to improvise without restraint on these two favourite compositions. The second half of the album also consists of two tracks and is an exhibition of synthesiser playing. These were some of the most advanced keyboard sounds on record at the time. Besides the Fender Rhodes electric piano, Herbie employed a clutch of ARP instruments: Pro Soloist, Odyssey, 2600, 3604 and PE-IV string ensemble. Unlike some of its predecessors such as the 2500, which were quite large, the Soloist was a light, portable instrument that could sit easily on top of an electric piano or organ. The Pro Soloist was introduced in 1972 and had 30 voices. The Odyssey was ARP's top-of-the-range instrument. A scaled-down version of the 2600, it became the top-selling ARP synthesiser during the mid-1970s.

The track *Nobu* (meaning 'prolong' or 'stretch' in Japanese) was not recorded anywhere else. It is supposed to have had a profound effect on later generations of DJs and electronic musicians and is considered by many to be the root of the genre of music called 'techno' that emanated from Detroit from the mid-1980s. DJ and producer Carl Craig, a leading figure in the world of techno music, said: "It opened up so many possibilities for me. I didn't think that it had been done twenty years before, to solo on top of a random sequence. The idea of it was so ahead of its time. God what was this guy on? Did he get in a time machine and see what we are doing today? The textures and qualities he used between synthesisers and Rhodes piano. It was spacey, it was thinking music, it was hallucinating music, it was just everything that encompasses what I do today." [42] The last track is an electronic version of *Cantaloupe Island* that features a repeating funky bass line over which Herbie improvises freely with the sounds available on the other instruments.

Herbie Hancock: *Man-Child* – 1975 (***)

It's surprising that with so many stars on duty for this album, so few of them are allowed to shine. It's just like the days of Miles Davis – but wait a minute - this is the days of Miles Davis! Hancock begins by inviting us to *Hang Up Your Hang Ups.* I'd like to give him the benefit of the doubt on this track for he sets off with a jumbojive in E major that sounds like he's hired both the Basie *and* Ellington bands and taught them all how to funk. The energy is bursting out of my hi-fi and, ignoring the somewhat erratic timekeeping, I start to sweat with excitement. I just wish he'd break loose from the drone of that E major chord. Is this perhaps the sound of my hang-up? First Bennie Maupin's tenor tries to break the curse for me and then, from 4.15, the band finally lets rip in a chromatic sequence of chords. The spell is broken; this *is* a great track after all. At 5.30, the team is continuing to tear up the bandstand, throwing everything but their guitar stands at this megafunk party when Herbie finally comes in on *acoustic piano,* detached and soaring above them like the superstar he is. The contrast is surreal in this musical context. Finally at seven and a half minutes the track is finished and I'm left in a perspiring heap to marvel at the spectacular music I've just heard.

As you might expect, the title *Sun Touch* indicates a more laid-back vibe and a total contrast. It also continues to draw upon the wide range of sounds and textures available to Herbie as they continuously evolve, like sunspots, through their five-minute cycle of relaxation. With *The Trailor* Herbie is focussing on the vibe as a canvas for his electronic paint. Trouble is, yet again we're stuck in an E-groove, cleverly androgynous between minor and major, and it's deep enough for us to be trapped there for nine and a half suicide-inducing minutes. I start to feel sorry for the bass and drums players having to grind out these desperately boring riffs. Bring on the days when bass and drum playing are turned into computerised sequences. I'm just starting to think that this is a band of robots when, at last, Paul Jackson makes his mark right at the very end of the track. Once more, we need to remember that there *were* a few bass players, such as Jackson, Alphonso Johnson and Stanley Clarke, already treading the path of slap and funky bass before the cataclysmic arrival of the 'Great One'. *Bubbles* goes some way to restoring my sanity. For me, it's a bubble bath, immersing me in warm, soft and lubricating music juice. At 1.45 the perfume of Wayne Shorter's soprano saxophone breaks through the humidity like a smile on the face of a tax inspector. And the sequence of chords is as slick as the soap used to blow the bubbles. I'm beautifully relaxed again. Nice one.

As I said, there doesn't seem much place for star musicians in Herbie's current style of music it seems, until Stevie Wonder makes a cameo appearance in *Steppin' In It*, a piece with more than an echo of *The Chameleon* about it. It's easy to forget just what a great harmonica player Stevie Wonder is when we listen to his own albums, which are filled with so many other things to rave about. On this track he simply plays harmonica like no other man on the planet. It's a true star performance. *Heartbeat* pulses fairly appropriately at first until the rhythmic complexity builds beyond anything related to human biology. By two minutes the piece is out of life support and growing rapidly in the warmth of the lab. This is a Hancock-inspired culture that pushes its boundaries better than anything else on this record.

I counted at least nineteen musicians used in the recording of this album. Only Herbie and Stevie Wonder break the surface of the waters in this jazz, although there are flashes of Wayne Shorter as we peer into the depths. This holistic style of music is influenced by the Davis philosophy to excise formal melody and traditional song structure, constrain individuals into a tighter band mix such that only occasional hints of solos are heard, and finally promote the single-note driven rhythm-based vibe as the focus of the music. Just how much this style was due to producer David Rubinson I don't know, so I have to blame the musician. Anyway, it works for Hancock and it may for you too. There is a lot of value here, but I cannot understand why anyone would buy a top of the range sports car and use it only for going to the shops. Well, I guess that's my hang-up and I'll have to learn to live with it.

Herbie Hancock: *Flood* – 1975 (****)

The album *Flood* (1975) was recorded live in Tokyo at the end of June 1975. Its rather dour, cataclysmic-looking artwork depicts Herbie's favoured topics – the extreme temporal links between the past and the future, the Universe, space travel and Africa, topics that are pretty hard to broaden on one album! By now the fusion floodgates were fully open and most of the world – Japan included – was rejoicing in the new sounds. *Flood* is a very good live album that presents the best known and loved tracks from Herbie's repertoire to date. For example, *Maiden Voyage* is introduced with a beautifully sensitive acoustic solo before the band turns it into a luxurious cruise through the fjords, assisted by some sweet flute playing from Maupin. *Actual Proof* follows seamlessly and develops into a highly charged rendition, notable for Paul Jackson's lively bass rhythm. He continues to impress in *Spank-a-Lee* with a seriously funky accompaniment that's full of many tricks and skills we shall soon attribute to Jaco. Bill Summers and Mike Clarke combine to provide a stunning percussive background, with the almost unnoticed Blackbird McKnight on guitar. By the time Herbie enters the fray the piece is boiling fiercely and an extended vibe provides the basis for a group solo, led by the eager Maupin on tenor. As live entertainment this must have really wowed the audience. The now familiar intro to the funky *Watermelon Man* leads into a fairly standard version of Herbie's best-known piece. Next is a thirteen-minute version of *Butterfly*, once again in a familiar format, but with the kind of extended improvisations we expect in live performance. Sadly, the beautiful creature is finally eaten by the fierce and funky *Chameleon*, but it all makes for good TV, as they say. This little scaly chap, however, has been subjected to some of Dr Hancock's electronic experimentations, which don't translate too well from live to recorded form. Nevertheless, it's a fair record of the mood of the gig. The final track is another extended vamp, this time of *Hang Up Your Hang Ups*. At last, Blackbird McKnight gets a chance to spread his wings on Melvin Ragin's guitar groove. It's the ideal opportunity for the band to work the crowd into a frenzy for the final number of the gig.

Herbie Hancock: *Secrets* – 1976 (***)

The middle of the 1970s was both a wonderful and a difficult time to be a musician. The jazz-rock hydra was sprouting new heads faster than many could understand. So much was happening in music and there were so many directions to run in, musicians could only guess which was likely to produce the best results. The truly innovative days for jazz-fusion were over and anyone wanting to continue in that genre needed a clear idea of what he wanted to do. But there was still plenty of scope to contribute to the evolution of music, especially with electronic instruments changing by the month. Herbie split his energies between his straight-ahead jazz and his funky dance music sounds, which are sharply focused on this album. He even said later that he was trying at this point *not* to make a jazz record! [43] He thought sometimes that he had not succeeded. In 1976, the Godfather, Miles Davis, had entered retirement, yet like Marlon

Brando's celluloid persona, his influence still loomed large over his extended family and Herbie was no exception.

I blow hot and cold over *Secrets*. When I'm hot, I love the exciting funky rhythms of the album, and there are some memorable tunes and beautiful well-selected electronic sounds from Hancock's keyboards. When I'm cold, I think the disc is best summed up with the phrase from its opening track, *Keep On Doin' It!* Some of this album is once again marred by long vamps that have promising starts followed by monotonous, repetitive sections. Davis's preference for everything to be 'wah wah' even creeps onto the disc with a guitar player who liked it so much he carries the name of it – Wah Wah Watson. (This was a pseudonym – his name was actually Melvin Ragin, whose name appears as co-writer on many of the album tracks during these years.) Hopes are high from the start of *Doin' It* as the superb funk builds from Ray Parker's guitar, but as the music grows I just want it to continue into something special and it doesn't. Thus, the bulk of the seven minutes is comprised of a very simple repeated phrase that finally evolves into a song. Thankfully, there is a simple middle section to break up the monotony; otherwise I would have killed myself before the piece finished.

The next track, *People Music*, is a big contrast with some really progressive music that Herbie crafts from the array of electronics at his disposal. His keyboard sounds are now mature and there's no chance these will date. The piece is thoughtfully funky without being 'in yer face' and there is a lot of variety and substance in the construction and the melodies.

Track three is a funk version of his popular number *Cantaloupe Island* (note my spelling – it's wrong on the sleeve!) It takes about two minutes to realise the piece's true identity for it is well disguised and interesting as a result. Throughout his career, Hancock has a propensity to recycle some of his numbers, but in the best jazz traditions he rings the changes on his compositions, making sure there is a reason for their re-working.

Track four is *Spider*, a frighteningly fast funk piece with conventional recording turned on its head to make sure that rhythm is the focus. The funk vibe is strong in the foreground whilst the lead noodlings are carried on very much in the background. There isn't much sign of melody here. There is evolution in the piece, but it's almost overwhelmed by the heavy dance rhythms, which are the primary purpose of the number.

Gentle Thoughts is another of the quieter, melodic numbers that, by being focused on the dance culture, has more repetition than it needs to. The rhythm of the piece is very much like Bill Withers' *Lovely Day* (1977). The B-section has a memorable hook that may well have influenced writers like Bob James a few years later. (Saying that someone sounds like Bob James is almost as bad as saying that Miles Davis sounds like Herb Alpert! It's no insult in my opinion: Bob James made some good music, and Herb Alpert could certainly play the trumpet.)

Swamp Rat is a fast funky number, which at first seems as if it has something to offer, but soon becomes dominated by a three minute Davis-style vamp as Benny Maupin blows a whole set of saxophone fuses. Perhaps that pushes your buttons – it doesn't push mine. To wrap it all up, Hancock chooses not to adopt the normal fade out and instead creates a strange ending that is totally out of character with the rest of the piece. He should have phoned Chick Corea for advice on this one.

Sansho Shima reminds us that Herbie is a Buddhist. The term is of Japanese origin and is used in Buddhism to mean obstacles and hindrances to the practice of Buddhism. Again, the start is interesting, and the flavour of the piece, though still funky at heart, is more abstract and adds novelty to the album. However, as the piece develops, the need to pursue a G-pedal point (i.e. use of G as the tonal focus) up a lengthy philosophical blind alley is mysterious, but, on reflection, is presumably Herbie's association with the Buddhist chant. Perhaps that's why I'm not a Buddhist.

It's at about this point in his career that Herbie was attracting particularly harsh criticism. Sounding like Bob James did not go down well with either the jazz puritans (they would have hated it, regardless) or those of a more jazz-fusion persuasion who now tried to keep the genre pure (whatever that meant). They thought Hancock was committing the worst crime of all - selling out to commercialism. Jazz-fusion was already poorly thought of, and without the obviously innovative music of *Headhunters* to drive him forward, this music did nothing to help his standing with those who could only view it as valueless. The fact that it was being perpetrated by a stalwart of Miles's Second Great Quintet made it even less palatable to these people. Worse was to come.

Herbie Hancock: *V.S.O.P.* – 1977 (***)

At the New York Newport Jazz Festival in 1976, promoter George Wein invited Hancock to play a 'Retrospective' of his music. A cynic might have said it was a way of saying 'forget all this fusion crap, let's get back to some *proper* jazz', but I won't say that. Herbie himself admits "There are people today who don't call the funk group a jazz group." [44] Amazingly, Herbie was successful in persuading all his former team-mates to meet up at the Festival on 29th June for a reunion concert under the banner of V.S.O.P. This is an odd choice of title that seems to derive from the name given to the best forms of cognac and means 'very superior old pale'. Deliciously, Herbie's very superior old pals came together for three different line-ups that night. Ron Carter, Tony Williams, Wayne Shorter and Freddie Hubbard re-formed the Miles Davis 1965 Quintet with Hubbard on trumpet, and it was this fivesome who formed the brandy-flavoured band. At this time, Miles was fully out of sight in his reclusive period that was to last for four years. On the sleeve notes to the album, Herbie paid tribute to Miles and dedicated the concert and the recording to his mentor. He must have had some indication of Miles's state of disillusionment and, as one of Miles's most fervent supporters must have been saddened by the prospect of Miles in retirement. The album has three tracks by this band: *Maiden Voyage*, *Nefertiti* and *Eye of the Hurricane*.

The second band was a reformation of the Mwandishi group with Eddie Henderson, Julian Priester, Bennie Maupin, Buster Williams and Billy Hart. The first track on the album is a good version of an old Hancock number called *Toys*, which appears on his album *Speak Like a Child* (1968). The second track is *You'll Know When You Get There* from the first Mwandishi album. Herbie loved this group: "When the Sextet was at its best, the whole group was like a living body. It was a music of the moment, no regular changes, bars or even tempo – but somehow, almost miraculously, the music would have a flow and order that made me feel like I was listening to the sound from all the planets. Trying to recapture that spirit was difficult, but it came off – it was really swinging." [44] But Herbie, what did it sound like when it *didn't* come off?

Finally, the promoter was forced to accept the funk band, with Ray Parker, Bennie Maupin, Wah Wah Watson, Paul Jackson, James Levi and Kenneth Nash playing *Hang Up Your Hang Ups* and *Spider*. Two chords more or less account for the two tracks and twenty-one minutes of music, which, I guess, makes this music with bars and tempo only twice as interesting as music with no changes, bars or tempo.

After the successful gig of '76, Hancock went on tour the following year with the V.S.O.P. band. There was constant speculation – wishful thinking, of course – that one day, Miles would join the group and reunite the classic band, but he never did. Too much water had flown under the bridge. By the end of the 70s Herbie was playing in a constantly changing line-up. Groupings included V.S.O.P., the Herbie Hancock Trio, Quartet and Quintet, as well as a clutch of solo and duet performances.

Ron Carter / Herbie Hancock / Tony Williams: *Third Plane* – 1978 (****)

Herbie spent the summer of 1977 in a continuation of his acoustic jazz incarnation as part of the V.S.O.P. band, now dubbed *The* Quintet (my italics). It was to be a most productive period and the band would reach a pinnacle of performance quality that, at last, we can enjoy today, thanks to a large number of fine recordings, despite the fact that, for too long, they have been rare. Tapes were not released for some years and only then in Japan. Only recently have the recordings become available for download.

On the 13th July 1977 Herbie was in his friend David Rubinson's studio, the Automatt in San Francisco with Tony Williams and Ron Carter to record a project of Ron's that would appear on the Milestone Records label entitled *Third Plane* (1978). Unusually for a bass player, Ron Carter had started early on what would become a long sequence of solo projects. Adopting a dedicated musical education in his teens that culminated with a Masters degree in music in 1961 from the Manhattan School of music, his early gigs were with Don Ellis and Eric Dolphy, for whom he appeared on *Out There* (1960) and *Far Cry* (1960). His recording career as a leader began with an album with Eric Dolphy and Mal Waldron entitled *Where?* (1961). These were followed by *Out Front* (1966) and *Uptown Conversation* (1969) whilst still working in Miles's band. Then, when Miles had embarked on his electric project Carter was faced with the challenge of whether to convert to electric bass or not. Although he did play electric bass for some of the early Davis experiments, Ron ultimately decided that he would remain an acoustic player, a choice that, to some extent, cemented his place in a region of jazz outside the fashionable jazz-fusion arena. Here, as one of the acknowledged truly great acoustic bass players, he refocused his career with no difficulty whatsoever. In great demand, he made appearances on sequences of albums by such great jazz pianists as McCoy Tyner and Horace Silver, as well as being the bassist-of-choice for acoustic projects by Herbie, Wayne and Tony. He was also able to record a long sequence of solo albums that continues to this day and is too extensive to discuss here.

This album begins with the title track, a very tuneful composition by Carter expressed as an acoustic swing piece. Herbie makes some utterly breathtaking selections of chords that turn what would otherwise have been a familiar melodic structure into something really exceptional. In contrast, the second track is a slow melody, also by Carter, entitled *Quiet Times* that traverses some beautiful landscapes and finishes with a group of harmonics that resonates exquisitely on bass and atmospherically on piano. This piece is an excellent demonstration of the highest levels of performance on acoustic bass that, because of its slow speed and clarity, can be clearly heard even by ears that are not used to listening to bass on record. *Lawra* is Tony's composition that is based upon a simple two-note motif to represent the girl's name in the title. Most of the piece consists of Herbie playing some sparse phrases whilst Ron's bass strides melodiously around the foreground. For his own piece even the irrepressible Tony Williams is somehow persuaded to stick to the script. The result is delightful.

The second half of the album begins with the old standard *Stella By Starlight*, a piece that the boys must have played hundreds of times with Miles, in which case, it is remarkable that the musicians still feel they have something fresh to say about the music. *United Blues* is a short Carter composition played in the standard 12-bar blues format with some nice variations and the comic main theme played by Ron and Herbie in unison. It's a swinging piece of fun. Finally comes Herbie's *Dolphin Dance*, a piece that appears frequently across the Hancock discography.

This is a very good acoustic trio album that allows Ron to have a much closer engagement with the listener than he could normally have in a quintet with sax and trumpet. Beautifully recorded with equipment that was an order of magnitude better than what he had been captured with in the 1960s, his bass was now sounding at its very best – almost electric in places – thanks especially to the 1992 remastering for the CD edition. As the focus of the instrumentation, Herbie is on magnificent form, and Tony Williams contributes enormously. There is always a danger of tracks on a piano trio album sounding same-ish, but that is never the case here.

Herbie Hancock: *The Herbie Hancock Trio* – 1977 (****)

In a continuation of what was clearly a very successful session, further tracks were recorded at the Automatt on the same day as the music that appeared on *Third Plane*. It is a great pity that this music was published only years later in Japan on a disc in which the words *The Herbie Hancock Trio* are the only ones printed almost unnoticeably in a very small box on the album's cover.

Apart from the final track, Miles Davis's *Milestones*, Herbie wrote all of the music. As on *Third Plane*, acoustic instruments are used throughout and there is no evidence of fusion or popular idioms other than the usual jazz mainstream format. We can deduce that, at the time of these recordings, the band was at a particular high point in its existence. Living closely together to facilitate the daily performances of a band on tour, these three friends had nevertheless established a deeper musical rapport than most. Here we are privileged to be able to listen to a jazz master-class as these musicians perform in a 'live' sense, but with the benefits of the latest and best studio recording technology. The album begins with two contrasting pieces that must have been performed enough times to be well-known to the musicians, yet still fresh enough to allow extended development in this context. *Watch It* appears uniquely on this disc and appears to be a mostly spontaneous piece with very little obvious prior organisation. It is simply delightful to hear how these three experts take a very simple idea and develop it in front of us in a demonstration of the very finest aspects of jazz performance.

A comparison of the version of *Speak Like A Child* originally recorded in March 1968 to the smooth accompaniment of horns and flutes, and the version that appears at track 2, now played as a piano trio, is worthwhile. The original was a very fine studio recording of a cleverly composed and constructed piece from the leading edge of late 60s jazz mainstream. This version is an order of magnitude further on, as the three men take it to an altogether higher level through a wonderful demonstration of the intimate understanding they now have. In the original, the main theme is a complex melody of evolving chords that offer no obvious root in a conventional key, yet remains traditionally harmonic. Played to a Latin rhythm, the simple, short child-like phrases are strung together in a not-too-logical order - just like a child. Being the main core of the piece, this is retained here, but developed and embossed with the benefit of nine years of hindsight. In the original, the main structure for improvisation oscillates over a two chord sequence – a simple ploy used in countless other jazz pieces. Here, the improvisation is so much more sophisticated, driven by the three men acting as a single unit. In particular, Ron Carter's playing is quite breathtaking as he demonstrates just how far an acoustic bass has been taken from the kind of work he played on the earlier version. The tone is penetrating and forward in the mix with extreme sonority and much slurring of notes as the jazz style is taken far beyond anything envisaged by the traditional European classical style of play. Tony Williams is constantly searching for new ways to provide accompaniment to the deep level of activity taking place alongside him. The first two tracks are both lengthy, the second being twice as long as its older sibling. This allows for a far more penetrating exploration of the music through this 'live' jazz improvisation.

In a sense, the performance is over with the passing of the first two enormously powerful tracks. They are followed by three shorter, seemingly less significant, though no less worthwhile tracks. *Watcha Waitin' For* is another Hancock composition that is unique to this album. An up-tempo swing piece, it passes through the usual processes of scrutiny with no special characteristics other than the same high level of performance and an ability to deliver satisfaction to its listeners. *Look* is the only recording of a slow waltz-time piece, again written by Herbie, which contrasts nicely with its neighbours and acts as a very pleasant palette-cleanser. Then, finally, *Milestones* begins in a way that is so fast and furious that you really wonder whether they can keep it up. Of course, they do. The familiar theme is soon past, even if the needs of jazz result in a little twisting of the melodic strands. After that, it moves quickly into a meaty period of improvisation that concludes with an exciting drum solo.

It goes without saying that Herbie's playing is utterly masterful on all counts. In the context of this music, Tony Williams' presence is obviously essential and luxuriously creative. However, I cannot help feeling that, important though he is, Tony is eclipsed by the truly outstanding performance of Ron Carter. On the evidence of this day's recordings, I feel he could have been almost as big a star as Herbie if the bass were a more significant instrument in the perception of listeners. This remarkable statement is assisted here, in part, by the extraordinarily clear recording of his beautiful instrument in Rubinson's studio, but also by the incomparable technique he demonstrates and his uncanny depth of understanding with his colleagues. Anyone who loves modern jazz should be very pleased to own this CD.

V.S.O.P.: *The Quintet* – 1977 (***)

It was only a few days after the San Francisco Automatt sessions that the band migrated down the coast to southern California for some live dates as part of the V.S.O.P. quintet tour. These too were recorded and selections from the tapes of two concerts at the famous Greek Theater, in the University of California at Berkeley and the San Diego Civic Theater, on 16th and 18th July respectively were released as a double vinyl album entitled *The Quintet* (1977).

One Of A Kind is a tune written by "Hubcap", a strange title that poorly disguises Hubbard as its creator. After a freely improvised opening led by Herbie, the repeating bass motif allows Herbie to continue his creativity to just over the one minute mark when the horns play the head in unison, supported by some fiery drumming from Tony. At 2.17, Hubbard is first soloist, clearly determined to establish the piece as a pot-boiler. His valve work, simmering and nimble, is edgy and inciting. From 5.10, Wayne's solo is played on soprano saxophone and develops a great energy and intensity that by 7 minutes into the piece has the band exploding with ideas. Even the return to the theme doesn't release the tension that continues through to the end. Herbie introduces *Third Plane* as "something we've just been working on." Somehow this version has lost the subtlety it had on the trio album. Gone are Herbie's delightfully innovative chords substituted by more energetic horn playing. Of course, we should admire the way Freddie and Wayne have learned the piece so consummately in such a short time. Herbie's tune *Jessica* is a slow ballad in waltz time that first appeared on *Fat Albert Rotunda* (1969). It was always an acoustically-focussed tune, and on the original version was played with the richer colours of combined front-line instruments. Here, the players share out the haunting melody, inspiring as they do so occasional shouts of delight from the audience. Fresh from their work on it for *Third Plane*, Williams' tune *Lawra* is next. Here it is significantly different, set up as a more energetic swing piece with two horns to accommodate, and unusually has Hubbard and Shorter improvising against each other. Tony is much freer here and plays a solo from 4.30 until 6.38 when Herbie comes in with a curious repeating motif that supports a bass solo through to 8.32 when the band reverts to the simple two-note main theme.

For the second half of the album, *Darts* is a fast straight-ahead piece written by Herbie that is in the modal style that leaves many ears wondering what happened to the melody. It's not surprising that this is its only appearance in Herbie's recorded repertoire. Wayne's composition *Dolores* first appeared on *Miles Smiles* (1966). It opens with Wayne playing a short soliloquy in the style of Wayne's cousin Dolores speaking. It is characterised by a prominent, instantly recognisable melody line, the rhythm and pitch of which is worked upon with enthusiasm at various times by the soloists. Next comes *Little Waltz*, a rare outing of a slow ballad with a strong and beautifully recorded solo by its composer, Ron Carter. Finally, *Byrdlike* is another Hubbard title that pays tribute to Freddie's friendship with and time in Donald Byrd's band. Fast and frantic, the piece makes an exciting and energetic finale to this very good value (71 minutes in length) album. It's well recorded and the band is on fine form, working together consistently on pieces yet also creating an envelope in which each musician could explore his own voice.

V.S.O.P.: *Tempest in the Colosseum* – 1977 (***)

By 23 July, the band was in Japan where they gave a concert at the Denen Colosseum, Tokyo under the same heading: V.S.O.P. – The Quintet. Silvert says that "more than 100,000 people turned out in just one month to see the V.S.O.P. quintet." [45] (I assume it was July 1977.) That was a remarkable statistic for a mainstream jazz group at the time, but merely reflected the stature achieved by this group of musicians. Certainly, by the look of the centrefold photos of the artwork for this CD, the statistic is eminently believable. Silvert went on to point out that, by working together in this essentially acoustic format, the band members were in some way repairing the damage caused to jazz by their participation elsewhere in the destructive forces of jazz-fusion. Even by 1977, the moaning about electric jazz-fusion was continuing...

Wayne and Freddie are cheered as they walk onto the stage and improvise to the backing of an as yet unrecognisable version of *Eye of the Hurricane*. Then at

2.17, the band is greeted with a cheer from the audience as the first theme is played. Played at a rate of 260-280 beats per minute, consistent with high velocity winds we might expect from a hurricane, it's now I realise this title is something of a misnomer for the piece because in the eye of a storm it is calm! But just like a hurricane causes great disintegration, the original theme is very fragmentary for this rendition as Hubbard leads off with a busy solo to 5.30 whereupon Shorter takes over. At 8.00 he takes us right into the eye of the storm. Then it's Herbie's turn to solo with Tony, who extemporises in alternate swashes of sound that are first brash and dominant, and then subdued, whilst swinging from his rapid cymbals. Throughout the whole enterprise, Ron keeps up the rigid tempo with his walking bass lines. At 11.40, Tony begins a four-minute solo, after which the piece ends with a last fragment of the theme.

Wayne wrote *Diana* for the daughter of Flora Purim and Airto Moreira. It's a beautiful, short, mostly out-of-tempo piece that is conventionally harmonic but which has an unconventional melodic lines played on soprano saxophone, a characteristic that makes it unpredictable to listen to and, sadly, unmemorable.

Eighty-One was Ron's tune originally recorded with Miles for his album *E.S.P.* (1965). Here it swings as a 12-bar through Freddie's solo, embarking on a period of double time at 4.15. Then, when Wayne plays his solo on soprano from 5.15, he begins with a wholly improvised section that finally returns to a 12-bar blues even as Wayne does his best to ignore the standard package behind. From 7.40, Ron does well to maintain the tempo as he single-mindedly solos to just the beat of Tony's sticks in the dangerous presence of a (notoriously unreliable) audience handclap. Herbie comes in at 8.55 and gets the trio back on track for his own solo. At first, it's minimalist, but then gradually fills out into a beautifully rhythmic performance that contains all the party tricks of a master pianist. His mounting energy draws the trio into a seething froth by 11.00, and the rhythm almost breaks down completely. Tony saves the day by shifting into his own brief solo and the band comes together at 11.45 for a final burst of the main theme.

Maiden Voyage opens with the familiar theme altered by a new bass line from Ron. At 1.48 the piece briefly takes on a fusion rhythm as Freddie leads off with his solo. The trio continues to play around with the song's original style. Tony, in particular, takes the band and soloist into new rhythmic territory from around 3.15 as Freddie improvises to 4.35 whereupon Herbie takes up the reins. Once again, Tony sets up yet more new rhythms for Herbie who flirts along with him to 6.30. At this point, the others drop out and Herbie plays on his own in a concerto-style cadenza to 8.35. His brilliance allows him to create a passage as tough, yet fluid, as any classical pianist, laced constantly with the themes of his composition. The main theme then repeats and develops into a whole-group improvisation around the ten-minute mark. It's not free jazz, as they hold on to the chord format and echo the motifs throughout. The piece moves to an end at 12 minutes without returning to the theme again.

Once again, Tony's piece *Lawra* is on the menu, played here at a pace of 250 bpm. Ron's driving pulse is prominent during the first part of the tune as Freddie and Wayne spar together. At 2.15, this sets up a long drum solo (it's his piece, after all) through to 7.12 by when there's just enough time to echo the double syllable theme a few times before ending.

The final piece is Freddie's composition *Red Clay*. It begins with a Spanish landscape and some harsh group improvisation that matches the parched terrain he presumably wishes to depict. At 1.20, Ron sets up the hard, driving tempo and the main theme is exposed by Freddie and Wayne. Freddie leads off the improvised section and impresses the Japanese audience with some very fast, accurate runs, some accurately pitched ear-splitters and some raspberries tossed into the mix like airy hand grenades. As Tony weakly tries to induce some new rhythmic energy, Wayne's tenor sax solo slithers across the keys like a snake might wriggle through a metal grill constructed to contain it. At 8.10, the snake even begins to bark. Herbie takes over from 8.30 and shows us that his runs are as fluid and friction-free as anyone else's. At 11.35, Ron brings the theme back for its curtain call.

This is a good, well-recorded acoustic live album with well-selected, slick and mostly improvised performances that allow us to make a good assessment of the way the band was playing at the time. There's not a sign of hesitation of mistakes as the boys are by now very familiar with the pieces, which have been played a lot over the preceding weeks. The numbers that are more familiar to us, in particular, show us that the themes, though barely intact and modified as we might expect from jazzers, are chopped right back to allow plenty of scope for improvisation. It's a masterful, complete band performance with no musician standing out above any other, whilst each gets his turn to shine in the spotlight.

Herbie Hancock: *Sunlight* – 1978 (***)

If you think the jazz puritans reaction to *Head Hunters* was bad, you've no idea how much they hated this album! It's worth remembering that his producer, David Rubinson, had been with him now for seven years or so. Having come from a key position in the organisation of the Fillmore West performance centre in San Francisco, Rubinson was very grounded in the music business and must have been a key figure in the project to 'commercialise Herbie'. Part of that process was an obvious plan use vocal albums to create a bridge between jazz-fusion and the large popular audience. The first three tracks of the five on

Sunlight (1978) are vocal tracks. The next album *Feets Don't Fail Me Now* (1979) had five vocal tracks, with only the final sixth track being an instrumental.

Herbie suffered especially badly with vitriolic reviews of this album, largely because of his use of a new sound effect called the Sennheiser vocoder VSM 201. By making any kind of vocal recording, Herbie was selling out to commerce, and when one of their number makes a record in a genre that jazzers have no respect for, an act of treachery has been committed. (Similar treatment was being meted out to Stanley Clarke, but he was younger and rather less important a figure in jazz at that time than Herbie.) But the issue that united a broad range of people, far wider than the jazz puritans alone, was Hancock's experiment with the notorious vocoder, an electronic device that converts the human voice into a sound associated with a robot. Even today, the vocoder has strong associations with *Sparky's Magic Piano* (1947), a children's audio story in which a piano speaks with a voice generated by a device called a Sonovox, an early version of the talk box.

The vocoder itself was not new at this point. *March, from A Clockwork Orange* by Wendy Carlos was the first recorded song to feature the use of a vocoder, and is often cited as the inspiration for many synthpop bands. After *Clockwork Orange* and Kraftwerk's *Autobahn* album of the early 1970s, the vocoder's sound became part of popular music's repertoire. Electric Light Orchestra tried it on *Mr Blue Sky*. Early devices were analogue and such vocoders are still manufactured. More recently, however, they have become digital in designs such as the "phase vocoder" where software is used to create the effect. Many performers have tried it: Cher used a Korg VC10 vocoder on her no 1 single *Believe* (1998) and Madonna on *Music* (2000). Joe Zawinul liked the vocoder enormously, because he felt that it converted his own inadequate singing voice into a new musical instrument.

The Sennheiser was an early mass-produced unit that Herbie adopted in his search for new sounds. Sennheiser was founded to manufacture electronic devices in the USA in 1945 by a German émigré electronics engineer, but a year later the company moved on to become a major manufacturer of sound devices such as microphones and headphones. The VSM sound effect vocoder appeared in 1978 and Herbie Hancock snapped one up to use on his new album.

I Thought it was You is a track by Herbie and Wah Wah Watson, with lyrics by Jeff Cohen and sung by Herbie using the vocoder. This is a superb, strong disco-dance number and we need to appreciate that, at this point in history, Herbie still needed real brass, woodwind and strings. It would not be long before a single keyboard could replace them all. The melody is memorable and the lyrics form only about half of the piece. There's also some really good (but unidentified) brass. At five minutes – presumably a generous limit for radio-play time - a second instrumental part commences that consists of a repeated phrase to wind up the disco vibe and give Herbie more opportunity for trying out new ideas. At around 7.30 you can hear him performing what is called scat singing on the vocoder. On this basis, these tracks combine music designed to be popular with music intended to be experimental. With so many new electronic tools at his fingertips, Herbie had endless permutations to play with.

Come Running to Me is the second of the three vocal tracks on this album, all sung using the vocoder. The melody of the piece is also directed towards a popular audience, but interspersed with significantly jazzier inflections. A middle section has Herbie improvising on Fender Rhodes electric piano, which now sounds very conventional, compared to some of the other electronic sounds he might have used. As before, the piece has a second part that develops a jazz vibe and keeps the music rooted in jazz rather than pop.

Sunlight is a funky trip with a good band backing Herbie's vocals. Paul Jackson (bass) and Ray Parker (guitar) supported by James Levi (drums) and Bill Summers (percussion) provide a lively backdrop, and a real brass section fills out the colour as the piece twists and turns. There's a lot of variety and an excellent soprano sax solo from Bennie Maupin, but it's too short, and that's a good indication that this is targeted at the airwaves. By five minutes, it's all over, but it does continue for a further two minutes as jazzers would expect it to. This song is the album's highlight.

The final two tracks are instrumentals. *No Means Yes* has Herbie with Bill Summers, Ray Parker, Harvey Mason and Paul Rekow (congas). There's a one-minute laid-back theme to start, after which it seems to shift up a gear and become deliberately funkier for a second theme. At 2.40 it falls into a middle section in which Herbie returns to Fender Rhodes for a substantial improvisation and the boys, led by the excellent Harvey Mason, wind it up towards a return to the main theme at 5.20.

Good Question is quite out of place here. Perhaps Herbie was having withdrawal symptoms through playing all this froth and wanted to get back to the serious business of jazz. Hancock uses the acoustic piano and only a few electronics. He is joined by Tony Williams and Jaco Pastorius, as well as Bill Summers and Paul Rekow. It's a complex piece and hard-core compared to the four preceding tracks, which is probably why he hired serious jazzers to play it. There's a one-minute exposition of a theme at the start, after which it moves into a faster hard-driving tempo that free-wheels along with little in the way of a theme to hang onto, except at the end when the original theme returns to conclude. Jaco, however, is not well recorded, but his presence is fulfilling. We hear plenty of Williams, of course, which is appropriate in this case, for it's a demanding blow from all sides. I should imagine that the disco dancers found this a little strange.

An interesting feature of this album from 1978 is that the package gives a significant description of Herbie's stage set-up, showing the arrangement of his banks of synthesisers. At this time, for a musician to be surrounded - indeed, almost enveloped by - great racks of keyboards and electronics with flashing lights was to be like Captain Kirk at the helm of the Starship Enterprise. It had become a kind of fashion statement for all the prog-rockers like Peter Gabriel, Rick Wakeman and Keith Emerson, flashily saying: "Look at all this high tech stuff I can play!" Herbie, of course, was the leading exponent of the electronic keyboard in jazz-fusion, whilst Jean-Michel Jarre was another in the avant-garde and electronic music genre.

The age of electronic instruments had truly arrived. A photograph of the set-up is supplemented by a diagram of the layout and shows a Micro-Moog, Mini-Moog, Poly-Moog, ARP Odyssey, Yamaha CP-30, Hohner D6 Clavinet, ARP String Ensemble, Sequential Circuits Prophet Synthesiser, ARP 2600, Yamaha Polyphonic Synthesiser and Oberheim Polyphonic Synthesiser. Once again the music was very progressive but proved to be unpopular with inertia-bound audiences.

Herbie: "The funny thing is the only place it was a hit was in England... We did a tour of Europe and we played in Germany and they booed us, they threw eggs and all kinds of things and we just had to wave with conviction, you know? We knew we were doing something that was daring. It was great when we played the first concert in London and all these girls were at the front of the stage and singing and waving their arms. It was very encouraging." [46]

The main focus for the discontent was, of course the vocoder. Kevin Legendre: "To me that doesn't sound cheesy, it doesn't sound disco as it's often derided. It sounds like a really interesting electronic colour that adds to the incredible range of electronic colours that you have on that album. If you think of all of the things he was using... this incredible bank of keyboards, and then the icing on the cake – some would say that it's the thing that really spoils it, but I don't hear it that way at all...he still brings his jazz sensibilities to it. What does he do with the vocoder? He ends up scatting and syncopating. So it's not some gimmick, as you find on a lot of disco records. When Herbie uses the vocoder he's obviously listened to King Pleasure, John Hendrix or some of the great scat singers. His musicality is not being diminished by the use of state-of-the-art technology. That's why it's so interesting." [47]

Herbie Hancock: *Feets Don't Fail Me Now* – 1979 (***)

The opening track is *You Bet Your Love*, a recording unashamedly aimed at the popular music market and none the worse for it. Annoyingly, not a single musician is named on the sleeve, but after a certain amount of searching the Internet we find uncorroborated reports that the basic band is James Gadson (drums), Bill Summers (percussion), Eddie Watkins (bass), Melvin Ragin and Ray Obiedo (guitar); guests include drummer Sheila Escovedo and Ray Parker Jr on his own composition *Ready Or Not*, whilst *Knee Deep* features the Headhunters with Freddie Washington on bass.

Because this track was released as a single it naturally attracted a lot of attention. One problem with the internet is that there is so little good textual material available on some subjects that when someone does write a review it gets copied around the bazaars. This can bias the results of a search. Nevertheless, it is an inescapable fact that this album got pasted with the glue that flowed freely when folks heard the opener track on their radios. Yet, as we shall see, the album is not all about the vocoder, neither is it only about disco music. (And what is so wrong with dancing?)

The more concise reviewers said that the album was "truly awful". Hancock had "ventured into disco schlock" and "Disco! It sounds like Disco! Disco SUCKS!" The more objective information sources such as Wikipedia wrote: "Throughout the 1970s, Hancock successfully flirted with various types of fusion - at one point he had four albums in the pop chart - but his ill-advised foray into disco on 1979's *Feets, Don't Fail Me Now* was a disaster."

Hancock injects the vocals through the vocoder, whilst the choral accompaniment is normally aspirated. Even allowing for the distorting effect of the electronics, Hancock makes a pretty good job of the melody and demonstrates some rather good blues lines. However, it's very difficult to ignore the unnatural sound of this robotic voice that makes so many people recoil in horror. Yet, I get the feeling that if the vocal had been replaced by saxophone, it would have received acclaim. The structure of the composition is well above the level of a standard pop song and there's plenty of interest. It's funky, disco music that over the years must have got a lot of people dancing. At about 3.20 there's a fracture in the music where a funky insert extends the basic piece beyond its compulsory three-minute radio lifespan. Hancock uses it to create a lively electric piano solo that becomes overdubbed with synthesiser and raises the track to a higher level. It really makes this piece worth a listen. Then at 5.12 the original theme returns and the track ends fairly predictably. Personally, I am not at all offended by this piece.

Trust Me is a superb vocal ballad – one of Herbie's best-known songs that he still plays today and additionally coloured here by vocoder textures. At 1.50, the piece becomes an instrumental in the same mould as many pieces of TV or film scores by cool jazz master Bob James, for example. Hancock's playing is laid back and melodic, which is another reason for attracting flak. This music is really great. Vocoder? Get over it! *Ready or Not* is largely a vocal number but does not feature the vocoder. It ends with some gutsy guitar playing that would make a lot of toes curl.

Tell Everybody is a very good disco number that begins with an excellent funk bass line before Hancock delivers more vocoder lines, but these are less weird electronics than they are earthy. How many rock singers have spent a long time trying to sing like this? Much of the singing is a dialogue between Hancock and his backing chorus. It's not high jazz, but it is good jazz-fusion. The middle section is a lengthy groove in the form of a worthwhile vamp that breaks out of its bag and delivers more excitement than we might expect. It's ten years on from the awful vamps Hancock was serving up on *Fat Albert Rotunda* (1969). This track deserves to be given more credit than it has received so far.

Honey From the Jar is a track that turns down the pace but turns up the funk. Though vocoder vocals continue to prevail above the female-led backing vocals, I find that you can get used to the unusual sound and once you do, you discover something that is really slinky and grease-saturated and is certainly appropriate to the original definition of the word 'funk'. Listen to the vocal itself, rather than the electronics, and you will hear lines that are worthy of many a famous R&B vocalist.

With *Knee Deep* it's back to basics. An instrumental track that can be judged purely on the basis of its contribution to the jazz-fusion repertoire, it is not without merit, although I find the repetitions are verging on the tedious. It would have benefited so much more from some sharper editing and splicing of its promising themes. And, unlike Pat Metheny, who never fails to provide me with something new when I think the music is about to end, this ends prematurely. Perhaps that's a good thing.

I reluctantly admit that you may not like this album, on the basis that the majority of the record-buying public is reported to detest it. However, I hope you are open-minded enough to read my arguments and give it a chance. It is certainly not high art, but I've given it three stars on the basis that it's lively and cheerful.

Herbie Hancock and Chick Corea: *An Evening With Herbie Hancock and Chick Corea In Concert* – 1978 (***)

By the end of the 1970s, Herbie and Chick had spent almost a decade fronted by arrays of electronic keyboards that were often experimental and extremely agricultural by today's standards. The initial burst of enthusiasm for jazz-rock fusion that both men had indulged in was over and they considered what projects to try next. Many observers, tired of electronic histrionics, requested that they perform some concerts of acoustic duets. Sure enough, both Herbie and Chick found that idea very acceptable, so in February 1978, they played some concerts in San Francisco, Los Angeles and Ann Arbor and recordings were made under the direction of Herbie's producer David Rubinson. Soon afterwards, Herbie's record company, Columbia, released a double vinyl album entitled *An Evening With Herbie Hancock and Chick Corea In Concert* (1978). Herbie and Chick then embarked upon a world tour that lasted until 1979. Since their album had proved commercially successful, it was followed up with a sister album on Chick's Polydor label, often listed simply as *Corea / Hancock*, but formally entitled *An Evening with Chick Corea and Herbie Hancock* (1979).

The 1978 album contains a balanced mixture of tracks. Herbie's *Maiden Voyage* is balanced by Chick's *La Fiesta*. There are two improvised pieces labelled *Button Up* and *February Moment*. The standards *Someday My Prince Will Come* and *Liza* refer to pieces that typically featured at Miles Davis performances.

The 1979 album adopts a similar theme of music selection. *Maiden Voyage* and *La Fiesta* appear for a second time, although taken from different concerts. *The Hook* is an improvised piece, whilst *Homecoming* and *Bouquet* are Chick's compositions. A piece of particular interest is the inclusion of a composition by the classical musician Béla Bartok called *Ostinato*, written specifically for two pianos. It's a very good example of just how versatile both men are – even in the classical environment

Herbie Hancock: *The Piano* – 1979 (***)

I have already discussed how Herbie has contributed to the birth and development of jazz-fusion and these aspects of the history of jazz are both interesting and essential reading for anyone who cares about its heritage. However, there are other aspects – beyond the field of jazz-fusion – to which Herbie Hancock has contributed immensely. This fascinating story is curious. It involves the very high esteem with which Herbie is held in Japan, to the extent that there was for many years, a large body of work did not emerge from the shores of that country, locked inside like some priceless treasure, too risky to expose to the wider world.

Herbie became very fond of touring in Japan and made frequent visits. He found himself taking part in experiments that helped to develop the entire recording industry thanks to his relationship with his recording company Columbia and its parent company Sony which was a leading player in the rapidly expanding market of consumer electronics.

It is worth reminding ourselves that, in the early days of recording, a musician's efforts were captured by a process whereby a needle vibrating at the frequencies of the music, cut a groove in a wax cylinder. Once made, there were no opportunities to edit or amend the recording and it required the performer to be confident enough to perform with as few errors as possible. Later, in the process of (literally) 'cutting' a disc, Herbie's producer, David Rubinson wrote "the state of the art for supreme recording quality was 'direct-to-disc'. This meant that a live performance was instantly and directly recorded, in real time, on a master acetate disc, which was immediately plated and used to stamp out a limited number of extremely high quality LP pressings. Not only were there no editing, fixing, or changes possible, but a performance had to fit exactly into the analog LP parameters, including time and amplitude." [48] In jazz, of course, a medium that relied heavily upon the unpredictability of improvisation, it was often very difficult to predict the length of a performance and errors could be a serious issue.

The Compact Disc as we know it today became commercially available in 1982, but it began as a development in the technology of the Laserdisc, a prototype of which was publicly demonstrated by the electrical company Phillips in Eindhoven, Netherlands, on 8 March 1979. Three years earlier, in September 1976, Sony had first publicly demonstrated an optical digital audio disc and then, in September 1978, their prototype disc had a 150 minute playing time, with music recorded at a 16-bit resolution and 44,056 Hz (44.1 kHz) sampling rate, a specification very similar to the one used today. Thanks to the efforts of his manager, David Rubinson, Herbie was invited to make a prototype CD using the equivalent of the old method of direct-to-disc recording. Sony's chief designer for the compact disc format and for the Walkman personal music player was Dr Toshi Doi, assisted by Yasohachi Itoh (whose name translates to eighty-eight!).

So, in Tokyo in October 1978 at the Sony studios, an album of solo piano music was recorded. It was a very rare occasion for Herbie as all of his officially released works had so far been made in the company of other musicians. Let us be in no doubt about the difficulty of the task that lay ahead. Rubinson: "For each side of the two-sided LP, Herbie had to play three - four songs, in real time, consecutively. Live. Perfectly. But not just perfectly, and not just exactly timed. For some people, the conditions would be an impediment; for Herbie they were not only a creative impetus, but in fact an amazing challenging catalyst of constraint, which actually elevated his creativity by imposing severe limits. The resulting performances were, in my opinion, better for having had the limitations themselves provide inspiration. That's what genius does." [48]

For those who like the sound of a master pianist performing solo on an acoustic grand piano this is essential listening, but the historical aspects to this recording make it even more interesting. Herbie selected a range of material, based again on an end-product that was two sides of a vinyl LP. On Side A he played three standards, *My Funny Valentine*, *Someday My Prince Will Come* and *On Green Dolphin Street*. For Side B he chose the originals *Harvest Time*, *Sonrisa*, *Manhattan Island* and *Blue Otani*. For many years, *The Piano* (1979) was available only in Japan and only in limited edition until it was re-mastered and released in the Columbia Legacy series in 2004.

Herbie Hancock: *Direct Step* - 1979 (***)

When he recorded *Dedication* (1974), Herbie divided his performance across two sides of vinyl split evenly with acoustic and electric music. In 1978, he did the same across two vinyl discs. At the same time as he recorded *The Piano* (1979), he also recorded an album with the Headhunters. Once again, the album, *Direct Step* (1979), was recorded for Sony (Japan) for release only in Japan and has largely remained in that country ever since. Once again, too, the album was recorded using the direct-to-disc system, hence the title of the album. At barely half an hour in length, there are just three tracks from the Headhunters, with Jackson, Summers and Maupin as usual, but this time with Ray Obiedo (guitar), Alphonse Mouzon (drums) and Webster Lewis (keyboards).

Butterfly is beautifully performed, although this time with an unusual change of tempo that allows Ray Obiedo to let loose on his guitar. We find the first outing on record of the band composition *Shiftless Shuffle*, a piece that is perhaps better performed on the album *Mr. Hands* (1980). Finally there is an excellent rendition of *I Thought It Was You*, very similar to the one on *Sunlight* (1977) but with an extended vamp at the end of its fifteen-minute length.

V.S.O.P.: *Live Under the Sky* – 1979 (****)

Columbia executive Bob Belden recalls how, in 1979, the record business was in dire straits and heading for a slump. [49] Not only was jazz itself suffering a major decline in popularity, but also sales of albums were declining because of the recognised deficiencies of the vinyl disc medium and the popularity of 'home taping'. Digitally recorded and stored music had become possible, but the technologies were still in their infancy. Belden concludes that the revival of interest in music - especially jazz - that took place in the early 1980s was due entirely to the invention of the CD. Vinyl technology and record decks had become *passé* in a new 'hi-tech' market that delivered music of superior quality. Customers' enjoyment was further enhanced with hardware that offered features such as instant track selection, random play and – above all - remote control. Curiously, the record-buying public was so taken with these advances in technology that they seemed entirely content to purchase CDs containing the same music they had bought earlier in vinyl formats. (People repeated this odd behaviour when videotapes were replaced with DVD!)

During a V.S.O.P. tour of Japan in July 1979, Herbie's producer David Rubinson once again worked closely with Sony's Japanese engineers to record two live concerts at the Denen Colosseum using the so-called 'direct-to-disc' method. So now V.S.O.P. too were guinea pigs - perhaps trail-blazers is a better word - but little they cared. They were BIG in Japan. They had all been involved with their own projects when Herbie called to invite them on another V.S.O.P. tour of Japan and Belden points out how much they must have wanted to do it. The most important thing was that they were received with rapturous enthusiasm by the Japanese audiences for music that was attracting little attention at home. (In 2004 Pat Metheny reported similar differences of response between audiences of different nationalities and the situation is unchanged today in 2010. [50]) The two albums were not released outside of Japan for over twenty years. The latest edition of the *Live Under the Sky* album is a treat for all lovers of acoustic mainstream jazz. An entire bonus disc of recordings from July 27 complements the original disc, which contains material from the first night, July 26. Apparently, the new digital method was sensitive enough to record the sound of the raindrops, an occupational hazard for all bands that try to play outdoors.

The notes to this album contain some interesting observations by Bob Belden that explain why much of Herbie's music of this period was not available to the wider world. Belden: "The touring band V.S.O.P. was controversial in that it was too modern sounding for the purists and too pure for the modernists. There was a schism in the musical community between popular styles overwhelming jazz musicians into playing softer, more commercial music and the codification of the avant-garde into a more 'democratic' form of expression. V.S.O.P. was the exact opposite of what each individual member was doing on his own at this time ... Much criticism came from those who felt that some of these artists ... had 'betrayed' jazz, that they had no 'right' to return to the flock. Columbia never issued this recording domestically." [51] It is shocking to think that, although the music on this and other albums was commercially acceptable in Japan, it was apparently unsellable in the musicians' home country.

Herbie Hancock: *Mr Hands* – 1980 (****)

So, back in the USA, Herbie continued with his own projects in his own way, regardless of critical comment. With the album *Mr Hands* (1980) it is clear that funk had at last come of age. Here at the beginning of a new decade is a collection of very different pieces that prove just how much the sub-genre has moved on in the four years that separate it from *Secrets* (1976). But much more than that, here is an intriguing album that demonstrates Herbie's early dedication to the advancement of music through technology. There is no question of this music sounding dated; the selection and creation of sound from the millions of different new sounds now made possible through the miracle of silicon is fully mature. There is no single band on the album. Herbie uses different groups of musicians for each of the six numbers, which superficially makes it seem like a *Best of* compilation, especially as there are no details of the recording dates or venues on the sleeve notes. There are no vocal numbers. This album is really about Herbie Hancock creating a panorama of musical colour with his own hands. There are fourteen instruments listed, and for the first time includes a 'modified Apple II computer'.

The album is a statement of intent, for although there is a clear aim to be a 'one-man band', he still hires the best musicians to support him. The opener is *Spiraling Prism*, an aptly titled gentle piece that cycles through a set of changes to create a steadily rising tension. Musicians Leon Chancler (drums) Bill Summers (percussion) and Byron Miller (bass) support Herbie's numerous keyboard variations.

Next Herbie plays in a trio piece, *Calypso*, with his friends Tony Williams and Ron Carter. In fact, Sheila Escovedo is credited on percussion but the sleeve notes proclaim that Herbie also makes the sound of steel drums so I am at a loss to know what she actually played on this track. An acoustic number, this track creates an imbalance on what might have been a jazz-fusion disc. Tony Williams' drumming is way over the top at times, especially with his use of cymbals, which often drown out the rest of the music.

Just Around the Corner is a far more appropriate and exciting addition to the running order. It starts with an excellent funky vibe from Freddie Washington's bass and Alphonze Mouzon on drums. The sleeve notes state that Wah Wah Watson is present too. I'm not sure if his odd name refers to his guitar style or his speech impediment, but with Herbie playing 'everything else' this track is a *tour de force* from Hancock, now a funk-master of the seventh dan.

A major bonus is the presence of Jaco Pastorius on *4 am*, a selection that shines brightly out of the album. Jaco is so far ahead of the game that the track is quite unforgettable for his bass playing, despite the very worthy contributions of the other bass players on this disc. The track is a sophisticated composition that requires significant discipline on the part of its players, as well as extraordinary talent. Thus, for someone whose reputation for self-destruction, insubordination and lack of self-control is unapproachable, Jaco demonstrates here every bit of the professionalism and artistic flair that Herbie would have expected from him. His impeccably clean and rhythmic lines are an absolute joy, right up to final seconds when I smile as he plays his trademark 'must have the last word' notes. Jaco and Herbie had worked together on Jaco's *Word of Mouth* (1981) album at around this time, and the added presence of the awesome Harvey Mason and Bill Summers turns this track into a special event.

Mason's clear edge over Williams (in this genre at least) is illustrated by the track with the least sensible title, *Shiftless Shuffle*. You should not be fooled into thinking that the track is any the worse for that. Far from being an aimless, medium tempo trot, this piece is more like a panic stricken stampede to the gangway on a blazing cruise ship as the amazing Mason and Summers, supported by bassist Paul Jackson, create a remarkable rhythmic storm behind Hancock's demanding keyboard lines. There is a strange rift in the rhythm at about 0.58, from which point Mason's drumming is quite extraordinary and drives everyone else along whilst not dominating as Williams does. The tension becomes feverish as the pace simply never lets up and you have to ask if there was ever a funky piece as hard-driven as this?

The tension is exquisitely released with Hancock's final coup – the delightful *Textures*, a track on which Hancock really does play everything. The sound of a Pastorius-like bass and silicon drums accompanies a really great Hancock melody that stays with you long after the record is over. There are some surprising changes of direction as the piece proceeds, all of which add to the 'tingle factor' of his creation. There is a great deal that is special on this album, but I particularly like the way he has (perhaps subconsciously?) juxtaposed each great musician with his electronic nemesis. If Herbie is going to demonstrate electronic bass, drums, sax, guitar, and everything else, why not use the whole album to do it? Why hire the likes of Williams, Carter, Pastorius & Co, only to put them alongside software and silicon? It's almost as if Herbie (in the nicest possible way) is cocking a snook at them and saying, "Hey guys look at this Brave New World of music that I'm into. You'd better watch your asses!" I can see his broad smile and hear his laugh as he does so. As if they didn't know already!

Herbie Hancock: *Monster* – 1980 (***)

Herbie's disco album formula was well developed by the time he released the album *Monster* (1980). Once again, he used his familiar band of Melvin "Wah Wah Watson" Ragin, Freddie Washington, Alphonze Mouzon with Sheila Escovedo (aka Sheila E) on percussion. With this collection of vocal music, the aim seems to have been to continue Herbie's career in jazz-pop. To achieve the variety of sound, style and content that producer David Rubinson had in mind, a number of guests were invited to join different tracks. The most notable was Carlos Santana on the excellent opening track, *Saturday Night*, a kind of Herbie equivalent to Elton John's great hit *Saturday Night's All Right For Fighting*. Santana is, as they say, a class act with a very high profile amongst many non-jazz listeners, and since the first track on any album is always the most commercially attractive, the album was clearly being held up in lights as an advertisement to the broader record-buying public. Again, a formula for the structure of the song was in place. The first three minutes is the standard fare that would appeal to radio DJs, and the next four minutes are given over to the instrumental solos. Greg Walker is the well-chosen vocalist, taking two cycles through the verse and chorus. Then comes the serious stuff.

Saturday Night has a Latin feel that clearly suits Santana's sensibilities and he surely lives up to it after the three-minute watershed. Herbie adopts a curious synthetic sound for his own solo that maintains the great disco rhythm whilst adding an unusual texture to the mix. The final part of the piece is a high-octane duel between the two main jousters, what is known in the trade as 'fours' – alternately played groups of four bars – between Carlos's trademark guitar voice and Herbie's terrific matching keyboard guitar sound.

Gavin Christopher was selected to sing *Stars in Your Eyes*, a slightly moodier groove piece that clings to D minor for its theme. Fortunately, the piece dips into a shallow basket of chord changes for its chorus section. Herbie is adding some slight sound effects during this phase of the song, but moves to a repeated clicky phrase from four minutes as he sets up a longer groove. The song moves back to the original verse/chorus format for the final two minutes. This is a piece that's all about the mood of the disco dance, rather than any attempt to push back boundaries of music and Herbie's contribution is more subdued.

Oren Waters takes the lead vocals for the up-tempo *Go For It*, once more cast in a disco rhythm thanks largely to Washington's slap bass style and Mouzon's funky beat. Herbie is busy adding the kind of parallel keyboard effects that we all take for granted these days. Once the FM radio's first four minutes are complete, Herbie comes in to set the jazzers buzzing with a great synth solo, before Waters returns with his siblings (Julia, Maxine and Luther) in the background for the re-run to the finish.

Gavin Christopher returns for *Don't Hold it In* which is another groove-based funk piece with some heavy guitar sounds from guest Randy Hansen. Herbie has also been experimenting with his buttons and has found some great new sounds on his keys. After a good guitar groove from Ragin at four minutes, Herbie starts what promises to be a great solo and then moves into a fantastic guitar duel with Hansen such that I struggle to tell the difference between the real and the synthetic guitar. (In fact, Herbie's is the first of each pair of lines.) From 6.00, it's back to the original theme with embellishments to negate the risk of repetition.

Making Love is a very pleasant tune with erotic lyrics. It makes a gentle contrast with the rest of the music and balances the styles nicely. This is followed by the more aggressively marketed last track, *It All Comes Round*, which sits on the rock side of the jazz-rock divide, largely because of the presence of Hendrix-impersonator Randy Hansen. Herbie doesn't appear to have much presence on this track, team-written by Ragin, Cohen and Rubinson. Bill Champlin is the lead vocalist, assisted by the Waters background singers. It's a good end to an album that can only be regarded as a solid collection of disco music, and it impressed many listeners that would not have walked round the corner to hear jazz played. If, therefore, it made jazz even a micron more accessible to the wider audience then its existence is justified. It is sad that this album, together with *Sunlight* (1978) and the subsequent *Magic Windows* (1981) (which make a neat three-record set of disco albums) is now difficult to buy.

The sleeve notes to my French edition of the CD claim that "Nulle trace de jazz dans Monster" (No trace of jazz in *Monster*.) [52] Well, the anonymous author doesn't appear to have much idea about the identity of jazz in jazz-fusion, for this is indeed a 1980s jazz-fusion album in a formula devised by Herbie. It was much hated by jazz puritans because of the sheer audacity of having one foot in the jazz camp. It was another step along the road to the complete absorption of jazz sensibilities into popular music – certainly not pure jazz, but quite different from the jazz-rock days of the Mahavishnu Orchestra and the jazz-funk days of the Headhunters.

Herbie Hancock: *Magic Windows* – 1981 (**)

The third album in the mini-series was *Magic Windows* (1981), with a further repeat of the winning disco formula. It may be one of the albums Mark Gilbert had in mind when he commented that some of Herbie's albums were 'as frothy as any dance music has a right to be,' which is a back-handed way of saying that albums such as this should not be judged alongside jazz albums because they appear worse than they are. This point was also made about *Future Shock* (1983) by Kevin Legendre. Gilbert followed up by saying that 'much of it has a satisfying substance.' [53]

It seems that the record company executives were worried that Herbie's accomplishments on records such as this would not be fully appreciated, so they included the following on the notes of his albums around this time: "There are no strings, brass, or other orchestral instruments on this album. All of these orchestrations are performed by Herbie Hancock on various synthesizers" Only a year before, Herbie had been using computers alongside real musicians. Now, like a football coach seeking a boost for his ailing team, he had substituted the human players with silicon chips from the bench.

Typical of the latest gear was the Fairlight CMI (Computer Musical Instrument), the first digital sampling synthesiser. Designed by Peter Vogel and Kim Ryrie, it was based on a dual microprocessor computer designed by Australian Tony Furse in the late 1970s. It was first used on Kate Bush's album *Never for Ever* (1980) and on Jean-Michel Jarre's *Magnetic Fields* (1981). A Fairlight CMI was used in Jan Hammer's music video for the theme song to the TV cops show *Miami Vice*. Well made, the Series I instrument with all options cost almost $1 million, so it was available only to the best-resourced musicians.

A good example is to be found on *Tonight's the Night*. Though it is a vocal number, there are two instrumental breaks that sound like a saxophone. The first was made on one of Herbie's many synthesisers (the great banks of keyboards are proudly displayed on the sleeve notes), the second from Michael Brecker's curved tenor tube. When you listen carefully, it is, of course, easy to tell the difference, but you could miss it otherwise. The number is in the mould of a typical 1980s middle-of-the-road easy listening vocal number that anyone who lived through the period would have heard countless times in shopping malls, airport lounges and hotel foyers. It's worth remembering that Herbie was at this time helping to create the entire sub-genre that later became more formally known as 'cool jazz', espoused by companies like GRP records and despised by the jazz puritans. The piece is a pleasant tune, well sung by Vicki Randle who seems not to have hit the big time despite her good performance.

The opening track, *Magic Number*, is a good enough disco piece but there is nothing of note about it at all. *Everybody's Broke* is a lowbrow number that introduces vocalist Gavin Christopher who tries humorous lyrics as a means of adding variety. *Help Yourself* is another vocal from Christopher, who is also credited with the 'brass arrangement concept'. *Satisfied with Love* is another ballad, well sung by Christopher and written by Herbie and Jean. The final track is *The Twilight Clone*, an instrumental piece with an oriental vibe. It reminds us that Herbie's music is really about jazz ideas painted with electronic colours and textures, and that the rest of this lightweight album is a flirtation – another short episode in a series a brief encounters with popular culture.

With the benefit of hindsight, it is easy for us to criticise this music as thin and lacking in substance, but there are several aspects to it. First, there is the composition – the idea. When a piece is credited to four or five people, we can only conclude that the idea was a thin one, criticised as such by a demanding producer and embellished by a committee of musicians in the studio five minutes before it was recorded. Then there is the musicianship involved. Clearly, Herbie demonstrates a great deal of skill in managing and playing all of the various keyboards, each with hundreds of sounds. However, when your name is Herbie Hancock, you have generous record company resources and the artistic clout to be able to hire the best musicians so that your ideas can be executed to the highest level. We know how much Herbie enjoys playing with the technology, but this is really just an example of 'boys' toys'. Posterity is not especially impressed with a battery of sounds that are simply imitations (often inferior) of the real thing. Herbie clearly made the right decision not to employ a regular band, for it is hard to say to a bassist or drummer that he is not required for the next track because it is planned to use electronics instead.

Herbie Hancock: *Herbie Hancock Trio with Ron Carter and Tony Williams* – 1981 (****)

Over the years, despite his great interest in playing fusion and other electronic forms of music, whenever possible, Herbie spent time with his old mates Ron Carter and Tony Williams to keep their mainstream jazz roots watered. In jazz, the piano trio is about the simplest kind of project you can have, especially when the music consists of well-known 'standards', so this was an uncomplicated project for Herbie entitled *Herbie Hancock Trio with Ron Carter and Tony Williams* (1981). A fresh set of selections includes Benny Golson's *Stable Mates*, and that old white standard *That Old Black Magic*. And it certainly is magic. Ron's lovely balled *A Slight Smile* is balanced by Tony's *La Maison Goree*, and the selections are completed by Herbie's familiar tune *Dolphin Dance*.

It's not exhibition stuff, but is nevertheless in the category that people would recognise as 'cocktail lounge' jazz. Warm tones and harmonies, user-friendly forms and melodies, and challenging but conventional improvisations: this is the kind of fare many listeners would be delighted to come home from work and listen to as they relax with a glass of wine. The band exhibits the kind of tightness that you would expect from a trio that has been intimate for nearly twenty years. Herbie's playing is quite superb: inspirational, precise. Tony is his usual ebullient self, placing himself firmly in the role of rhythmic innovator. Yes, he follows leads set by Ron and Herbie, but is equally likely to drive the pace and style in his own direction as wait for others to do it for him. He's loud and brash, but knows when to be quiet too. Ron is also outstanding: evolutionary, never repetitive, but also now bursting with digital clarity.

This was another album recorded in Tokyo by Sony on their new digital recording system. (We need to remember that the system it replaced was based upon analogue magnetic tape.) Sony was keen to continue with its policy of making recordings at the cutting edge of technology. Even today, it seems that the Japanese edition is the only one available. Now, I am not one who subscribes to the view that analogue recordings are somehow (even mysteriously) better than digital ones. The science is simple: a sound signal can be represented to perfection with a binary code, as long as the sampling rate is fast enough. The ultimate sound reproduction we hear is not limited by what is on the CD, but rather by the quality of the speakers we are using. What I am trying to say is that this digital recording quality is as excellent as you could expect to get and the sound of each member of the band is crystal clear. It makes this a highly desirable CD of top-quality acoustic mainstream jazz and makes an excellent companion to *The Herbie Hancock Trio* (1977).

Herbie Hancock: *Herbie Hancock Quartet* – 1982 (***)

Another album, recorded in Japan and having had restricted distribution is simply titled *Herbie Hancock Quartet* (1982). As this is one of only two occasions when Herbie can be heard on a recording with controversial trumpeter, Wynton Marsalis, it is, in itself, a curiosity for reasons I will explain.

The second of six sons, Wynton Marsalis was born in 1961 in New Orleans to Dolores and Ellis Marsalis Jr., a music teacher and pianist. His elder brother Branford (b1960) is also a leading jazz musician. Wynton got his first trumpet at the age of six, and at eight years old he performed traditional New Orleans music in a church band. Like Herbie, he was invited to perform with a major orchestra, the New Orleans Philharmonic, at 14. During his high school years Marsalis was a member of numerous classical music ensembles, whilst also playing in jazz bands. He moved to New York City to attend the Juilliard School of Music in 1978, and in 1980 he followed a familiar course for budding jazz stars by joining Art Blakey's Jazz Messengers. In 1981, he joined Herbie's acoustic quartet and toured throughout the USA and Japan, as well as performing at the Newport Jazz Festival. It was during this tour that this album was recorded using the very latest digital equipment.

Today, Wynton Marsalis is a household name in the world of jazz, though not necessarily for the right reasons. In the late 1990s, Marsalis became famous for his outspoken views on jazz – in effect, he appointed himself a leader of the jazz puritan movement. Seriously critical of the free jazz and fusion movements, he whipped up a storm of criticism by promoting traditional values in jazz. This kind of backward-facing viewpoint merely invoked the retort that his views were regressive and counter to the Davis argument of jazz being about "living in the moment", in other words, anything is fine as long as you are being instantly creative and original. Wynton's academic approach to jazz flew directly in the face of the loose style and musical philosophy that Miles (and others like Coltrane and Coleman too) had developed. Many music fans chose Davis & Co. over Marsalis.

His biggest exposure came with his involvement in the US PBS TV series *Jazz*, written and produced by Ken Burns. Marsalis's role as a 'senior consultant' seemed to have introduced a backward-facing bias to the programmes that many informed observers felt diminished this major work. His own generous number of appearances came across as an immodest attempt at self-promotion. Raising his head above the parapet in this way, Marsalis might have expected to get shot at by snipers, but perhaps he never expected to be met by a wall of machine gun fire. As so often happens, the criticism quickly got personal, to the extent that many senior, well-qualified observers even denigrated his skills as a trumpeter and his place as a leading jazz musician. Keith Jarrett described him as no more than a "talented high school player" [54]

Pierre Sprey, president of jazz record company Mapleshade Records, said: "When Marsalis was nineteen, he was a fine jazz trumpeter ... But he was getting his tail beat off every night in Art Blakey's band. I don't think he could keep up. And finally he retreated to safe waters. He's a good classical trumpeter and thus he sees jazz as being a classical Music. He has no clue what's going on now." [55]

Ake, asking how we should interpret Wynton's self-defined position, made this observation: "Has the role of the contemporary jazz musician, like that of many of his or her counterparts in the European classical tradition, become that of the interpreter, reviving works and styles from bygone eras? If so, this would represent a very untraditional shift in jazz performance aesthetics as they have developed thus far. For an enduring hallmark of jazz musicians over the course of the twentieth century has been their desire to continually draw on and reshape the sounds, tunes and genres around them." [56]

For those not interested in the politics of the debate, this album makes a good addition to a collection of wholesome acoustic mainstream jazz. In the light of Jarrett's critique of Marsalis, I should be careful in saying that Marsalis plays well on the record. However, I hardly think that Herbie would have chosen him to join his tour with Ron and Tony if Wynton had not been a top-notch player. There is a generous scattering of tunes from the Miles Davis catalogue, such as

Well You Needn't, *'Round Midnight*, *Pee Wee*, *I Fall in Love Too Easily*, and *Sorcerer*, as well as Herbie's own standard, *Eye of the Hurricane*. It is worth remembering that this recording took place some five years before Wynton, after hoping to be invited to jam with Miles at the Montreal Jazz Festival, was infamously dismissed from the stage with the curt order to "get the fuck off". [57] Perhaps the album selections would have been different if the record had been made in 1987!

Herbie Hancock: *Lite Me Up* - 1982 (***)

Later in his career, Herbie said that he had tried to make a record that was not a jazz record. Well, this is it – or perhaps I should say another of them. *Lite Me Up* (1982) is an album of vocal tracks, with Herbie singing some of the songs without the protective disguise of his vocoder on every one, although the vocoder is used on a couple. He needn't have worried: his voice is fine. Most people would describe the album as a pop record, some in disparaging tones. Now, when the project was being worked on, I have no doubt that Herbie was hoping for a hit record in the album charts, and why should we blame him for that?

Setting aside the music for the moment, this record astonishes me for one thing – its musicians! Herbie went to the Californian coast to join up with top-notch session guys who were playing on all the best crossover music of the time. Herbie's main assistant on the album was songwriter/ keyboardist Rod Temperton who had played with the funk band Heatwave. Temperton was an original member at the band's inception in 1976. In January 1977 they reached a high spot in the UK charts with *Boogie Nights*. The ensuing album *Too Hot to Handle* and the single release *Always and Forever* were also big hits. Then Temperton quit the band in 1978 to concentrate on his solo career as a songwriter. It proved to be a good decision. His career sparkled with hits written for a host of top acts. Temperton worked with Quincy Jones, one of the most successful musicians ever and a major reason for Michael Jackson's success. As he worked with Herbie, Temperton was hot from working on Michael Jackson's *Thriller* (1982), one of the greatest pop albums of all time. Not only did Temperton write the title track, but also *Baby Be Mine* and *The Lady in My Life*. Temperton wrote six of the eight tracks on *Lite Me Up*, three of them co-written with Herbie, but it didn't stop there. Along with Temperton came most of the team that had made the *Thriller* album: Michael Boddicker was a superb keyboard programmer, Larry Williams played sax and woodwinds, Narada Michael Walden played drums. Then there were David Foster (keyboards) and Jeff Porcaro (drums). Jerry Hey (trumpet) and Bill Reichenbach (trombone) appear with their team of fabulous horn players. These guys were the finest of their ilk, providing unbelievably tight, quick-fire brass punctuation that characterised many of the *Thriller* tracks. How could Herbie have chosen a better team? On the face of it, it is remarkable that this album was not a #1 smash hit. All of the ingredients were there – 28 musicians and singers, many of them the best in the business, performing music written by Michael Jackson's favourite composer.

Lite Me Up! is a good up-tempo pop song that meets all the criteria for a hit record, except that it didn't make it. Steve Lukather plays guitar on this track, which alone is worth reporting. Track 2 is *The Bomb*, a good song with silly lyrics that is as good as the opener. At 1.50 the piece sounds as if it has come from the cutting room floor of the *Thriller* production room, but the keyboard solo that follows it is a Herbie special. *Gettin' to the Good Part* is a good album track in which Herbie returns to his vocoder; you'll either love it or hate it, but the song is pretty good. *Paradise* sees another new guest in the studio, Jay Graydon (guitar), who, along with David Foster, Abe Laboriel (bass) and Jeff Porcaro (drums) were all working with the great singer Al Jarreau at around this time. Unsurprisingly, this piece is very much like their music, and equally as good. Surprisingly, Herbie sings the lead vocals *without* the disguise of the vocoder.

Can't Hide Your Love is another track that Herbie sings himself, aided by a different team of musicians underpinned with Walden's drums, Randy Jackson's bass and guitar work from Carrado Rustici. *The Fun Tracks* is a Temperton piece, sung by Wayne Anthony that fades into insignificance when the album's over, eclipsed by better material around it. *Motor Mouth* isn't a lot better, sung again by Wayne Anthony and with more vocoder. The final track is *Give It All Your Heart* in which vocoder Herbie is joined in his fetish by Patrice Rushen. This funky piece is better from a fusion viewpoint and there is finally an extended Rhodes piano solo and some colourful brass at the end.

Temperton's team is unquestionably professional and produces some good pop music, which is what Hancock wanted, but the best music occurs when Al Jarreau's team led by Jay Graydon take charge. Although the sleeve notes, as usual, list a large array of electronic gear that Herbie used in the recordings, sadly, there isn't much evidence of clever, innovative keyboards on the album except in a few brief bridge sections. *Lite Me Up* is a good pop album, but anyone expecting jazz will be disappointed.

Herbie Hancock: *Future Shock* – 1983 (***)

Herbie re-emerged as a pop sensation with the release of his album *Future Shock* (1983), which included *Rockit*. This song won him a Grammy for best R&B Instrumental, and the music video that accompanied it won 5 MTV

Awards. In September 2005, Herbie told Steve Wright [58] that it "somehow resonated with the general public." By now, the term 'fusion' had become useless for describing a musical genre. It seemed more appropriate to talk of 'crossover' in which artists from one genre introduce their fans to the music from another genre. *Future Shock*, and in particular the opening track *Rockit*, became a big hit for Herbie, but once again the critics hated it. He told Wright: "Well for the most part the jazz fans either liked the record or didn't like it but they never said anything about my right to make whatever record I wanna make. But somehow the critics – many of them were really irate about it, you know, how could you do this? Well I never signed in blood that I even had to be a musician much less to be a jazz musician. I'm a human being! I can do what I like." [58]

In hip-hop, Herbie was surprised to find quite a bit of sympathy for his work: "I noticed a lot of people in the hip-hop scene have a great respect for jazz and have incorporated by sampling some elements that come from jazz." [58]

Future Shock was a collaboration between Herbie and two musicians Bill Laswell (bass) and Michael Beinhorn (keyboards) from the New York band, Material. It took fusion music in an entirely new direction and, as Hancock admits, was a really lucky break for him. It brought the new genre of hip-hop out of the closet and had a major impact upon the music scene way beyond the realms of jazz.

With *Rockit* and *Earth Beat* Laswell says that Herbie was trying to achieve an entirely new kind of sound that was 'radically hip' and that they aimed to create a 'big kind of fusion' with many electronic and rhythmic influences [59]. *Rockit* begins with a heavily synthesised drum track built up from sequencers, as well as a variety of electronic sounds and real percussion. At 0.45, Hancock comes in with a synthetic theme that is quickly memorable and from then on it's fairly small variations on the theme. From 2.52 to 3.57 we hear an early demonstration of the use of turntables as musical instruments by Grand Mixer DST. From 4.00 to 4.42 there's an improvised section using a variety of effects and then the final section is a brief improvisation by Herbie. The music is invigorating and a lot of fun, and it's clear where much of the hip-hop music of today derives from.

The title track is the only one not credited to the musicians playing the music. Second on the album is the funky *Future Shock*, composed by Mayfield. It is a kind of 1980s protest song featuring a vocal by Dwight Jackson Jr. Pete Cosey, a graduate from Miles's mid-70s fusion band, delivers a substantial raunchy guitar solo, whilst the rest of the band stick fairly closely to the script.

The unhelpfully titled *TFS* is a trio piece with Hancock, Laswell and Beinhorn.

Over a solid rock drum rhythm, the music moves along conventionally to a striking arrangement of a good theme. This track is probably the album's highlight for the more conventionally minded listener.

As mentioned above, *Earth Beat* belongs in the same slot as *Rockit* in its conception. It has the same musicians and the same kind of direction and effects, but being slower is clearly not as commercial. The middle of the track contains lots of extraterrestrial electronic sounds, but the track mostly goes nowhere beyond low orbit. On the other hand, *Autodrive* is in a higher gear and really flies. The same trio of musicians that appeared on *TFS* can surely make good music together. At last, Herbie makes a sustained effort to deliver some serious jazz piano amidst the rocking, but it's short and the track is dominated by a really thrusting theme that, for me, makes this track the best on the album.

Rough is disappointing. Maybe this sounded really new at the time, and its repetitiveness influenced generations of young musicians to do the same. However, I have never found pleasure in simply playing the same stuff over and over. Where's the skill? Where's the ingenuity? There's no serious musicianship here and it's clear from the other music that these guys can really play, so why don't they? They make a reasonable groove, but that's all. It's pointless as it stands and an otherwise good record is spoiled by a very poor track.

On the Columbia Legacy reissue disc, the bonus track is a megamix of *Rockit*. This is a total waste of time and simply tells me why it was not included on the original disc, but who declines a bonus?

There's nothing beautiful about this record and I guess that that also tells me why I don't like hip-hop music. Maybe I'm just an old fuddy-duddy, but I like to think not. There are some good grooves and themes. Though the bass playing is clearly very interesting, it's acoustically dull and disappointing that it has not been recorded well. As a collection, the music really does hang together under the "sci-fi" wrappers it has been given. As jazz, the content is weak, but viewed from outside of the jazz genre, it is probably a very exciting record that other people would give more stars than I have. It is certainly a very memorable collection of music that is worth a try, especially if you are inclined towards the kind of popular music emanating from New York around the mid to late 1980s.

Herbie acknowledges that he was fortunate in being in the right place at the right time with the right people. [60] Laswell had been the real driving force behind the music, made even more exciting by Grandmixer DST's first use of a turntable in this way. Never before had jazz been merged with the hip-hop sounds of the street. It was exactly the kind of thing Miles Davis had been looking for ten years earlier. Yet even Laswell didn't appreciate at first the power of what he had created. Bill Laswell: "I didn't know what we really had until I played it when I stopped at a stereo store on the way to the airport in LA. I had a cassette of two songs and I was looking at speakers and I had some time to kill and I said 'Let me hear this speaker, let me hear this speaker', and he would play something like *Kansas* and I would say, no, play this. And he played that song, *Rockit*, and there was a moment where you turned around and there was like fifty kids going '*What is that?*' And then we knew." [61]

Rockit won a Grammy for best instrumental in 1983, assisted in its elevation by a stunning new style of pop video produced by Kevin Godly for MTV – another ground-breaker. Herbie was now a true pop superstar, but at the cost of yet more criticism from the jazz establishment. Kevin Legendre had a good answer to the critics: "The problem is because he is defined as a jazz artist we tend to assess…everything that he does according to jazz criteria. We are looking at him through that prism specifically, when in fact there are times when we shouldn't at all. I hear *Rockit* as a funk tune or a hip-hop tune. I don't hear it as a jazz tune, even though there is jazz knowledge in there... You dance to *Rockit*, it's so important. When jazz critics say 'Oh, well I don't hear much in there and it's not very exciting' I say 'You're not supposed to just listen to it, you're supposed to dance to it. Get up off your ass and dance to this music. That's why it works." [62]

Herbie Hancock: *Sound System* – 1984 (***)

In 1984, the Organising Committee for the Los Angeles Olympic Games approached Herbie to write some music for the field events. Clearly such high profile challenges inspire artists to think deeply about their commission. In Herbie's case, he decided to look for music that would illustrate the 'Roots of Man'. [63] Once again, Herbie's strong African heritage came to the front of his musical consciousness and just happened to coincide with his meeting an African musician called Foday Musa Suso.

As a boy in his native Gambia, Suso had learned many musical instruments, but concentrated on the kora, a 21-string musical instrument traditionally played by the Mandinga people of West Africa. The kora is the specialist instrument of people known as Griots or Jali. (In French, griots, are wandering troubadours, oral historians, chroniclers and praise singers who, while low down in the social hierarchy of the Mandinga, have long been respected in West African societies as repositories of history and tradition. In some ways they are analogous to the travelling American blues singers of the 1920s and 30s.) Suso claims to be descended from a line of Griots lasting for some 700 years. An acclaimed master of the kora, Suso's instrument is superficially similar to a guitar or a sitar, having a large rounded sound box at one end and making a delicate harp-like sound. Suso spent his early adulthood travelling and playing throughout Europe before returning to Africa in the mid-70s to teach at the University of Ghana. By 1977 Suso was living in Chicago, where he formed a fusion ensemble called the Mandingo Griot Society, with percussionist Adam Rudolph and Hamid Drake. The band specialised in the genre now known as World Music, although at that time it was recognised simply as an ethnic African music.

So, in 1984, Hancock followed up the great commercial success of *Future Shock* (1983) and the hit single *Rockit* with *Sound System* (1984). His formula was once more spot-on target for he won a second Grammy for the title track. *Sound-System* must have been an explosion of the mind as well as the ears for contemporary listeners. The advances in electronic keyboards, begun in the 70s, were now happening at a great pace. Similar changes to percussion instruments were only now taking off. Simmons drums were sets of hexagonal pads configured as electronic drums. They became available from the early 1980s. Another electronic percussion system was the DMX, released in 1980 and contained 24 percussion instrument samples. The unit was capable of creating unusual rhythms and time signatures. It stored 100 sequences and 50 'songs' in memory, and could deliver its sounds via 8 outputs, so different drum sounds could be processed separately. The DMX could also be synchronised to a DSX sequencer.

One of the most remarkable - and little recognised - of Herbie's achievements is the blending of traditional African with futuristic concepts in his music. The cover art for *Flood* (1975) advertises this perfectly with Africans in traditional dress juxtaposed with a space-suited Herbie, but in terms of the music itself it is probably best illustrated on this album by the inclusion of his new musical colleagues Foday Musa Suso and associates. Thanks to his Olympic commission, he had by now begun to work with Suso, and in doing so had discovered a new collection of sounds with which he could expand upon the new turf he had cut on *Future Shock*. Of course, John McLaughlin's work in blending the guitar with music played by traditional Indian musicians was well known, but Herbie's addition of the kora to Bill Laswell's futuristic sounds was a step into the unknown. It would also not be the last time, for ten years later Herbie would be revisiting this music with his album *Dis Is Da Drum* (1994).

Karabali tries to compensate for its monochrome predecessor with a more traditional structure and content and allows Herbie the chance to play something creative. The title becomes the subject of a hypnotic chant that embeds itself into your brain on first hearing it. Nevertheless, the music is interesting, made more so by the presence of Wayne Shorter's imaginative soprano sax work.

First on the menu is *Hardrock*, a title that accurately describes some of the guitar work from Nick Skopelitis and Henry Kaiser. However, it's not the guitar that's the star, so much as the robotic Laswell sounds that introduce this next stage in the eightyfication of jazz. Like it or not, this sound, and that of the following track, was destined to transform popular black music.

Metal Beat is the panel-beaters' anthem and it does exactly what it says on the tin, as they say. It is a tribute to metal bashers everywhere that this piece hammers itself into shape before our very ears. However, not only is it entirely devoid of melody, which some would argue is a perfectly valid approach to composition, but also it has no musical notes at all for long periods. There is vocalisation, rather than singing, and Bernard Fowler's voice sounds, at times, like a robot's version of the French kid's song, *Frère Jacques*. It's also true that this is an example of what has now become very familiar to those of us who listen to the popular airwaves. My own approach is to support music with as much colour as the artist can squeeze into it so this grey piece rates at the bottom of my scale of interest. No less than eleven names are credited as contributing to this track. It's hard to imagine what they all did apart from make sharp contacts with their favourite metal. For me, this is not aerospace titanium, but plumber's lead.

In contrast (thankfully), Herbie's Olympic song *Junku* is an opportunity for us to appreciate the beauty of Suso's kora and the amazing way in which its traditional sound has been juxtaposed with the sound of silicon. Likewise, *People Are Changing* is a much more traditional piece of music with Bernard Fowler (vocal) combining with Herbie and Anton Fier (percussion) to present a very acceptable song, even if the lyrics are somewhat unimaginative.

For once, the title track comes last. The piece is rich in creativity, with an imaginative blend of traditional and modern instrumentation. Despite its superficial similarity to computer-generated music, this is the music of a band, admittedly overdubbed, but played by humans nevertheless. Besides Laswell's bass and digital DMX drums, Anton Fier plays Simmons drums - those small hexagonal pads that replace the traditional drum kit and act as triggers for the chosen electronic sounds. Suso appears on his kora, as well as playing the talking drum, a popular percussion instrument that originates from West Africa. The technique involves squeezing the tuning ropes while striking the head with a small bent wooden mallet. The variations in tension of the skin cause the pitch to vary widely and produce a special sound. Suso's fellow-member of the Mandingo Griot Society, Hamid Drake, plays cymbals. More percussion is provided by Aiyb Diend, not forgetting D. St's scratching. Nicky Skopelitis plays guitar, and Toshinori Kondo plays a very appropriate trumpet solo. All this takes place to Hancock's now usual keyboards. The composition is structured and exciting and well deserves its Grammy.

Herbie Hancock: *The Herbie Hancock Trio In Concert* – 1984 (***)

The Herbie Hancock Trio In Concert (1984) appears to be an 'unofficial' release of a recording made in July 1984 at the Estival Lugano, Switzerland. Also available as a DVD, once again, it is an acoustic piano trio performance and is of interest mainly because of the presence of drummer Billy Cobham. In the early 1970s, Cobham was drummer for the first Mahavishnu Orchestra, with which band he made three astonishing albums: *The Inner Mounting Flame* (1971), *Birds of Fire* (1973) and *Between Nothingness and Eternity* (1973). It was thanks to these albums that he became the favourite for many as the world's greatest drummer. Of this album, Bailey wrote: "It is perhaps Cobham who captures most of the attention here. Long well known for his contributions to Fusion and other electric jazz, Cobham proves that he is perfectly at home in the close quarters of the acoustic trio. Known long for his BIG sound, he plays with a well-cultivated grace and light touch." [64] Cobham shows off his chops straight away in the opening track, a version of *Eye of the Hurricane* that is even faster than usual. *First Trip* is a swinging, nine minutes of delightful, inventive music. Then comes a group of solo tracks: *Willow Weep For Me* is an improvisation by Ron Carter; Herbie's *Dolphin Dance* is also performed entirely solo, emphasising his creative genius, as if that were necessary. Track 4 is a drum solo entitled *Ili's Treasure*. The album then returns to the trio format. *Princess* is a long, contemplative ballad that is new to Herbie's repertoire, whilst *Walking* is an up tempo rendition of the Miles Davis favourite. The recording quality of the album is not as good as we might expect and the inaccurate package is a disappointment. Nevertheless, this is an intriguing album.

Herbie Hancock and Foday Musa Suso: *Village Life* – 1985 (***)

In 1984, Suso joined Herbie's international tour to promote *Sound System* and, when it was over, the two men entered a recording studio in Tokyo Japan on 7-9 August 1984 where *Village Life* was recorded with the help of Bill Laswell as co-producer. It coincided with the time that Herbie discovered the brand new Yamaha DX-1 synthesiser. Herbie: "I was initially going to play acoustic piano accompanying Suso, but a couple of days before the sessions, I was taken on a tour of the Yamaha factory and that's when I saw the DX-1 synthesiser. I just had to have it right away. That's all I play on the album. There are no overdubs at all. I loved the chance to explore the direction I was being pointed at in *Future Shock*, using sound – noise even – as dynamic elements in the music. Traditional African instruments are not tuned like a piano The DX-1 allows for de-tuning, to more closely match the intonation of Suso's kora." [65]

Besides the African content, Herbie beautifully brings the wonders of the new instrument to the foreground with the short third track *Early Warning* and the commencement of the final track, *Kanatente*. A series of four duets, the album is more directed towards African music than it is jazz, and as such does not fall naturally into the jazz-fusion category, despite the presence of Herbie and his new toy. The music is as happy and as lively as you would expect from knowledge of its origins.

Dexter Gordon: *Round Midnight* (CD and DVD) – 1986 (***)

In 1986, Herbie was commissioned to write the score for the movie *Round Midnight*. (In deference to the ability of the apostrophe to constantly screw things up, it appears to have been deliberately omitted by the film company.) This was an entirely different project to those Herbie had worked on in the 1960s and 70s. This was a film about jazz – a very realistic portrayal of a fictional tenor sax man, Dale Turner (played by Dexter Gordon) who is failing rapidly thanks to the usual problems caused by the demon drink. Offered the chance of rehabilitation in Paris (where, as a black man he finds the respect he deserves), the main character begins a battle to save not only his career but his life.

Director Bertrand Tavernier could hardly have made a better choice for his musical director. The film required music from the acoustic mainstream genre of jazz, and Herbie's compositions, coupled with the musicians he chose to perform them, were perfect for the film. Gordon (1923-90) was a giant of jazz in the period of interest, most notably engaging in titanic saxophone duels with his friend and rival Wardell Gray. Though the movie is aimed at (though not based on) the lives of Bud Powell and Lester Young, it could also be a metaphor for Gordon himself. By 1985, in his early 60s, he was a scarred campaigner, and this is reflected in his appearance on this record. Perhaps, recognising that listeners might not appreciate Gordon in his prime, the CD re-issuers included a version of *'Round Midnight* played in December 1976 at the Village Vanguard Jazz Club. It featured Gordon in far finer fettle; any weaknesses he may have had in 1986 are disguised by the way Herbie orchestrates his contributions. Herbie also hired Wayne Shorter to play soprano and tenor saxophone.

In the sleeve notes to the album, Tavernier explains how he had planned to record all of the music live during filming and played in a facsimile of New York's Blue Note Jazz Club. He decided not to use the traditional method of recording the music in a studio and then playing it back to musicians who mime during filming. This worried Herbie at first, but was later shown to be absolutely correct, despite some logistical difficulties during the filming process.

The album contains a mix of classic jazz tunes and Herbie originals. It opens with a deliciously sexy version of Monk's *'Round Midnight*, using Bobby McFerrin's vocal as a lead instrument to supplement the usual Herbie/Ron/Tony trio line-up. A highlight is a beautiful version of *Body and Soul* in which Dexter and Herbie are joined by Pierre Michelot (bass), Billy Higgins (drums) and John McLaughlin (guitar). The Gershwin tune *How Long Has This Been Going On* was sung by Lonette McKee (who also performed it with excellence in the film), whilst a brilliant version of *Rhythm-A-Ning* was played – at a sedate tempo - by Dexter with Cedar Walton, Ron Carter, Tony Williams and Freddie Hubbard.

Herbie also added some compositions of his own: *Still Time*, a beautiful ballad with Michelot, Higgins and Wayne Shorter on soprano sax. *Chan's Song (Never Said)* features an encore for the opening quartet in which McFerrin adds his distinctive vocal colour to Herbie's rather sad song. The movie performance of this piece – with Gordon instead of McFerrin - is a highlight of the film. *Bérangère's Nightmare* is an aural depiction of some stressful moments when Dexter's character goes missing. Gordon appears (supported by Shorter) on Herbie's band version of Bud Powell's *Una Noche Con Francis*. Kenny Dorham's composition *Fair Weather* achieved much praise thanks to Herbie's selection of Chet Baker to sing it. After the release of *Chet Baker Sings* (1953) Baker, a much loved trumpet exponent of cool jazz, had attracted much criticism from the jazz puritans for his decision to sing on recordings. Of course, Herbie has never shown any sign of critical judgement about other people's artistic decisions and was thrilled to get Baker's vocal presence on this tune.

The album is completed by a duet with Herbie and vibraphone player Bobby Hutcherson, *Minuit aux Champs-Elysées* and a rendition of Rowles' composition *The Peacocks* made even more colourful by Wayne's appropriately selected soprano saxophone sound.

Viewers of the DVD who love mainstream jazz will probably find the movie very enjoyable, even if the story is somewhat predictable. Gordon's musical performances in the film are quite satisfying and the film has added poignancy when we realise that Dexter Gordon died just a few years after the film was completed. If nothing else, there's some good entertainment to be obtained from playing 'spot the jazz musician'. Herbie himself has a significant role as pianist in Dale Turner's band, and there are appearances by many of the real musicians who play this music. All of the music from the album (except for the final track) is to be found in the film, although some of it is in small snatches. Listeners may also be amused as Herbie's monogram – *Watermelon Man* – occurs at several points in the film. Almost all of the music was played live for the filming, but the album music was recorded separately in the studio and the musicians playing on CD do not always correspond to those seen in the film.

Dexter Gordon: *The Other Side of Round Midnight* – 1986 (***)

Unusually, a second album of music to the film *Round Midnight* was released slightly after the official movie soundtrack CD. Whilst the original was a Columbia publication, the second album was released on the Blue Note label and seems to have resulted from the involvement of producer Michael Cuscuna with Blue Note Records. Under Herbie's direction, there was so much music generated for the film that the soundtrack album could not accommodate it all. This album used some of that remaining material and the disc makes a very good companion to the Columbia release, even if Herbie's great involvement is not given a fair representation in this package.

Not all of the contents of the album can be found in the movie, however. The old standard *As Time Goes By* features prominently at an early stage in the film, whilst the scene in the recording studio during which *'Round Midnight* is recorded with two double basses occurs towards the end of the film. The track *Tivoli* was the only music used in the film that was not recorded live for the film and movie viewers will at once detect this by the mismatch in what they see and what they hear. Also, two different bands were used in the recordings.

The track *Call Sheet Blues*, which does not appear in the film, was an entirely spontaneous recording and its players Herbie, Wayne, Ron Carter and Billy Higgins were awarded a Grammy for "Best Instrumental Composition." Then, a few weeks later, Herbie won an Academy Award for "Best Score". For a musician to be awarded an Oscar is a great achievement and a high point of Herbie's career, even though there were more great moments still to come.

Herbie Hancock and Foday Muso Susa: *Jazz Africa* – 1987 (***)

In 1986, Herbie continued his partnership with Gambian kora virtuoso Foday Musa Suso. In particular, they formed a band that came together on 2nd December for a musical event at Bill Graham's Wiltern Theatre in Los Angeles. The gig was filmed for TV by Jack Lewis under a broader umbrella project entitled *Jazzvisions*, a series of seven concerts that covered a wide spectrum of jazz genres. The swinging (and very rare) live album *Jazz Africa* (1987) is a record of selections from the single concert with that name. Besides Herbie and Suso, the band consisted mostly of percussionists: Aiyb Dieng, Hamid Drake, Armando Peraza and Adam Rudolph, together with guitarist Abdul Hakeem and bassist Joe Thomas. Although clearly dominated by African influences in the kora-focused tracks *Kumbasora* and *Jimbasing*, there is plenty of American jazz-fusion from electric instruments in the tracks *Debo* and *Cigarette Lighter* as well as the pervasive Latin jazz influence of Cuban bongo specialist Armando

Peraza. The album is a rare snapshot of an early eclectic kind of world music in which Herbie is seems to be more of a participant than a leader.

Herbie Hancock: *Perfect Machine* – 1988 (***)

They say good (or bad) things come in threes. *Perfect Machine* (1988) is the third album in the series of what, during the intervening period after the release of *Future Shock* had become 'techno-pop'. It didn't seem to help Hancock's career, however, for after this he left Columbia to whom he had been contracted since 1973. In 1999, in a strange interview with Bob Belden, Laswell suggested that: "...the initial records just honestly were over his head and he didn't know what we were really doing. And with the initial success of the single, then he became obviously attracted to his own success." [65] To continue to say, in the same interview, that *"Future Shock - Rockit* - put me on the map, but it's not a map I really care to be on..." is an odd thing to say in the circumstances.

The album is a tighter, more defined project in which there are far fewer humans involved with its creation. Hancock, of course, plays a large number of keyboards, assisted by Jeff Bova's computer programming skills, whilst Laswell has disappeared from the floor of the studio into the producer's box. Even though Laswell's name does not appear amongst the performers, his mark is all over the record. Since the last album, countless hours of human endeavour have been expended in design of electronic circuitry, but D. St.'s turntable scratching continues to be a mainline instrument. It must be nice to be so indispensable. Leon 'Sugarfoot' Bonner adds vocals and Nicky Skopelitis moves from guitar to Fairlight drums. The identity of a vocalist and keyboardist called 'Micro Wave' is unknown.

On the legacy CD, the six tracks - *Perfect Machine, Obsession, Vibe Alive, Beat Wise, Maiden Voyage/ B. Bop* and *Chemical Residue* - are supplemented by two bonus tracks, commercial mixes of *Vibe Alive* and *Beat Wise*. Apart from *Chemical Residue*, which is due to Herbie alone, all tracks are credited to the main contributing musicians.

Perfect Machine is certainly good enough to become the robot's signature tune, providing he's friendly, for this one doesn't feel evil. His vocoder speech is a bit remedial, which I guess makes him a little less than perfect, but the track is interesting. According to Isaac Asimov, the laws of robotics demand that they are friendly to humans. *Obsession* is the more disturbing of the two tracks, its electronic vocals sounding as if they could come from one of the less likeable characters from a murder movie. I wouldn't like to meet him on a dark night, but that's the nature of the portrayal and Hancock has got it just right.

The next two tracks *Vibe Alive* and *Beat Wise* are compositions of dance music intended to find commercial success, and the lengthier mixes are added as bonus tracks on the latest CD. Apparently, both failed to make an impact on the charts, which is a pity for the music is quite compulsive. One criticism applied to it is that Laswell is so determined to stamp his own electric/rhythmic imprints on the music that Hancock's keyboard skills are pushed well into the background. Whilst you can find justification for this argument, it's hard to imagine that Herbie didn't agree with it.

Herbie is a practising Buddhist, not a Hindu, so there are no sacred cows in his music. Thus, it's no surprise that, arguably, his greatest piece *Maiden Voyage* is sacrificed to Laswell on this album – it had to happen sooner or later! This one is fused to another piece called *B. Bop* that is well matched with *Maiden Voyage* – it needs to be. The two pieces in seamless symbiosis make a delightful change, despite the fact that, at times, there are so many effects being tossed in that the 'boys toys' syndrome seems appropriate again.

Chemical Residue smacks of the alchemist's shop, with the apprentice working away in the dark corner of the dusty, cobweb-covered laboratory as he tries to convert a fresh sample of lead into gold. The flasks bubble and hiss gently as the alchemist devises the magic formula. Somehow, it's a great relief to be free at last from the earlier robotic mechanics as we stand in awe of the great man, working his spells. And the result? Why pure gold, of course!

Herbie Hancock: *A Tribute To Miles* – 1994 (****)

Miles Davis died on 28 September 1991; the music world was stunned. He had become noticeably weaker during the summer, but he had been gigging right up to 25 August . Indeed, it was lucky that Herbie (along with many other Miles alumni) was available to take part in a unique reunion concert with Miles in Paris on 10 July 1991, during which Herbie got to play *Watermelon Man* with Miles and the band. This gig is now available on a DVD entitled *Miles Davis at La Villette* (2001). Although Miles's state of health had always been poor, the end of this great life still took everyone by surprise. Herbie must have felt the loss as much as anybody: they had worked closely together for a decade or so, and had been close friends since 1962. Miles's presence loomed large in the life of anyone who had come into close contact with him.

In 1992, Herbie joined the other members of the Second Great Quintet - Ron Carter, Tony Williams and Wayne Shorter - for an extensive world tour. They took with them Wallace Roney in Davis's role, just as Roney had done at the famous Montreux Festival on 8 July 1991, a wonderful performance preserved on the Warners album, *Miles & Quincy: Live at Montreux* (1993).

A Tribute To Miles (1994) is an album of pieces played on the tour: two were live recordings, the remaining five captured in the studio. The first track is *So What (Live)*, a fast (and furious) interpretation of the famous piece from *Kind of Blue* (1959). It's played quite aggressively and not at all similar to the well-known cool form that it had on the original record. This group of musicians didn't play the original in any case, although they may have played it live many times with Miles. Roney makes a very good attempt at sounding like Miles, as he does on much of this recording. It was never the intention of these guys to look backwards at the music and each selection is played in the 1992 moment, as Miles would certainly have wished. Roney is very much the guest: each of the others contributed a composition to the recording. It's curious that they should have chosen no less than three pieces from Miles's album *E.S.P.* (1965). Herbie's *Little One* also appeared on his own *Maiden Voyage* (1965). Likewise, Ron's piece *RJ* appeared on *E.S.P.* and although the theme is recognisable, it's a much more energetic (and brief) version on this record. *Eighty-One* is credited to both Ron and to Miles and this version is more chilled and superbly moody. Wayne's tune *Pinocchio* appears on Miles's *Nefertiti* (1967) and is very recognisable here with its haunting melody. Tony wrote *Elegy* especially for the occasion, as his own special and very beautiful tribute to Miles. It appears not to have been recorded elsewhere. The final track is *All Blues (live)*, once again taken from *Kind of Blue*. It was one of Miles's favourites, if there could be such a thing, as he often included it in his performances, and it's played as close to the original as we could possibly expect, even allowing for the occasional diversion, particularly towards the end of Wayne's solo.

This was a joint project, and it would have been outside the scope of each man's recording contract. As a result, Herbie's friend Quincy Jones agreed to publish *A Tribute to Miles* (1994) on his own Qwest Records label. This company, allied to Warner Brothers, was active during the period 1980-2000. At the 37th Annual Grammy Awards in February 1994, the album won a Grammy for Best Jazz Instrumental Performance, Individual or Group.

Herbie Hancock: *The Herbie Hancock Quartet Live* – 1994 (***)

Two albums that feature quite strongly in Herbie's discography are not in the official list. These are both live recordings issued in the same year by the Jazz Door label and they are a trio recording called *Live in New York* (1994) and *The Herbie Hancock Quartet Live* (1994). It turns out that the second of these albums was recorded first. Indeed, the four tracks contained on the Quartet album span four years. The third track *Sorcerer* features alto saxophone player Greg Osby and was recorded in Belgrade on 31 October 1988. The other tracks were recorded in New York on 23 May 1992. The common feature is Herbie's trio partners, Buster Williams on bass and Al Foster on drums. Nothing else is common about this album.

Just One of Those Things is an extended 25-minute blow-out that features some intense playing by all those on stage, but in particular the formidable tenor saxophone player Michael Brecker. Herbie had been friends with Michael for years, but their successful careers had prevented them from interacting much on record. Jaco Pastorius had succeeded in bringing them together on his debut album *Jaco Pastorius* (1976), and Herbie had invited Michael to play on his album *Magic Windows* (1981). The two men would remain close right up to Michael's death in 2007 and would make many more recordings together.

Air Dancing is aptly titled as Michael skips his way through this piece with breath control that's as important to his performance as leg muscles to a bullfrog. Buster's solo is especially attractive, as we might expect from the composer of the piece. The lyrical melody and pensive mood make a wonderful display case for the immense skills of bassman Williams. Buster was also present in the band when Larry Coryell played it live for his own album *Air Dancing* (1988).

Sorcerer is a lively version of Herbie's composition used on the Miles Davis *Sorcerer* (1967) album. Osby is a relative unknown musician who acquits himself extremely well in this stellar company and whose lighter alto pitch and tone make a refreshing change to the more masculine and gutsy tenor sound. Al Foster gets the chance to play a solo and reminds us just what an asset he was to Miles's band of the 1970s and 80s.

Jammin' is a mistitled and much faster version of the classic Charlie Parker tune *Moose the Mooche* played at the breathtaking pace of 288 bpm. It's a lot of fun as Bobby McFerrin introduces his own brand of vocal gymnastics. His vocal chords spar with the other musicians in remarkable ways. The interaction of Brecker and McFerrin causes me to want to replay the track just to reassure myself that my ears do not deceive me as the theatre takes on the characteristics of an aviary. McFerrin's approach to jazz vocals may not be to everyone's taste, but it is undeniably unique. Meanwhile the quartet is on fire for this one.

It's a pity that this album is somewhat fragmented by the time gap between the tracks, the more so because of the way they are sequenced on the CD. Fortunately, listeners are not made too aware of this as we relax and enjoy this superb music, for the atmosphere and ambience of the two venues is rather similar. We just need to be grateful that the recordings exist at all, especially in view of their quality and scarcity.

Herbie Hancock Trio: *Live In New York* – 1994 (****)

This trio album documents Herbie's 1993 tour in which he invited two relatively unknown musicians to join him, Jeff Littleton (bass) and Gene Jackson (drums). Jeff Littleton (b1950) is based in Los Angeles where for ten years since 1998 he has been a member of the Taumbu International Ensemble. Jackson (b1961) graduated from Berklee Music College where he shared an apartment with Branford Marsalis. He kicked off his career with a successful spell working with both Kevin and Robin Eubanks. He was introduced to Herbie in late 1991 largely thanks to friendship with fellow drummer Terri Lynne Carrington. He played frequently in Herbie's touring quartet between 1991 and February 2000, although this is his only appearance on record.

There are two jazz standards on this record, both by Cole Porter: the album opens with *I Love You*, whilst *Just One of Those Things* brings it to a close. After a little over one chorus, we are off on a hair-raising ride with the trio in the first piece, and, just like boy racers, our boys seem hell-bent on giving us a thrill. Each takes turns behind the wheel, each with his own course to follow and each successfully impressing us with his skills. Clearly, Herbie would not have hired Jeff and Gene for this outing if they were not up to the task. By the final three minutes of this energetic piece you can actually smell the testosterone on their breath.

One Finger Snap gets off to an energetic start with yet more wheel-spin. It's now thirty years since this piece first appeared as the opener on *Empyrean Isles* (1964) and there's no sign of Herbie taking his foot off the gas in this one. By three minutes into this sixteen-minute cycle of the Indianapolis brickyard, the trio has got the engine up to full revs. Just like the entrance to the pit lane, the familiar theme returns periodically where we inspect our progress, and the activity in the pits may appear to be an opportunity for us to catch our breath, but don't expect much respite from the energy and excitement of the event. Littleton's solo is sonorous and beautifully constructed, then it's out for another lap before it's Jackson's turn to supply new rubber. The last few laps are taken at full pelt as the engine threatens to explode. As we cross the line the chequered flag is something of a relief and it's the crowd that explodes with sheer enthusiasm for what it has witnessed.

The familiar *Cantaloupe Island* appears next, in yet another new guise. Herbie continues to find ever more variations in what was always the cutest of syncopated rhythms. Now his brilliance is even better displayed as he not only inserts syncopation on syncopation but then, as if that were not enough, layers-in entirely new chords to boot! He makes Jackson's job seem simple, but of course, all this is done with the help of Jackson (and Littleton) whose underlying support is critical to the success of this great piece. By five minutes into the piece, this Island is the funkiest, liveliest place on Earth. Herbie is playing with deep intensity, and it is greatly to the credit of his two colleagues that they follow him closely through the many twists and turns of the steep-sided valleys that make up this exotic place. No other solos here - just Herbie at his brilliant best.

Maiden Voyage seems to be an ever-present item on the agenda, to the extent that when I see it listed yet again on an album I wish he would choose something else. Yet I should have learned by now that Herbie's incredible genius cannot fail to create something entirely new from something he has played hundreds, perhaps thousands, of times before. This version opens with a long and very thoughtful improvisation. By four minutes it is so thoughtful that he begins to confuse the audience who clap during a period of silence. There's an interaction between player and audience as the latter shows obvious amusement and Herbie starts to delve into the guts of the piano, in the manner of Chick Corea. At times the solo takes on the level of performance of a classical music specialist. The familiar theme emerges by 7.30; by 12 minutes into the piece, Herbie is once more at full stretch, his arpeggios flooding the piano keyboard like water pouring from a sprinkler system activated by the intense heat being generated in the room. The cooling of the water is effective, for the piece now subsides into quietness and yet another delivery is over.

It's back to the racetrack for *Just One of Those Things* where you can even hear the pistons pounding the cylinder interiors during the opening minute. Then, as the green light shows at 1.20, the car suddenly becomes as smooth as fresh tarmac as it draws away from the start-line and embarks on another octane-fuelled loop of this historic jazz circuit.

This is a very good album, well recorded and with some exceptionally imaginative interpretations of the selected music. The members of the trio are beautifully enmeshed in each other's creativity and it is remarkable that Herbie's two colleagues are not better known. The record is one of the most energetic collections of Herbie's live music in which songs are presented in a package that is highly-charged – even aggressive in many places. This disc is not on the list of 'official' Herbie Hancock albums, but it is well worth collecting as an example of dynamic, forceful, imaginative live performance.

Herbie Hancock: *Dis Is Da Drum* – 1994 (****)

In 1994 Hancock made a unique deal with PolyGram Records that allowed him to appear on many labels. For example, he could record jazz for Verve whilst his pop albums would be released on the Mercury label. The first of the pop-targeted albums was *Dis Is Da Drum* (1994) in which Herbie returned to hip-hop, but with a collection of material very much focussed on West African drum rhythms. The album is interesting because, although it is a Herbie Hancock record, it is also very much a collective production from a group of new generation musicians thoroughly grounded in computer-generated hip-hop music. Will 'Roc' Griffin is all over this album, yet he seems to have done nothing else musically. That's a very strange observation considering the great influence he must have had in making this sound so good. Many of Herbie's old friends are present as well as some new ones. They all help to make this a novel blend of musical genres and an excellent 1990s jazz-fusion album. There are places on the record where genuine African sounds are used to compare and contrast alongside the computerised American ones. All of the tracks apart from *Butterfly* are group efforts, written, arranged, played, recorded and produced by the musicians themselves.

Call it 95 is a throbbing opener that gets your feet tapping from the very start. It's totally modern sound is gripping. Herbie takes an acoustic solo amidst the electronics, and Wallace Roney makes an atonal guest spot that is a welcome, fresh sound in such a modern context.

The title track is next, although as far as I can tell the words are spoken correctly and not Africanised as the title suggests. A couple of spoken lines are used at the start: "This is the drum that brings the good spirit to possess you or drives away the bad spirit. This is the drum that creates a hypnotic influence over its listeners, so it is said." From these words, a shortened version is constructed and used for a repeated spoken line throughout the song: "This is the drum that brings the good spirit, this is the drum." It really adds feeling to this great piece. As the music starts, the sound of Africa breaks out at once as an introduction, and the main theme starts at 0.34. Despite all the effects and electronics, there is a standard structure to this piece. As you might expect, the theme is hypnotic enough to supplant itself into your brain for some time after listening to it, and there is a strong predominance of drums throughout. Hancock takes a mid-section synth solo at 2.50. After a reprise of the theme, the piece is over and straight into a short drum solo track entitled *Shooz*. The complicated sleeve notes indicate that Will 'Roc' Griffin' built the piece from samples played by Airto Moreira and Bill Summers. It's only just over a minute long and followed by *The Melody (on the Deuce by 44)*. This is a rap number performed by Chil Factor with an injection of jazz from Herbie. Griffin clearly has a big input to the piece which has all the kind of effects we know and love from rap music.

Mojuba is another track of the same ilk as *Call it 95*. Delicious blends of jazz with the sound of Africa, these tracks are a great success on the album. They are fun, lively, danceable, tuneful and interesting. *Mojuba* even has a middle section with synthetic brass, just before it breaks into another acoustic piano solo. Listen to it with a good bass system and you will be amazed at the resonance of the bass drum.

Butterfly is a recycled version of a particularly nice Hancock composition that first appeared twenty years earlier on *Thrust* (1974) and, in its new guise, it fits beautifully on this album. Hubert Laws takes the luscious flute part. And, just in case you didn't get enough, there's a re-mixed version as a bonus track. *Juju* makes a good attempt at depicting an African landscape, complete with thunderclaps, which is a bit disconcerting when, like I did, you listen to it whilst driving in thundery weather. *Hump* opens with a short burst from Wallace Roney, before taking on a stomping beat and some richly colourful brass arrangements. This is great 1990s jazz-fusion. Gil Evans would have loved this. *Come and See Me* is a 90s-style development of the dance-funk-disco music Herbie spent so long with in the 70s and 80s. Strong on rhythm, light on melodies, token solos, it is still fit-for-purpose and bears repeated listening.

The album's highlight is *Rubber Soul*, oddly named in view of the extremely famous (unrelated) Beatles album. The piece starts innocuously after a brief out-of-tempo intro and develops a stunning vibe with the most delicate pastel colours that entice you into the piece like a shimmering lake in the desert that turns out to be a mirage. As the piece progresses, there are some gentle solos, notably from a muted Roney trumpet and Maupin's tenor sax. It doesn't really go anywhere, but the vibe is so beautiful I just want it to go on and on...

The album concludes with *Bo Ba Be Da*. In the language business this is called onomatopoeia, that is, when you use words to imitate a sound. There's no doubt that this was how Herbie described the main theme to the guys who had to play it. Once again, a hot hip-hop groove rides shotgun alongside a cool jazz theme, embellished with electronic effects and a constant input from Herbie who never really solos, but is always in the driving seat. Don't spare the drummers, Herbie. This one's a great success.

Herbie Hancock: *The New Standard* – 1995 (****)

From the start of his career, Herbie Hancock was infused with the tradition of mainstream jazz whereby classic songs – so-called ''standards' - from the broader American music industry known colloquially as Tin Pan Alley are given jazz interpretations. During the course of Herbie's career, the music business had changed enormously, mostly due to the emergence of rock and pop music and the many genres and styles they encompassed. Herbie had now come to realise that perhaps something that was missing from his catalogue of recordings was an appreciative look at material from the 'modern' era. It was with this in mind that he embarked upon a new project that became known as *The New Standard* (1995). He found himself with an all-star band including John Scofield (guitar), Dave Holland (bass), Jack DeJohnette (drums), Don Alias (percussion) and Michael Brecker interpreting pop songs by Nirvana, Stevie Wonder, the Beatles, Prince, the Eagles, Simon and Garfunkel, Peter Gabriel and others.

The brilliant opening track is a version of Don Henley's sad song *New York Minute*, first recorded on his album *The End of Innocence* (1989) and later by the Eagles on *Hell Freezes Over* (1994). Despite the acceleration in pace from the slow plod of the original, Herbie's version loses none of the angst and atmosphere. Herbie's brilliant translation of the simple pop chords into luxurious sonic adventures is a joy to hear and provides an exciting foundation to the rich swinging improvisations that follow.

Mercy Street is a very poignant song taken from Peter Gabriel's album *So* (1986). The conversion of this wonderful pop song into a piece of exquisite modern jazz is breathtaking. (Herbie would do this again with another of Gabriel's tunes *Don't Give Up* on his album *The Imagine Project* 2010.) Herbie shows how, with the aid of a strong Latin rhythm from Alias and de Johnette, this music can be transformed into a rich tapestry of musical colour. Originally inspired by the tragic American poet Anne Sexton, it seems almost irreverent to make this music joyful, but this is such a multi-faceted rendition that somehow the source's creative strands have intertwined sympathetically: the end therefore justifies the means. No far-out soloing here – just beautiful music.

We might expect the presence of a Beatles' tune on the album and here it is. This time, it's *Norwegian Wood*, the familiar melody first outlined by Dave Holland and then shaded exquisitely in Sco-blue. The later colourful fills are rendered by Herbie's brush, which drips with luscious pastel shades and is supported by a well-controlled orchestra. The final passes involve Mike Brecker in unison with Sco and Herbie and to the accompaniment of some Gil Evans-type harmonies are as satisfying as anything on the record.

Another song that was very topical in 1994 was the gentle ballad *When Can I See You*, a hit single taken from the album by Babyface, *For the Cool In You* (1994). Babyface was the nickname of Kenneth Edmonds, given to him during his time as a teenager in Bootsy Collins' funk band. The song became his biggest hit on the Billboard Hot 100 chart where it reached #4. The song earned him his first Grammy for "Best Male R&B Vocal Performance." Played here with a Latin rhythm and a string accompaniment to Herbie's acoustic piano and Brecker's wistful soprano saxophone tones, the song takes on a new identity and well illustrates just how the jazz philosophy can be used to enrich the wider world of music.

Stevie Wonder's *You've Got It Bad Girl* is an ideal choice for conversion into a high-energy, dynamic piece of mainstream. Taken from Stevie's remarkable album *Talking Book* (1972) the piece had already achieved the status of a 'New Standard' without Herbie's help. Here it is presented as a straight-ahead piece of modern jazz.

Love is Stronger Than Pride was the opening track to the album *Stronger Than Pride* (1988) by Sade Adu, the lead singer of the English band Sade. Once again, a remarkably beautiful piece of music is converted into something different but equally attractive by this interpretation with the help of John Scofield's unusual guitar tones and Michael Brecker's thrusting presence. The addition of extra brass rounds off this excellent and, at times, incredibly funky track.

Scarborough Fair is actually an English traditional folk tune rendered universally popular by Simon and Garfunkel. Achieving fabled status by its appearance on their album *Parsley, Sage, Rosemary and Thyme* (1966) and in the film *The Graduate* (1968), it was a dangerous choice in that it could be a disappointment to many listeners who are hooked on the sound of the original. It's a matter of opinion whether this version succeeds, but it's given the traditional jazz treatment, along the lines of the simplest form of Coltrane's *My Favourite Things*. Of course, with Brecker leading off the solo, it might be expected that the tension would be ratcheted up to an intense level. However, he is unusually restrained, this time acting as an aperitif for Sco's rocking guitar licks. In the end, unlike Coltrane's discovery, the cave of exploration for this number seems unusually dead-ended and perhaps the tune's over-familiarity renders the result disappointing. What worked for S&G doesn't do the job here.

The mood is changed entirely for Prince's *Thieves in the Temple*, taken from the album *Graffiti Bridge* (1990) where it was added at the last minute and became the most successful song on the album. Here, Herbie serves it up as a strong dose of funk, very much in parallel with his own music, which (who knows?) may have formerly inspired the artist, known as *Watermelon Man*.

All Apologies is a song written by Kurt Cobain and originally performed by the American grunge band Nirvana. It's selection goes to show once more how wide is Herbie's appreciation of the music scene. Cobain apparently summarised its sound as "peaceful, happy, comfort" and dedicated it to his wife and daughter, which is contrast to what many of us remember about the tragic life of this rock superstar. There's a strong blues element running through its melody that Herbie draws on to the odd accompaniment of Scofield's electric sitar. It all adds up to great variety and entertainment of this very good album.

Another high point was the award of a Grammy for the "Best Instrumental Composition" on *Manhattan (Island Of Lights And Love)*. Like the track, it was a fitting finale to a beautiful project.

Herbie Hancock and Wayne Shorter: *1+1* – 1997 (***)

Perhaps inspired by being appointed Artistic Director of the Thelonius Monk Institute of Jazz at the Music Center of Los Angeles, in 1997, Herbie joined forces with his great friend Wayne Shorter for a major new project that would make a key mark in the sands of music history. I have not here written much about Wayne Shorter, and I intend to put that right in another book about him. However, to do justice to this masterpiece, it is necessary to discuss him here in more detail. First, I shall reproduce some lines from the album *1+1* (1997), which are key to an understanding of this difficult and challenging work. "In this recording, the artists call upon the full palette of their musical resources to paint life's stories with all the texture or emotion and intensity of color – a process demanding the performance equivalent of a leap into the unknown. Musical images emerge and evolve into character and story, leading the listener on an inner journey. This is a monumental, historic collaboration - but these words insufficiently describe the daring performances by Herbie Hancock and Wayne Shorter which have been captured here. This is the evanescent made eternal." [66]

My guess is that Wayne had a big contribution to these words. In particular, the last sentence is typical of the man. Wayne and Herbie are well matched in skills, for both composition and performance. However, Wayne has made a particular focus of his compositions, all of which are carefully and precisely scripted, yet which maintain the improvisational element that constitutes the jazz ethos. In the pantheon of jazz saxophone players, Wayne is perhaps one of the less comprehensible, unless perhaps you share his special ability to encapsulate imagery into sound, and *vice versa*. Besides Wayne himself, it was Joni Mitchell who has perhaps recognised and made the greatest use of this skill in many of her albums. In Wayne's playing, Joni could hear all of the visual elements she wished to portray with her music. The causal listener will find Wayne's playing harsh, even – dare I say it - tuneless at times, though not on this album where he is at his most melodic. Both a tenor and a soprano player, Wayne uses only the latter instrument here. His playing is generally without vibrato, except where he wishes to soften the effect, and it can be as sharp (as in cutting) as a razor-blade. What surprises some is that he is also often sharp (as in pitch), for Wayne is a jazz player. He has extended his playing beyond the mere restrictions of the formal Western system of music into the regions between the standard notation – what jazzers call playing in the cracks. This is in perfect agreement with the age-old tradition of the blues whereby performers would make use of a blues scale in which some of the notes were not to be found on the piano keyboard. It is of course, also the tradition in the music of the far and middle-east and Wayne would see only advantage in using it.

A surprise on this album is the decision not to use any rhythm players in an age when a percussionist, at the very least, seems an essential component of any jazz project. However, there is great freedom in going drumless. The music here is liberated by the complete release from fixed tempos and allows these two masters of music to interact to the fullest extent, altering their tempo at will to suit the interpretation of the moment. The other surprise on the album is the decision to adopt what I describe as conventional harmonies. There is no resort here to abstraction of any kind, or to the kind of modal melodies that seem to hang in the air and leave me completely unsatisfied.

This is music that is written, seriously arranged, yet improvised. As the notes say, it is "the evanescent made eternal", in other words, music of the moment encapsulated into permanence by the process of recording. These tracks are 'stories' from the wide world around us. Some are obvious. *Aung San Suu Kyi* is an unambiguous, approachable track. Most people are familiar with the popular political leader of Burma who was then (and is still) being kept under house arrest by the ruling military junta. *Hale-Bopp, Hip Hop* is named after the heavenly comet, first discovered in 1995, and which sailed past the Earth on 1 April 1997. This musical portrait is similarly straightforward as we hear it emerge from the void and disappear the same way. The addition of the words *Hip Hop* to the title is at the same time both amusing, inspired and entirely pertinent – again, something from Wayne's back pocket.

Some tracks are based on mythical characters. *Meridianne – A Wood Sylph* may not exist, but she is no more difficult to imagine than a comet, thanks to the kind of movies we watched as children. The track entitled *Sonrisa* (Spanish for smile) is also available for our own individual interpretation. Some tracks are more personal, as with *Diana*, or *Joanna's Theme*. Unfortunately, we are unable to enjoy the deepest meanings of this music since we do not know the people involved.

An opportunistic joining of two comprehensible words, as in *Manhattan Lorelei*, gives rise to all kinds of mental images. *Manhattan* needs no further words from me; *Lorelei* could be many things from a fictional comic character to a rock sample. The farther a subject title submerges itself into the abstract, the more enigmatic the confluence of words, the more delight I can imagine spreading across Wayne's face. *Memory of Enchantment* continues with the theme of ideas from childhood imagination, whilst the pair of tracks *Visitor From Nowhere* and

Visitor from Nowhere do nothing but tantalise me because I feel they should be related, yet I am unable to find the link.

I feel certain that this album is a masterpiece, but somehow it leaves me unmoved. For all the hints we are given about the ideas behind the music, there is so little that remains in my heart when the CD stops turning. I have come to the conclusion that this kind of music is an extrapolation of the Miles Davis philosophy of 'living in the moment.' It is fundamentally appropriate to jazz, a music form based strongly on improvisation. Miles was obsessed with playing fresh music – not clichés. This can work in live performances, but not on record. There is a clear paradox: how can music be - at the same time - both composed and improvised? Once a CD is played for a second and subsequent times, surely the improvised music is no longer fresh? This music is undeniably melodic, yet there is almost total absence of recognisable tune. We are bereft of the usual gravitational pull of the musical key. Together, this leaves no imprint on my brain once it is over. I believe that in this style, both Wayne and Herbie are demonstrating how music can sound fresh on each listening.

The song *Aung San Suu Kyi* won the Grammy Award for Best Instrumental Composition. It is, of course, the composition that is closest to the traditional melodic and harmonic form, which demonstrates, to me at least, that the panel was less impressed with the other music on this album. This is an album I will play occasionally for the rest of my life, but it is not one of my favourites.

Herbie Hancock: *Gershwin's World* – 1998 (****)

The year 1998 was the centenary of the birth of one of the truly great American songwriters, George Gershwin. Born into a family of Russian-Jewish extraction, Gershwin took up the piano from the age of ten and quickly taught himself to play in all the popular styles of the day, influenced especially by the exponents of stride and ragtime piano such as James P Johnson and Scott Joplin. He left school at 15 to take up a career in the part of New York City that was known as Tin Pan Alley. According to Greenberg, Tin Pan Alley "...is said to have taken its name from the jangling, tinny sound (likened to the clattering of kitchen pans) issuing from dozens of upright pianos being incessantly pounded in a small area of New York centred around 28th St, from 6th Ave to Broadway. This was the city's main entertainment district, crammed with vaudeville theatres and music halls." [67] Gershwin was a 'song-plugger' or a 'piano pounder', which meant that he was paid to perform the songs currently being promoted by his employer, one of a group of music companies who provided the music for the musical shows being performed no more than a few blocks away. We notice that it was not amongst the duties of a song-plugger to actually *write* the songs – merely to perform them to whoever came to listen. Nevertheless, Gershwin was an avid composer of the music for songs, working in partnership with a lyricist (his older brother Ira, from 1924 onwards). As always, serendipity plays a large part in getting started in show business, and it was playing his own song *Swanee* to the Broadway star Al Jolson at a party in 1919 that got Gershwin his big break. Jolson loved the song, used it in his show and the song sold two million copies in the first year. It put Gershwin on the road to a phenomenally successful career as a writer of songs for Broadway shows.

George Gershwin was different from all others of his kind. Besides an extraordinary skill on the piano, gained from endlessly transposing and transforming songs on Tin Pan Alley from 1913 to 1919, he had a genius for finding the most attractive songs - what was described as his "ability to clothe words with apt key changes and harmonic surprises." [68] Songs such as *Somebody Loves Me* or *Embraceable You* could be "built almost entirely of simple scales and perfectly balanced little phrases – one of his favourite formulas." [69] Listeners were frequently "drawn into a song by some new harmonic surprise." [70] At the piano, George would "draw out a lovely melody like a golden thread, then juggle it, twist it and toss it around mischievously, weave it into unexpected intricate patterns, and hurl it into a cascade of ever-changing rhythms and counterpoints." [71] But the characteristic of Gerswhin's music that had the most importance for us was his use of the 'blue' scale, an effect that had the result of making his music sound like jazz. It was the first time of significance that a white composer had successfully achieved it, and his name became forever associated with it by his use of the title *Rhapsody in Blue* for a piece of music written for the concert orchestra in 1924. English musician and conductor Simon Rattle considered the opening bars as defining the very sound of New York, a "collision between the yearning voice of blues singer Bessie Smith and the Yiddish folk tunes of Gershwin's forebears in old Russia." [72]

In 1923, Gerswhin was invited to accompany the leading classical singer Eva Gauthier in a recital at the Aeolian Hall in New York. The recital, which included a number of his own songs was a resounding success. For the first time, an audience was subjected to a blend of classical with popular music tinged with jazz. One critic wrote: "He (Gershwin) is the beginning of sophisticated jazz." For the first time, "the show tunes of Kern, Berlin and Gershwin, were fair game for recital audiences to experience in venues hallowed by the songs of Schubert, Schuman and Brahms. And because of the quality of his tunes and the ear-catching inventiveness of his piano-playing, Gershwin was nominated their standard bearer in making this crossover an exciting and culturally acceptable process." [73] Cultural acceptability was essential for, just as in the early days of rock 'n' roll, older people associated jazz with depravity – crime, drugs, alcohol abuse and prostitution.

So we see that George Gershwin was an early exponent of music fusion, something that Herbie had espoused for much of his own career. It was absolutely appropriate for this piano genius to celebrate the centenary of an earlier one.

For his final rendition of *Embraceable You*, Herbie does exactly what Mamoulian said of Gershwin in the quotation above. Herbie describes his own philosophy: "Anyone can play the straight Gershwin tunes. Out intentions were to reach inside to the core of each piece in search of the composer's original impulses, and to take those elements and recompose and reconstruct them in our own way." [74] Many people might start with the classic version by Ella Fitzgerald with the Nelson Riddle Orchestra, a complete set of which is to be found on *Ella Fitzgerald Sings the George and Ira Gershwin Songbook* (1959). The combination of her pure voice and Riddle's exquisite orchestration is perfect and, when compared to Herbie's version you might be forgiven for choosing Ella's song over Herbie's. However, it is essential to realise that the notes of Ella's version are not the ones Gershwin wrote; Ella and Nelson recomposed and reconstructed them in their own way. Like Picasso, Herbie is deconstructing Gershwin's music and rebuilding it into something that is his own artist's impression, not just of the music, but the life and times of Gershwin. That is exactly how powerful a medium jazz can be. Even more than that, Herbie is being true to the philosophy he learned from Miles Davis: that of 'living in the moment'. Superficially it seems obvious. If Herbie were to play it again here and now it would sound different because he is clearly living in a different moment, he has learned new things and has different feelings about the music since he last played it. More important is the possibility that his style is an answer to the paradox of playing recorded jazz: each time you listen to it, it sounds the same. This intense style of jazz overcomes that because each time you listen to it, you do not remember precisely what you heard last time. The improvisation process is so intense that the result is very difficult for a human to remember accurately. Therefore the next time you hear it, it still sounds fresh. This is the very essence of Miles's philosophy of living in the moment.

The album is *not* a collection of Gershwin's music alone. Entitled *Gershwin's World*, it encompasses the musical spirit of the times. As Herbie says: "There's a thread that binds them all together – that thread is jazz and George Gershwin." [74] Besides some obvious selections from the glorious Gershwin catalogue, Herbie and his producer Robert Sadin included the *St Louis Blues* by the great bluesman W. C. Handy. Also *Blueberry Rhyme* by James P Johnson, whose stride piano style greatly influenced Gershwin as a pianist. Johnson (1894-1955) was an undisputed father of the jazz piano. [75] Duke Ellington was a close contemporary of Gershwin, hence the inclusion of *Cotton Tail*.

But Herbie was also interested in "rekindling my participation with classical music." [74] Last, but by no means least are the selections that represent the overlap with contemporary classical music. Track 6 is *Lullaby*, a piece that was Gershwin's first recorded attempt at musical composition in something other than a song format. It is a single movement written in 1919 for a string quartet as an exercise in orchestration whilst he was formally studying music with Edward Kilenyi. Gershwin did not attempt to publish or promote the piece. It received its first public performance only in 1963 when the brilliant harmonica player Larry Adler arranged and performed it at the Edinburgh Festival. In its original form it was performed by the Julliard String Quartet in 1967 and published in 1968. On this album we have a beautiful reconstruction for Herbie's piano, accompanied by the Orpheus Chamber Orchestra. Remember, this is not Gershwin's actual music: it's a wonderful piece of jazz-classical fusion.

Gershwin originally planned to write twenty-four preludes, but by the time the music was eventually published, only three were left. The second, marked *Andante con moto e poco rubato* (slowly, with movement and a flexible tempo) is the *Prelude in C# minor* Herbie chose to receive his own interpretation. Oddly, these pieces, originally written for solo piano have been re-arranged in many forms for small groups of instruments. This makes Herbie's arrangement here entirely justifiable, even if, as classical puritans, we did not subscribe to the general principle. In any case, Gershwin's original is a loose format that comes in two distinct and seemingly unrelated sections. This sextet of soprano, piano, cello, bass, guitar and percussion distil the essence of Gershwin's idea and condense the vapours into something that is beautiful, atmospheric and very jazzy. Gershwin's own description of the piece as "a sort of blues lullaby" is a useful link to bridge the space between the original and this version.

A poignant note appears affixed to the track entitled *Concerto for Piano and Orchestra in G, 2nd movement*. Herbie dedicated the recording to his great friend Tony Williams who passed away on 23 February 1997 at the time the music was performed. This well-known classical piece by Maurice Ravel was one of the few from the standard classical repertoire that had attracted great interest from the jazz world because of the jazzy musical colour it contained. Not only had Gershwin been a great fan of Ravel, but he had even (unsuccessfully) sought lessons from the great man. It is said that when Ravel found out what Gershwin was earning, he suggested that Gershwin should be giving *him* lessons! On this record, Herbie takes the second movement straight from the score and makes a wonderful performance alongside the Orpheus Chamber Orchestra.

Now on a roll, and reaping the rewards of his 'godfather' status, the album was voted the 'Best Jazz Instrumental Performance, Individual Or Group.' Herbie Robert Sadin and Stevie Wonder also received a Grammy for Best Instrumental Arrangement Accompanying Vocal for their work on *St Louis Blues*.

Headhunters: *Return of the Headhunters* – 1998 (****)

In 1998, Herbie made a guest appearance on an album by his original Headhunters band. He plays on four of the ten tunes. *Funk Hunter* is a very colourful funk extravaganza with a memorable tune and a great solo from Herbie. *Skank It* is short but slick funk and should get most juices flowing. *Watch Your Back* is a strong commercial tune that combines some great funk, a vocal from lead singer N'dea Davenport and a rap from Trevant Hardson. Herbie has some terrific electronic sounds here. Herbie's final contribution is to PP Head, another superb funky party in which he gets the first solo spot and Maupin plays more luscious tenor sax.

Billy Childs takes Herbie's place on the remaining six tunes. *Frankie and Kevin* is a slow ballad with Childs playing a delicious acoustic piano solo and Maupin blowing some great tenor saxophone licks. *Premonition* begins with some beautiful atmospheric sounds before a gentle rhythm is established and Maupin's bass clarinet is the very expressive lead instrument for the first part of this fine piece of music. From 4.30, the piece takes on a more energetic guise with Childs soloing on electric piano before the music reverts at 6.00 to the original format. *Tip Toe* is mostly about an explosion of rhythmic energy from Jackson and Clark as they back a vocal sung by N'dea Davenport. At 2.50 the piece jerks into a full-blown, if brief, funk-fest before Davenport returns for the final verse. Mike Clark's clever drumming is on show again at the start of *Two But Not Two* which develops into a clever group jam. How much of this excellent track is improvised is hard to tell, but it's very loose and lively. *Kwanzaa* is full of energetic jazz juices, more electronic and less funky than other tracks with a very strong syncopated rhythm that features another good solo from Childs and finally fades out with Clark's sticks burning up his skins. The final track has the title *6/8 – 7/8* that reflects the peculiar metre pervading the main body of the piece. Maupin is strong on soprano sax, but it's very much a strong band piece.

This is a very good album that is imaginative, yet retains a good sense of being commercial. The members of the band composed all of the tunes that contain a great variety of sounds, textures, rhythms and large dollops of jazz-fusion colour. It seems a shame that Herbie couldn't have played on all of these great tracks. Paul Jackson's funk bass is a real highlight of this album, although Mike Clark makes a real impact and the whole band is very much together as a unit.

Herbie Hancock: *Future 2 Future* – 2001 (****)

As with other musicians who seem to feel that they are working at the cutting edge, Herbie has often turned to 'sci-fi' themes for his titles and artwork. The cover of this album features a stern Hancock looking like a scientist from an 'anonymous government department' who has arrived to collect the body of E.T. and sanitise the area afterwards.

Future 2 Future is a very good album that features Herbie with a nucleus of musicians including Bill Laswell, veteran drummer Jack de Johnette from the straight-ahead/ free jazz genres, Wayne Shorter and newcomer acoustic bassist Charnett Moffett. These musicians form the basis for around half of the tracks with the other tracks used as experiments with several of the new breed of musicians who work with scratched vinyl, turntables and computers. Lastly, there are several vocalists who make a range of contributions.

Hebero is a musical idea split into two parts. A collaboration between Herbie and Carl Craig, *Part I* is presented at the head of the album - a fusion of primitive rhythms from the past with futuristic electronic musings. *Part II* appears at track 8 and is a clear development of the first part. An explanation for the whole album – or perhaps just a hint of one – appears in the second track, *Wisdom* as the child's voice of Elenni Davis-Knight asserts that "Knowledge corresponds to the past: it is technology. Wisdom is the future: it is philosophy." Thus, we begin to wonder if this is a themed album? These thirty seconds of wise words are presumably some of the sources of inspiration for Herbie – a long practising Buddhist, and they make a good aperitif to the rest of the album.

The Essence follows straight on and would seem to be the focal point of the album, intended to extend the philosophical content still further. On my edition, there is even a second CD consisting of nine different mixes of this same track so Herbie must have considered it important! It is a very commercial number with a significant vocal sung by Chaka Khan and is absolutely fine as a stand-alone track, but is certainly enhanced because of the tracks that surround it. Here is an example of how the modern practice of listening to a random sequence of downloaded MP3 tracks impoverishes music. Imaginative sequencing of tracks on an album frequently enhances the benefit of music. Charnett Moffett plays acoustic bass competently throughout to an accompaniment of drums and turntable from Grandmixer (or is that Grandscratcher?) DXT.

This is Rob Swift is a remarkable creation demonstrating the named artist's considerable skills in working with a turntable and, no doubt, endless patience cutting and pasting on a computer. The focus of the music is a great groove set up by Hancock and Laswell, with Jack de Johnette playing drums like you never heard him before, unless it was a mistake on the sleeve notes and it was really someone else! The equivalent of the lead vocal consists of samples taken from quaint promotional or instructional recordings that feature several male voices speaking short phrases. These are chopped and spliced into the music in such a way as to be relevant and even comic, but which tantalisingly transform into garbled noise just as the voice is about to complete a meaningful sentence. At 2.48, Herbie begins a very cool solo on electric piano whilst Swift's accompaniment of digestive hics and burps subtly fills out the groove that continues behind. At 5.00 the patronising voice of a 1950s CBS telecaster emerges to inform us that the sounds are exciting, before being digested into the pancreatic juices of Hancock's groove. The effects on this track are stunning. It may not be music to everyone's ears, but this is true 21st century jazz-fusion.

Herbie joins forces with Gerald Simpson on *Black Gravity* to produce a superb piece of wholly synthetic art, except for some short sections played on acoustic grand piano. My drummer friends always hate pieces like this because it puts them out of work, but this track is excellent. It has variety, interest and lots of colour. Its only downside is that they did not know how to end it.

The track *Tony Williams* serves to remind me why I dislike lyrics with my jazz. Just when someone serves me up some words that seem to inspire me, as do the words of *Wisdom*, then along comes someone who spoils everything. Tony's death was the inspiration for this music and the words are targeted at his perceived greatness in the annals of jazz drumming. Lyrics such as these toe a line that teeters on the edge of sickening pretentiousness. Somehow, I feel they do him a disservice, although Williams was a proponent of the free-jazz movement and Herbie no doubt feels he would have liked them. So be it. The music features Williams' posthumous drumming and, along with Bill Laswell, Herbie creates a thrusting framework over which Wayne Shorter does his thing on soprano saxophone – not tenor as listed in the sleeve notes. I forgive this track its vocal, for it is deep in concept and magnetic in execution.

Be Still continues with the quartet format, along with a vocal from Imani Uzuri whose lyrics fortunately do not distract from the music. It is the most immediately accessible track for those listeners with ears that are more used to cool jazz and is, as a result, the least significant track on the album, despite some nice playing from Wayne Shorter.

Ionosphere shifts us up two gears in both speed and height with some frantic sampled drum beats set up by Karsh Kale. We are transported from the Earthly forest floor of *Be Still* into the rarefied atmosphere reached only by metallic blackbirds. And then, as if absorbed by the force field from a passing alien ship we find ourselves seamlessly flying with the second part of *Hebero*. The vocals are in the style of a Buddhist chant, which may turn you on if you are that way inclined, but the music is both challenging and rewarding anyway. The penultimate track *Alphabeta* has Jack de Johnette providing a rhythm in the style of a rock drummer whilst giving a jazz cymbal accompaniment – a new and unusual take on jazz-rock fusion. To this backing Herbie paints a complex landscape of electronic sounds. Despite its abstract nature, the result is quite pleasing on the ear.

Virtual Hornets is also remarkable, though for an unusual reason. This composition was included as the major work on the album *Sextant* (1973) about which I have already written. Here the piece is entirely reborn – not that there was a great deal to work with in the first place. The original, you may recall, was what Bob Belden described in the 1998 sleeve notes as a 'hardcore groove'. Pretty much everything else was improvised. On this version, the groove is enhanced and played straight through with little interruption, unlike the original that was punctuated with bridging sections. The piece actually has what might be called a theme, generally played and developed throughout by Herbie, whilst Moffett adds some very good acoustic bass. As a whole, the piece does not have the nasty sting of those hornets of 1973; the creatures still seem to buzz around, but they've gained a more mature, less aggressive behaviour in their old age. Wayne Shorter, who can always be relied upon to create something meaningful, takes on the main soloing role. Here he plays a style that is breathy and directional, but lurches either side of the path of traditional harmony for that added edge. From being something I actively disliked on *Sextant*, this version is one of the better tracks on the album.

As a whole, *Future 2 Future* is one of Herbie's best albums, especially as it is one of the finest examples of modern jazz-fusion. Appearing 18 years after *Future Shock*, this form of the genre is extremely well refined on this album and Herbie demonstrates yet again why he is such an all-round jazz musician.

Herbie Hancock / Michael Brecker / Roy Hargrove: *Directions in Music* – 2002 (*****)

Despite his irresistible urge to continue to develop new music based in electronics, as he did with *Future 2 Future* (2001), it is clear now that, as Herbie moved past his sixtieth year and into the 21st century, Miles Davis would never be far from his thoughts. Yet again, he chose to continue with his love of acoustic jazz in a further celebration, this time of both Miles Davis and John Coltrane. Both men were born in 1926, so in 2001 Herbie decided to create a project to celebrate the 75th anniversary of their birth. For this ambitious project Herbie invited Michael Brecker to represent Coltrane's tenor saxophone and Roy Hargrove to represent Miles. Hargrove (b1969) had been carving a somewhat narrow groove with his own quartet on the New York jazz scene since 1989, and had already won a Grammy for *Habana* (1997) with a band called Crisol. Even so, it was a huge accolade for Roy to be invited to join such stellar company here where his exceptional talent gained a new level of recognition in the acoustic jazz mainstream. Over the coming years, he would continue to play in Herbie's bands, as well as continue working with his own small group. Bass and drums were provided by the brilliant partnership of John Patitucci and Brian Blade, two men who had become first choice for Wayne Shorter's own quartet. Although the packaging of the project focuses on the three leading players, we should not underestimate the contributions made by this remarkable pairing.

As Herbie points out in the sleeve notes to this album, "We're not just playing the original chords of these pieces, but really moving beyond that, using our powers of concentration and our hearts and our trust in the ability of the others to respond to whatever happens and work outside the box. This philosophy is very much in keeping with what I believe to be the true spirit of Miles Davis and John Coltrane." [76] Herbie had, of course, always subscribed to this tenet – another he had learned from Miles. Herbie has frequently pointed out that Miles used to say that he employed musicians to experiment on the bandstand, not in rehearsal rooms, and this ethos is carried forward by this live recording in Toronto entitled *Directions in Music* (2002).

The album opens with Herbie's piece *The Sorcerer*, which he first played with Miles on the classic 1967 album of the same name. In other arenas, such a choice would be regarded as standard fare, but with these musicians there's no such interpretation. This version moves on as inevitably as any of the repeated recordings of Herbie's back catalogue.

So What / Impressions are two jazz compositions credited respectively to Miles and Trane that have enormous presence in the jazz repertoire. The chord sequence of both of these two famous pieces is identical: 16 bars of Dm7, 8 bars of Ebm7 and 8 bars of Dm7. This, of course, makes them easy to blend into one, as happens on this track. Both Miles and Trane would have been familiar with a cover version by Ahmad Jamal in 1955 of *Pavanne* by Morton Gould and this is indeed the origin of both songs. [77]

Transition (1965) was an album by Coltrane that bridged his traditional quartet work and some of the more experimental music of his last years. The title track is used as the basis for this band to develop. The theme is fast and penetrating and quickly lost as each soloist gives his take on the ideas. According to Wikipedia, the original Coltrane composition "exhibits an operatic dramatisation of the human search for meaning." [78] It now becomes clearer just how challenging it must have been for these three musicians (Brecker, especially) to take on the playing of this music and even dare to hope that they might approach it. Somehow, this kind of work could never be comparable with the playing of just another version of *Someday My Prince Will Come,* for example.

My Ship is in the same slow, beautiful vein as the original on *Miles Ahead* (1957), except that here it is given the slightest swing that pushes it into new territory. Hargrove's flügelhorn is at its luxurious best for this sweet music.

It is not enough, however, merely to reinterpret the music of the two icons. Instead, these musicians brought their own music to the project. Thus, Hargrove wrote the piece entitled *The Poet* with Miles in mind, saying that the piece was inspired by the Miles Davis quintet of the 1960s "when they were getting into a sound that went beyond traditional structure." [79] Brecker wrote *D Trane*, which he said was "loosely based on a West African clave rhythmic structure and was influenced by Coltrane's compositions that drew upon African music." [80] As you listen to this rendition, it is quite possible to understand how this music could actually better represent the intellectual ideals of Coltrane's *Transition*. This piece is rightly positioned as the final track on the album, for it is a massive performance on the part of all those involved, and a *tour de force* for Brecker that draws a huge response from the audience.

The track entitled *Misstery* is a joint composition by Hancock, Brecker and Hargrove that adds a welcome freshness to a running order that contains plenty of well-known items. Yet, even as we ponder the up-coming *Naima*, a very well known piece from Trane's repertoire, we can have no idea what treat is in store. For any musician to stand alone on stage and perform Coltrane's *Naima* is daring in the extreme and beyond most sane players of the saxophone. For Michael Brecker to do so is a demonstration of his stratospheric pinnacle of achievement on his instrument. Even allowing for the fact that he must have wood-shedded this piece on countless occasions, it is a demonstration of tenor saxophone performance at an unparalleled level and, under any circumstances, we should feel privileged to listen. I could hardly imagine a better tribute to Trane.

There have been many tributes to Coltrane and Miles, not forgetting Herbie's own involvement with *A Tribute to Miles* (1994), and there will be many more in the future, but this must rank as one of the finest of all time. The whole concept of this album is a considerable challenge for everyone involved. As I have suggested above, it surely challenged its musicians. The members of the band, however, have the great advantage of knowing everything there is to know about the project – of knowing the origins of the music and playing it and developing it night after night on the bandstand. They even know it so well that they feel able to compose their own music in advance. Thus, as with Brecker's *D Trane* or Hargrove's *The Poet*, we should never underestimate the challenge of presenting to the other musicians a self-penned work that might dare to approach the work of the two dead masters. During the performances, the musicians also experience and feel the intimate personal interactions, even if they are transitory and vary nightly with each re-working of a piece. For them to work together in such a way as to make it seem as if they are playing some perfectly scripted score even as they dodge and weave through the music in ways that are new even to them, is jazz craft at the highest level.

The album challenges us too, though not nearly as much. The great contradiction of music that is built upon improvisation, however, is in its permanence on a recording. We surely appreciate it more when we gain an understanding of the task at hand, yet the value of an improvised work must be lost in the repetition? I am at a loss to understand how the audience exposed to this for the first time could have gained anything more than the immediacy of living in their own personal moments. Some, unfamiliar with the music being performed and of the artists in question, must surely gain little other than the instant aural experience, which they cannot be guaranteed to like. We, on the other hand, have the advantage of additional information such as I give you here, as well as the opportunity to listen again and to enjoy the moments we may have missed the first time around or to better understand those we did not miss first time around. Clearly, the benefit of retrospect pays dividends for the immense artistic achievement on this album, which is then better recognised. As a result, the album was rewarded by the decision of the jazz peer group when it not only won a Grammy for the 'Best Jazz Instrumental Album', but got Herbie a personal Grammy for the 'Best Jazz Instrumental Solo' on *My Ship*. For all of these reasons, as well as for the sheer audacity of the idea and of the execution, I feel obliged to give this album a five star rating, but be under no illusion that this is an album for the easy-listener.

Herbie Hancock: Gig at the Lighthouse Centre, Poole, 3 May 2005

Unlike geriatric rockers who fill stadiums to the sound of 'Greatest Hits Rehashed', jazzers rarely rest on the laurels of their previous incarnations, though they sometimes feel old, just like the rest of us. "Everything in this band's new – except me!" proclaimed the great man at this rather subdued gig at the Lighthouse Centre, Poole. Since the band was titled, the Herbie Hancock Quartet, then clearly he was its longest serving member, but of course the joke was about his age. So is he feeling his age? Well, it would seem not – at least, not in music. Here was a man who was not going to be rushed. After an entrance that was a lot later than most other gigs I have been to, the suspense was prolonged when he strangely began shuffling through his music as if to decide what he was going to play first. Maybe he was making a point to those members of the audience who are still incapable of understanding what time things should start. Then, there were a peculiar couple of minutes lost as he arduously manipulated the mechanism that raised and lowered the seat of his piano stool, as if it he had just set foot in the building and his roadies had let him down.

The music too was a slow starter. Despite the powerful presence of a stunningly beautiful concert grand piano centre stage, electronics played a central role in the sound of this band. The diminutive drummer Richie Barshay sat astride an appropriately small kit, the smallest piece of which was a digibox of tiny geometry but gargantuan proportions. He proceeded to play it as if he had been doing so since the day he was born, which was roughly one third of the number of Hancock's years. But don't be fooled into thinking that here was a clash of the cultures – a musical mutton dressed as lamb. Hancock has always been at the forefront of jazz, first by his electric piano playing on Miles Davis's *Bitches Brew* (1969) in the earliest days of jazz-rock fusion and then by wholeheartedly indulging in funk and adopting electronic sounds on his chart-topping album *Head Hunters* (1974). Even now, weeks after his sixty-fifth birthday, he has a greater appreciation of (and skill with) electronic musical instruments played by seriously clever musicians half his age. Yet throughout all the showmanship and razzamatazz, Hancock has always been the consummate pianist, preferring (according to John Harle [2]) to practice his scales and arpeggios alone on his days off.

Thus, the concert began with the creation of a timeless, atmospheric vibe through a combination of mysterious hand gestures from Barshay and a series of menu selections on Hancock's computer. Herbie's quizzical left handed twiddles were translated into an enigmatic sequence of sounds generated from his right hand on a chaste white slab that languished carelessly on the top surface of the concert grand piano. As the soundscape continued its metamorphosis, we became aware that the fascinating guitar-player, Benin-born Lionel Loueke, was indeed making music, although of a kind we are not used to hearing from the strings of this instrument. Here too the electronic revolution had arrived. The instrument in question had the superficial appearance of a Spanish acoustic guitar, but whose ghostly body was indeed a mere outline, an apology for the replacement of its stately sound by a constantly changing portfolio of effects controlled, not from the player's hands, but his feet. Constant pedalling to a remote silicon chip today replaces the percussive sound of finger-plucked stings with all manner of legato notes that fill appropriate spaces in the electronic facade. Against such a backdrop, bassist Dave Carpenter inevitably looked as old as Methuselah, bowing his antique string bass in the style of a Wagnerian orchestra member.

As for the music, well, it was superbly coherent and mostly intended to soothe and relax us, rather than to stimulate us into involuntary foot and hand movements. Pieces were long and presented with almost no gaps between them, though we did get an introduction to the band at an arbitrary midpoint in the evening. The music derived from the pens of most of the players and was in formats that could not be unravelled at first hearing. The range of sounds was far in excess of what you would expect from a mere quartet. With the electronics firmly under control, we were introduced to everything from the abstract to the material, from the sound of a brass line-up to a vocal chorus. This was modern jazz at its complex best – very tonal, never aggressive, constantly intriguing. We were always aware of being present at something special. Jazz on this night had moved on yet again, safe in the hands of one of its elder statesmen.

Change on stage is met with change in the audiences. Gone are the days when audiences listened in motionless silence to the delectable offerings they have paid handsomely to witness. In its place is a crowd that is constantly concerned with the next event on its list of bodily input and output. I hesitate even to consider the day when more than half the audience decides to get the beer in during the quiet moments of Herbie's *Maiden Voyage* piano solo at the start of the last piece. As it is, the few who do so should be loudly reminded of the privilege they should feel at being present during one of the high moments of modern jazz. Time moves on, and this final piece of the six presented to us was as majestic as we might dare to expect. I was reminded that in these days of celebrity worship, the celebs themselves constantly change their appearance, trying to hide their identity from the inquisitive masses. In *Maiden Voyage* Hancock holds the responsibility for a musical celebrity, barely recognisable from its last appearance in public, but retaining all the characteristics that put it there in the first place. Perhaps *Chameleon* might have been a more appropriate piece to air, but on second thoughts, perhaps not. It had already been well covered by the Dorset Youth Jazz Band in the foyer beforehand.

Attendance at a gig like this always has an air of the surreal about it. You don't know any of the music, and you know only one of the musicians. After sitting back and letting the creativity wash over you for two hours, what remains? Well, certain knowledge that you have witnessed something very special. Hancock may not be in his physical prime – he may exhibit some of the crankiness of a pensioner, but his musical acumen is as sharp as ever. The seamless integration of cutting edge electronics into the traditional quartet format, alongside master craftsmanship at the piano is a joy and a privilege to behold. This was not a night for displays of technical wizardry on any given instrument. It was a night for fine art, perfectly presented and of the highest calibre. It was a display of skilled musical thought transformed into beautiful aural landscapes.

It was also a demonstration of the widening disparity between the evolution of the minds of those on stage and those off it. The end of the gig was celebrated not just with polite (though never over-enthusiastic) applause, but also with a strategic withdrawal of an embarrassingly large proportion of the audience heading for the last bus. I suppose it is inevitable that a man's fame, rather than his music, is the draw for a gig such as this. Once the audience had been weeded down to the real music aficionados, the encore consisted of a guitar solo from the gifted and highly original Loueke, who played a beautifully rhythmic African-style number punctuated with vocals in the style of Richard Bono. Though somewhat out of place in the context of the rest of the show, what are such occasions for if not to allow young up-and-coming musicians to promenade their licks? Here is one young man with a great future ahead of him. Finally, the band pressed its 'swing buttons' and concluded with an up-tempo number faster by far than anything they had played all night. An appearance of this number earlier in the schedule might have invoked a greater show of satisfaction from those who had left, but who cares? Like Kilroy, I was there.

Herbie Hancock: *Possibilities* – 2005 (****)

In 2005 Herbie made yet another change of direction. In a step forward from *The New Standard* (1994), his presentation in the jazz genre of a collection of songs from the popular genre, Herbie got the musicians themselves to play and sing alongside him: songs by some of his favourite artists such as Sting, Stevie Wonder, Paul Simon and Annie Lennox.

The highlight of the album for me is a stunning version by Christina Aguilera of the Carpenters' beautiful song *A Song for You*. I'm sure Hancock would have preferred to have Karen's exquisite voice perform it, but after Carpenter, and the incomparable Ella Fitzgerald, Aguilera has one of the finest voices around today. She uses it to illustrate wonderfully just how the modern vocal style, derived from singers such as Witney Houston and Maria Carey, draws on the jazz legacy. The melody she sings has only a passing resemblance to the Karen Carpenter version but is a master-class in improvisation that both Carpenter and Fitzgerald would have admired.

Not especially noted for their love of jazz, Stevie Wonder (*I Just Called to Say I Love You*) and Paul Simon (*I Do it For Your Love*), must have been slightly stunned by what Herbie planned to do with their material, for both songs are substantially changed. Carlos Santana's song *Safiatou* takes on an even more Latin feel than it had in 1999, and I'm not sure that Herbie has improved it. However, the blues is well represented by the terrific numbers on tracks one and seven. The first is *Stitched Up* with John Mayer, the second *When Love comes to Town*, which features Johnny Lang and Joss Stone. Sting, the included artist probably most at home with jazz, sings *Sister Moon*, a jazz choice that is a bit straight-laced for all but the most up-market New York cocktail-bars.

The album was dubbed a "disappointing 'Starbucks' album" [81] and spends a rather disproportionate amount of time lingering with the sentimental rather than the swinging, which is almost entirely unrepresented. It could be argued that Herbie is doing something new again, not only for himself, but by encouraging the artists to experiment with things they themselves may not have tried before. Unfortunately, when they don't appear as comfortable with the material as Herbie does, it sounds to some as if the selection of artists was not quite right.

Kevin Legendre: "I think the *Possibilities* album was probably an impossible dream. I don't think it quite worked. I think he was trying to go in too many different directions. I'm not sure that the guests were right. The reason why he did *Possibilities* is the same reason why he did *Rockit*, which I love, it's the same reason why he did *Head Hunters* because he's thinking beyond the parameters of what other people might define for him as a 'jazz' musician. You're only supposed to do this, you're not supposed to use a vocoder, you're not supposed to work with a hip-hop producer you're not supposed to work with mainstream pop vocalists. 'To hell with that!' he's saying. 'I'll do what I want.' That's why he's changed things." [62]

In a world where almost everything has been tried already, Herbie is indeed looking for yet another new approach. I believe he pulled it off. Jazz-fusion is not really a factor on this more conventional record, but it is a sufficiently unusual album to make it a favourite with many listeners and I recommend it wholeheartedly.

Herbie Hancock: The Roundhouse Gig, Saturday 11 November 2006

The Roundhouse on Chalk Farm Road in London's Camden Town seemed to be an unlikely location for a Herbie Hancock gig, but it was quite a coup for its management as Herbie flew in from Switzerland to play this venue on a warm Saturday night in November 2006. I had visited the website during September to buy tickets and was dismayed to discover that the bulk of the tickets were for standing customers; the seating tickets had sold out long ago. From thereon, I tried unsuccessfully to buy seats through every agency I could contact. When the day arrived, Chris and I simply turned up to see what we could find. At four in the afternoon there was still nothing available at the box office. As I waited in the hope that there might be some returned, a black limo deposited three men onto the pavement outside and I recognised Lionel Louecke. In the surprise of the moment, an image of his beautiful guitar came into my mind and, shaking his hand, I asked him if he had brought it with him. I had been very impressed with his guitar when I saw him play in Poole over two years ago. It was little more than a fingerboard attached to a curved piece of wood having the outline of a guitar shape. Based on a Spanish nylon string design it was necessarily wholly electric because of its non-existent sound box. I wanted one badly. The tall gentleman from Benin beamed down on me and said yes. As we exchanged some pleasantries, I became aware that the other band members had gone inside; Herbie had not yet arrived. It was very soon after that one of the friendly staff received news that two standing tickets had been returned. I took a deep breath. I didn't know how my ageing legs and back muscles would respond to hours of standing, but I bought the tickets and was immediately grateful. It was my lucky day after all. Little did I realise just how lucky I was…

I should have guessed the plan. Standing is what young people do at gigs, isn't it? Standing allows larger audiences – it was rumoured amongst the waiting queues that some three thousand people were expected at this one, including a bus load of junior school kids sponsored by an American bank! Standing, so it is said, provides a better atmosphere and invites body movements. Dancing? Surely not. Was this a sign that the gig would be a return to the old rocking Herbie? With support from Vinnie Colaiuta, one-time Zappa band member and now one of the great jazz-fusion session drummers, and Nathan East, an electric bass player from the same background, I should have known that this was indeed Herbie's signal for the audience to prepare to rock. Only a musician of Herbie's stature can succeed in the "decriminalisation of jazz-funk". No-one else would dare.

As we claimed our places at the very front of the auditorium I was stunned by the venue. It was like being inside a brand-new structure, built by I. K. Brunel to the plans of H. G. Wells, a kind of Victorian flying saucer. With little sign of the middle-aged nerds like me who populate jazz events these days, the audience was now overwhelmingly young. It was heart-warming to speak to many young people who were not jazz fans, but who had come to find out what this music was all about because they had heard their dads play Herbie Hancock records. As the ranks of photographers grew in the pit below the stage it was beyond doubt that this was to be a rock-style concert, with Herbie Hancock the star. To my surprise, I was, after all, delighted to be standing and not seated. The seats around the rear were remote from the stage and behind pillars supporting the roof of the UFO. Here amidst the crush at the front, there was real atmosphere the like of which I had long ago forgotten since the days when I stood to watch English professional football.

The opener was *Watermelon Man* - with a twist" that, according to Herbie, was a bonus feature provided by Lionel's twisted imagination. "He's mad" he kept telling us, although he meant it in the nicest possible way, and later amended his description to "genius". What he actually meant was that Lionel was 'gifted', one of those very rare individuals who can take a great jazz standard like *Watermelon Man* and turn it into something new. The result was stunning! The crowd went wild for one of the rockiest of jazz tunes, created when rock music was still an embryonic figment of most imaginations. We were soon fired-up to Mach two by Herbie's solo on his Roland neck-slung keyboard that Chris had noticed possessed the shape of a can opener. Another indicator of what was in store was Vinnie's appearance on stage dressed in sweatband, tracksuit bottoms and vest, like he was ready for a workout. And that's just what he did to his kit, with microsecond-impeccable timing. In fact, as he finished his first solo I thought I saw coffee brewing on the drum skins.

When Herbie quickly reminded us of his last album from 2005, the collaborative *Possibilities*, recorded with a host of great singers from all genres, I immediately wondered if he would conjure up some surprise guest vocalists. He didn't but it didn't matter. Yet even when he introduced the bluesy *When Love Comes to Town*, I still didn't quite expect the entire gig to be jazz-fusion, a genre that everyone was telling me was dead and buried. In fact, the band played three numbers from the album, along with its brilliant opener *Stitched Up* and Stevie Wonder's *I Just Called to Say I Love You* with vocals provided by Nathan East. Needless to say, Herbie's new synth gave a good imitation of Stevie's harmonica. Of all of these great numbers, I shall never forget during *Stitched Up* being rocked like never before by a concert grand piano. Only Elton John has got near it. Herbie pulled an unusual oldie out of the bag when the song *Touch Me* resurfaced in a beautiful modern ballad form. With the aid of some gorgeous sounds from Herbie's keyboard and Lionel's guitar there was no need to blow cobwebs from his old vocoder - thankfully!

Around the halfway point, Herbie introduced what he called a Lionel 'soup', in which the young guitar genius cleverly used electronics to cook up an amazing broth of vocals, percussion and guitar playing. It brought a completely new meaning to the term 'one-man band' and reminded me of Jaco's circus-style antics during the Weather Report gigs of the late seventies. *Cantaloupe Island* rounded off the formal part of the show, by which time we were all screaming for more, so the band, who were thoroughly enjoying themselves, duly gave us a twenty minute three-part encore of *Chameleon*, two parts of which were twisted enough to be Louecke-inspired.

By the time I took my seat on the underground train, I had been standing for five hours, but it had been one of the great events of my many years of gigs. At sixty-six years of age, Herbie can still rock the crowd with the best of them, and like his great friend Miles, can still attract the young ears jazz needs.

Herbie Hancock: *River, The Joni Letters* – 2007 (*****)

With *River, The Joni Letters*, Herbie seemed to prick the conscience of the music industry. It was as if his album made them realise that they had not paid due respect to Joni Mitchell's priceless contributions to music. Any informed observer will know that Mitchell's artistry has been of far greater value than the mere music content of her songs, even allowing for their incomparable beauty. Her poetry had said as much as any other writer about modern America and the sufferings of its citizens in their day-to-day relationships. The lyrics to her songs, spread over nineteen varied, perceptive, original studio albums, form a body of work that Herbie had decided to call *The Joni Letters*. Using her own (often difficult) autobiographical commentaries as reference material for the human condition, Joni's writings to the world had covered subjects crossing the entire spectrum of human activity, subjects that were sometimes painful yet always recognisable to her listeners. By 2007, when she had all but retired from music, she had been offered a share of the awards from her industry that was perhaps modest when compared to the achievements of other far less penetrating artists. Starting out as a 'folk singer', her talent was quickly recognised with a Grammy for 'Best Folk Performance' for *Clouds* (1969). Next came the comparatively insignificant 'Best Arrangement Accompanying Vocalists' for *Down to You* (1974). Then it was a long wait until *Turbulent Indigo* (1995) which won 'Best Pop Album'. This was indeed an honour, yet her massive contributions during 21 intervening years had been ignored. At least her paintings (which had adorned all of her album covers) were now responsible for 'Best Recording Package' on *Turbulent Indigo*. Two more awards followed: 'Best Traditional Pop Vocal Album' for *Both Sides Now* (2000) and 'Best Pop Instrumental Performance' for *One Week Last Summer* (2007). Despite these awards, there seemed to be so much that remained unsaid by her peers. Herbie's piercing project finally burst that insulating bubble.

As any music student will tell you, Joni Mitchell is unique – a writer, poet, artist and musician who, in the best traditions of fusion, has blended her skills to form a creative force of great stature. Identified mostly in the domain of popular music, she is one of the very few of her ilk to make a serious impression in the world of jazz – the crossover in that direction being much trickier than the reverse motion. With a number of other top jazz musicians, Herbie had participated in Joni's wonderful project with Charlie Mingus that resulted in the album *Mingus* (1979) and he had also played in her band at gigs promoting its release. Herbie and Joni had been firm friends ever since. Herbie Hancock's recognition that it was time for a careful jazz study of Joni's music (he'd done a similar thing with George Gershwin ten years earlier) seemed to catch the music Mafia by surprise. Indeed, they were so surprised that, once the wonder of hearing this beautiful album had really sunk in, they felt obliged to make this their 'Album of the Year' – not just the best *jazz* album, or the best *pop* album, but *best album*! It was an unexpected coup for Herbie and, indirectly at least, the ultimate accolade for Joni herself. The realisation of Herbie's project was a truly immense album of music that seemed to encapsulate perfectly not just the career of a unique musician, but also the messages, the diaries, the observations and analyses from a lifetime of work.

The team Herbie chose to execute the project could not have been better. Having worked with her since *Don Juan's Reckless Daughter* (1977), Wayne Shorter knows Joni's music as well as anyone. She felt that Wayne was the only musician who could so perfectly encapsulate her thoughts into music. Herbie and Wayne had been close friends for so long that they were in total musical symbiosis. Herbie's choice of Lionel Louecke and Vinnine Colaiuta was not just a result of them being friends and current band colleagues, but of Herbie's complete confidence that each would be able to contribute the kind of sympathetic responses to the music of the moment. Finally, Herbie knew that Dave Holland was simply the best acoustic bass player around who would not only provide solid support, but also respond perfectly to the changes caused by their inspirations.

A particularly clever move was Herbie's choice of Larry Klein for co-producer. Although he was Joni's ex-husband, they were still good friends and Klein had proved himself to be a very competent musician and producer who clearly knew Joni's music very well indeed. Herbie and Larry had earlier worked together with Joni and Wayne when in June 1989 they had formed a 'superband' with ex-Police drummer Andy Summers to perform at a UN-organised benefit performance. Herbie and Larry were also part of Joni's band when she did her *Both Sides Now* tour in 2002. Klein is a talented jazz musician who, early in his career, played bass guitar on a number of Freddie Hubbard's albums. Klein had harboured ambitions to become a record producer and was able to realise his ambitions starting with Joni's albums *Wild Things Run Fast* (1982) and *Dog Eat Dog* (1986). Since then he has been involved with many artists, including Rebecca Pidgeon, Madeleine Peyroux, Tracey Chapman and Luciana Sousa. He seems to have made a specialisation of producing the work of female singer-songwriters: he married Sousa in 2006. It's interesting to note that Joni herself was kept (or kept herself) at a distance from the project. Apart from singing on one track – *Tea Leaf Prophecy* - she rightly makes no other obvious contribution.

Herbie's strategy was a development of the one he had successfully used on *Possibilities* (2005). Here he combined the use of carefully selected vocalists, each matched with a song from Joni's repertoire, and instrumental interpretations that, in some way, described Joni's music as well as any of the paintings she herself uses for her album cover artwork. *Court and Spark* was matched to Norah Jones and used to open the album. Tina Turner was an inspirational choice for *Edith and the Kingpin*, for not only was Tina's voice perfect for the role, but her difficult lifetime experiences made her the perfect candidate to sing of the violent, seedy world described therein. Corinne Bailey Rae exhibits the wonderful childlike naivete of young love required to capture the mood for *River*. A poor choice was Luciana Sousa, whose tone was too close (and quite inferior) to Joni's. When the philosophy is to exploit the jazz and to celebrate the differences it allows, the restrictions imposed by the selection of Sousa is unforgiveable. It's a great shame because *Amelia* is one of the truly great Mitchell compositions and everything else about this rendition is superb. The album concludes with Leonard Cohen reciting the lyrics to *The Jungle Line*, another of Joni's brilliant indictments of modern society. Cohen's drawl is somehow the perfect embodiment of tone and timbre for the role and Herbie's solo piano accompaniment draws every last gram of emotion from the weeping wounds left by centuries of oppression, racism, war, death and hate.

Between these Mitchell milestones is a scattering of other instrumental portraits, not necessarily written by her, but which nonetheless, contain the essence of what she was about. Her important song *Both Sides Now* is given the full Herbie/Wayne treatment. Try playing this version back-to-back with the original and you will notice only the barest similarity, yet the inescapable conclusion is that this version embraces everything the original does. Somehow, the melodic constructs of Wayne and Herbie compensate for the absence of those lyrics that explain that, no matter how you look at it, love is quite incomprehensible. "*Sweet Bird* – its title taken from the Tennessee Williams play *Sweet Bird of Youth* [is] a gentle meditation on transience and inevitability." [82] Of course, it's a delightful self-reference and the version here by Herbie is as captivating as a meeting with the maestro herself. Wayne's impression of Joni compares her to *Nefertiti*. Both women he sees as highly influential, both at the pinnacle of their own hierarchies. This distillation of the original composition written for Miles Davis's *Nefertiti* (1968) reflects the years of acquisition of wisdom and experience of living. It is immensely richer as a result. But life at the top can be very lonely, and the track *Solitude* has some deep significance in Joni's life, selected by Herbie for reasons that are not obvious. Certainly, for all her successes, Joni portrays herself as a sad, lonely figure. Loving the company of men, but unable to enjoy the lifelong company of just one man created its own sadness that she narrated in her many songs. Perhaps the greatest hole in her life was estrangement from her daughter, mercifully now at an end. Originally written by Duke Ellington and first recorded in 1934, *Solitude* is played here by the trio of Herbie, Vinnie and Dave, who retain the beautiful character of this great jazz standard.

I view Herbie Hancock as a musical Picasso. This master painter takes an expression or a thought and wraps it in the entire context in which it has been placed. Then he distils the essences into their constituent colours and condenses them onto his canvas in ways that leave us in awe of his perception and skill. That does not mean that any of his music is easy. As we saw in his album with Wayne, *1 +1* (1997) and *Gershwin's World* (1998), Herbie's analysis, like a theoretical paper by Russell or Einstein, is the result of the purest of thought and the deepest philosophy. This is a science that has been arrived at after nearly fifty years of immersion in and devotion to his chosen field of study. It is, therefore (unsurprisingly) hard to comprehend. But it stands for all time. That is why, at last, and with a proper display of recognition, the Grammy award for 'Album of the Year' (2007) was given to Herbie Hancock and Larry Klein. In the history of the Grammys, only once before had the top prize gone to a jazz album – to Stan Getz and Joao Gilberto for their album *Getz / Gilberto* (1964). It is probably the greatest award a jazz musician could receive, equivalent to the 'Best Film' Academy Award in the film industry. It was a magnificent achievement, and I wish to take nothing away from Herbie when I add that it was won thanks to the brilliant music of Joni Mitchell. Jazz purists will hate the thought that *Getz / Gilberto* (1964) was an early Brazilian-jazz-fusion album. They will be madder still when they realise that *River, The Joni Letters* (2007) was a pop-folk-jazz fusion.

Classical Herbie

In an interview at the rehearsals for the Ceremony for the 50th Grammy Awards Herbie said: "I was completely stunned when I was nominated for 'Album of the Year' I mean, it never happens for jazz." [83] He was standing alongside the Chinese classical music superstar Lang Lang as they rehearsed a piece for the show. Lang had also received a nomination and someone in the organisation had made the obvious suggestion: "Hey! Why don't these two guys play a duet?"

Herbie is not well known for his performances of classical music. At the 2008 Grammys, Herbie and Lang Lang played a six-minute adaptation of George Gershwin's *Rhapsody In Blue* for two pianos. They quickly became friends. It became clear to both men that there was scope for them to work together in some way. Their successful performance had shown that they could play classical music together, but what of Lang Lang and jazz? It wasn't long before Lang Lang was taking themes from *Rhapsody in Blue* and improvising over them. The circle was complete.

Their diaries were busy for months ahead. For example, in August 2008, Lang Lang played at the opening ceremony of the Beijing Olympics watched by an estimated 5 billion people. Finally, in 2009, Herbie and Lang went on a tour of Europe and the USA playing some classical music pieces. Herbie, "Before the tour I was both delighted and frightened to death, considering that he's the consummate classical pianist. I haven't been playing classical music since I was 18, and I spent the last two months practising three or four hours a day." [84] Herbie had clearly forgotten the odd occasions when he had recorded pieces from the classical repertoire. There was Béla Bartok's *Ostinato* that appeared on the album *Corea/Hancock* (1979). Much later, there was the second movement of *Ravel's Piano Concerto in G*, recorded for *Gershwin's World* (1998). But the plans he made with Lang Lang were of an altogether different level of participation. And there was the added pressure of playing alongside a premier league classical pianist. Amongst other pieces, some of which required Lang Lang to improvise, the two men played a John Mauceri arrangement of Gershwin's *Rhapsody In Blue* and the *Concerto for Two Pianos and Orchestra* by Ralph Vaughan Williams. For a four-handed arrangement of Maurice Ravel's difficult *Mother Goose Suite*, they sat side by side, shoulder to shoulder. Lang said of Herbie: "He really plays classical music brilliantly, like the Vaughan Williams, which requires a great deal of confidence and technique." [84] As if we didn't know that already, the project with Lang Lang clearly shows that Herbie is capable of playing in any genre and context.

Herbie Hancock's Headhunters: *Watermelon Man* (DVD)– 2008 (***)

This is a good DVD of a concert on 20 August 2005 in Tokyo, Japan. The band is very exciting as Herbie is joined by Marcus Miller (bass), Roy Hargrove (trumpet, flügelhorn) Terri Lyne Carrington (drums), Lionel Louecke (guitar), Melvin 'Wah Wah Watson' Ragin (guitar) and Munyungo Jackson (percussion).

The music gets off to a great start as *Watermelon Man* is given the same kind of treatment that it received on the original *Head Hunters* (1974) album. *Spider* is next, a piece familiar to Wah Wah Watson as it comes from the album *Secrets* (1976) that he played on. Herbie introduces *Safiatou* as the track he played with Carlos Santana on the *Possibilities* (2005) album and it is Lionel Louecke's task to fill Santana's shoes – a tall order that is fulfilled very satisfactorily as he plays in the finger-picking style. The music retains its strong Latin rhythm thanks to Jackson's lively percussion and Carrington's imaginative drumming. Perhaps the most remarkable piece on the video is Herbie's other mid-70s blockbuster *Actual Proof* from *Thrust* (1974). The band deals with the stunning rhythmic complexity as if it's a nursery rhyme. Only Wah Wah Watson looks in any way perplexed as he struggles to find anything to go wah-wah to in this one. Herbie is at his very best as he hustles between his acoustic and electric keyboards to deliver his solos. Watson is much more at home playing *Hang Up Your Hang*

Ups as the band now delivers its funky monochordal backing.

It's not a DVD that pushes back boundaries, but it is a rare opportunity to witness a very recent version of Herbie's jazz-fusion band. There are a number of memorable aspects of the DVD. It's a strong performance from Roy Hargrove who delivers some very rich tones from his various horns, some of which are nicely intercepted with electronics. Amazing dexterity and apparently little effort is shown by Lionel Louecke, who also takes the opportunity to sing in the style of his recently released albums of West African world music. The rhythm section is wonderful thanks to Marcus Miller's rock-solid bass lines and fabulous funk, Terri Lyne Carrington's beautiful professional job on drums and Munyungo Jackson's imaginative use of kit. It's rather disappointing for Wah Wah Watson who, on the DVD at least, contributes minimally. Herbie's mastery of what looks like a complex array of electronics is very impressive, and his playing is unceasingly creative. Even on the most familiar compositions he continues to find new things to say with a facility that is bewildering.

Herbie Hancock: *The Imagine Project* – 2010 (*****)

The idea of a common humanity goes back to early religious history, but from time to time undergoes a resurgence of interest and is cast into new forms. In 1824, Beethoven wrote a setting for the poem *Ode to Joy* as a celebration of the ideal of unity and brotherhood of all humankind. Many have argued that religious disagreement has too often been the cause of war, not its cure. It was really only in the 20th century that thoughtful minds began to conceive a united world unlimited by national boundary or religion. "Imagine there's no countries ... and no religion too." The catastrophe of two World Wars and the very real possibility of nuclear Armageddon led to a new peace movement in which John Lennon and his wife Yoko Ono became prominent members in the late 1960s. At the same time, Apollo astronauts taking photographs of the Earth from space drew our attention to the fragility of our tiny planet. In time, this new-found innocence and understanding of our place in the Universe helped us form a context for the scale of the disaster facing us today as we fight to save the planet.

Amongst all of the compositions that John Lennon penned for the Beatles, *Imagine* is now probably his most significant song. It was once voted third in the list of 500 greatest songs of all time by *Rolling Stone* magazine and Lennon would, I'm sure, be glad to know that one of his most cherished creations is recognisable to a large percentage of the people on the planet. In his lyrics Lennon described humans belonging to one country, one world, one people. It was another part of the transformation of developed world cultures by the power of popular music and musicians. We had moved on from cheap love songs to powerful statements about the future of the human race. Even today, as I write this, I watch Glastonbury 2010 in which Stevie Wonder exhorts his audience to treat everyone as equal, whilst from behind a Greenpeace banner the band Faithless proclaims a similar philosophy with its stirring song *We Come 1*. Herbie Hancock's latest album project is clearly not and never could be unique; it's not even new. Nevertheless, the idea of an entire themed album of altruism and lofty ideas for humankind is somewhat unusual. Whatever! In the words of Peter Gabriel: "Don't Give Up."

Herbie's latest album *The Imagine Project* (2010), once again co-produced with Larry Klein, is a collection of carefully selected world music, performed by the musicians of the world and recorded in studios around the world. It is ambitious and eclectic and yet another example of jazz-fusion. Herbie embraces the world's musical cultures, either fusing them (as in *Imagine* or *Tamatant Tilay / Exodus*) or adapting the original ethos of a song into a new one (as in *The Times They Are A' Changin'*). In other songs, the lyrics are powerful enough to convey their message with no change to the setting necessary (as in *Space Captain* or *A Change Is Gonna Come*). Herbie's choices are not always obvious, which adds greatly to the album's interest, but they are always sincere and appropriate. And the choice of musicians is utterly brilliant. Who but Herbie could have matched Dave Matthews with the Beatles' tune *Tomorrow Never Knows*, probably the only time this amazing piece has been covered apart from the original. There is a fresh currency about many of the singers he chooses to present his material.

Imagine begins with a gentle introduction in which Pink and Seal share the plaintive vocal with only Herbie's grieving piano for accompaniment. It's a sad start. The lyrics are engraved upon our hearts. Before we have even started our journey, we all know the problem: no world leader with the power to change things seems to listen. At the utterance of "...And the world will be as one" there is a spine-tingling outbreak of rhythm and melodic stardust as American soul and R&B singer India.Arie exhorts us all to see sense. Superficially, the song is simple, but at 3.40 is transformed into a humming African fiesta from an entirely new band of African musicians called Konono No 1. Oumou Sangare is another vocalist who sings in front of the African band and the splicing together is beautifully seamless giving new meaning to the idea of jazz-fusion. Another highlight – one of many in this great opening song - is the unexpected sophisticated lead guitar sound of Jeff Beck who plays a fitting solo.

This wonderful beginning is followed by Peter Gabriel's *Don't Give Up*, originally sung in a duet with Kate Bush and here given a similar two-headed vocalisation by Pink (stylised to P!NK) and John Legend. Pink's outstanding voice and artistry has attracted huge attention since her debut in 2000. *Billboard* named her as the Number 1 Pop Song Artist of the decade (2000-10), whilst

Legend has had considerable success, winning six Grammys since launching his career with his debut album *Get Lifted* (2004). Gabriel's original recording was, for many observers, unbeatable and although changes are evident to the harmonic setting for *Don't Give Up*, the Hancock version is still breathtaking. Legend's intonation in the verses sounds quite like Gabriel's original vocal. As Pink substitutes her own charm for the incomparable Kate Bush in the chorus, the backdrop devised by George Whitty is stunning. Australian Tal Wilkenfeld is on bass, whilst Dean Parks plays a beautiful guitar solo. Herbie's playing in this moving track is mostly minimalist with every note like a tear running down the cheek of a child.

Tempo De Amor is a piece from Brazil, led on vocals by Maria do Céu Whitaker Poças, who abbreviates her name in the Brazilian tradition to Céu or CéU. The song dates back to a collaboration between two of that country's great musicians, Baden Powell and Vinicius Moraes. As the American love of the Bossa Nova was starting to pass, they produced a more refined collection of African-Brazilian fusions called *Os Afro-Sambas* (1966). The song taken from that album, *Tempo De Amor* (also known as *Samba Do Veloso*) is puzzling for the presence of what sounds exactly like a guitar yet is not listed in the credits. If this is Herbie playing yet another keyboard then he has moved forward again. His solo is on acoustic piano and is juicily jazzy to the slinky cool Brazilian backwash. Despite this uncertainty, the music and Portuguese lyrics are both refreshing and fun.

On first hearing, *Space Captain* seems a strange title for the fourth track, but the lyrics have real significance within the confines of *The Imagine Project*. This is a song written by Matthew Moore and made famous by Joe Cocker, first on his live album *Mad Dogs and Englishmen* (1970) and then on *Space Captain* (1972). Here, the piece is sung by blues and soul artist Susan Tedeschi. Susan's husband, Derek Trucks, contributes some fine southern-style guitar work in a kind of 'B. B. King meets Jimmy Page' style, with much slurring and sliding. It's in the gospel/soul genre with the fine tradition of Hammond B-3 organ and there's a lot of variations of mood and tension in the song as it goes from uproarious vocal-fest to near silence with some staccato punctuation of solo guitar and piano.

Dylan's song *The Times They Are A' Changin'* is an obvious choice for the album. A well-known anthem of the 1960s cultural revolution, it has lyrics of such significance that they are universally applicable. The decision to meld the song into an Irish folk setting is inspired. Lead vocals are from multi-award winning Lisa Hannigan who has had much success both in her native Ireland and in the USA. Her voice is urgent and earthy. Here, she joins forces with the famous Irish band, The Chieftains, who contribute their own natural sounds whilst never dominating the piece, for this is a true fusion piece. The musical designer wrappings raise the song out of its rural setting to a pseudo-spiritual level. There's no sign of the Irish jig; instead, a dreamy waltz-time as Herbie's piano sounds hang in the air above the piece like some beneficent spirit. Lionel Louecke's guitar inclusions are well matched to Herbie's contributions as the other musicians go about the business of performing the Dylan piece straight. The overlaid dreaminess is enhanced by the presence of the sound of the African kora played by Toumain Diabete. The ethnic fiddle and tin whistle are heard just before the Chieftains come together for a concerted run through the piece in Gaelic, at which point the fusion is most clearly comprised of elements from the traditional Irish folk and improvised jazz from the New World.

La Tierra is sung by Colombian-born Latin-rock artist Juan Esteban Aristizabal, aka Juanes. This is a slick mix of mostly American musicians joining with the Miami Spanish sound. The strong Latin rhythm are medium paced and Herbie for once takes on a significant solo that he clearly has fun with, especially when the medium tempo is doubled up.

The next piece could be interpreted as a representation of one of the world's most intractable problems. As we all know, the Middle East is the focus of the sadly conflicting religions of Islam and Judaism. *Tamatant Tilay / Exodus* sounds like a fusion of the sounds of Arab and Jewish peoples. Two songs are woven together in such a clever way that you can't hear the joins. K'naan takes the first vocals for *Tamatant Tilay*, a happy song that arouses images of friendly folk all across the north African / Middle Eastern landscapes. Of course, the parallel biblical theme of *Exodus*, sung by Los Lobos, is relevant not just to ancient struggles of the Jews in the Red Sea region but to the current global migrations of people from the world's poor regions to the rich. Of great relevance is the constant rhythmic pulse of this music that implies the trudge of tired limbs across endless stretches of sandy, arid land.

Tomorrow Never Knows has a philosophical theme about 'Life, the Universe and Everything'. Written by Lennon-McCartney at a time when they were being subjected to the theisms and transcendental meditation techniques of Maharishi Mahesh Yogi, this version possesses all the auras of the original. Dave Matthews gravel voice is particularly well chosen to present the lyrics and the backdrop present in the Beatles' experiments with magnetic tapes is well covered on this piece. In view of the fact that Herbie visited the Abbey Road studios in north London during the recording of *Don't Give Up*, it's a shame that Herbie couldn't have recorded *Tomorrow Never Knows* in the studio where it was originally recorded. Now that would have been a nice touch!

A Change Is Gonna Come was written by soul music pioneer, Sam Cooke, a prominent member of the American Civil Rights Movement. Cooke was much influenced by Dylan's *Blowin' In The Wind* and penned his song in 1963, shortly before he was shot dead. The song became a Civil Rights anthem and was voted number 12 in *Rolling Stone's* 500 Best Songs list. Here it is played by a very strong group of musicians comprised of Vinnie Colaiuta, Paulinho da Costa, Dean Parks and Tal Wilkenfeld. Lyrics are delivered by the remarkable James Morrison who came to prominence with his hit single *You Give Me Something* (2006) and debut album *Undiscovered* (2006). He sings with great poignancy and tells a wonderful story in his few brief lines. There is an especially beautiful way in which Herbie's piano lines encapsulate the vocals, his expansive, thoughtful notes as meaningful as anything sung by Morrison. There's an extended piano solo for the final part of this long track during which all of the musicians (without Parks) are improvising and interacting in extraordinary ways. As it comes to clean and satisfying end, we become aware that this is very remarkable track.

The final track is *The Song Goes On*, an Indian jazz-fusion with a mixture of Indian and American musicians overdubbed from studios in Mumbai and LA. Chaka Khan takes the lead for the English language lyrics whilst the Indian lyrics are sung by K. S. Chithra. Herbie's buddy Wayne Shorter contributes some colourful soprano sax splashes.

Herbie's partnership with Larry Klein that began years ago has now paid him rich dividends. Clearly deep thought has gone into the planning of this album which is a step up from the somewhat similar *Possibilities* (2005). This is especially significant in the current musical environment with vocal jazz suffering as great an identity crisis as mainstream instrumental jazz. With a rapidly falling level of popularity, certainly in the USA and UK, the association of vocal jazz with these songs from other cultures is a brave effort to keep jazz music alive by continuing to work with aspects of jazz-fusion. Herbie is not presenting mere pop music. He is moulding jazz itself, persuading singers who have little or no associations with jazz, to sing close to or inside the jazz idiom. In so doing, he is developing his own forms of vocal jazz music, whilst retaining the feel of the popular genres within them. And his own contributions to the art of piano playing are refined to new levels of perfection on this disc. At numerous times, the careful listener must agree that Herbie's piano work is not accompaniment in the usual sense, but is a symbiosis of expression with his guest musicians at the very highest level. The piano is surely as close to the human voice as it is possible to get.

Another especially good aspect to the album is the fusion not just of musical genres, but of the musicians themselves. On most tracks we find musicians that have come together for this project, even if, at times, it is done by recording them in different studios. By definition, non-English lyrics remove something from the verbal message of the record, but the gain from having songs from other cultures, sung by musicians from those cultures, is complete compensation. There are some omissions: there's nothing from China or Japan, for example. However, we can't expect Herbie to include every culture. Where would it end? Should he have included some Vietnamese fishermen's lullabies or Volga boatmen football anthems? Overall, *The Imagine Project* is an excellent album with fine ambitions, which continues to push boundaries of jazz-fusion and the art of jazz piano, yet remains accessible to many listeners.

Concluding Remarks

Herbie Hancock is an extremely successful, major-league jazz musician who, whilst remaining within the jazz environment has broken out of it frequently enough for him to become a household name. After Davis, Ellington and Armstrong, he is probably the most famous jazz musician of the modern era. There was a good line in unspoken humour associated with Herbie's cameo appearance as a cocktail lounge pianist in the Robert Redford / Demie Moore movie *Indecent Proposal* (1993): only someone as rich as John Gage (Redford's character) could afford Herbie Hancock for a party aboard his private yacht! Despite the fact that his forays into the world of 'frothy' popular music made him a wealthy man and attracted the scorn of all those who secretly wished they could do the same but didn't, Herbie always retained his 'feets' in other camps too and was able to produce music of substance in all his ventures. In 1992, referring to Herbie's risk-taking in pop, Mark Gilbert said, "there is plainly no law of aesthetics which says that financial motive cancels out creativity." [53]

Herbie is a master of the keyboard in whatever form - electronic or acoustic - and I here nominate him as the best pianist / keyboardist in jazz. There is much justification for that conclusion. First, he is expert in the use of keyboard and computer technology in jazz improvisation, for which he has done as much if not more than anyone else in jazz. Jazz critic Gary Giddins said: "When Herbie discovered electric instruments he was like a kid at the circus. It's very important to realise that he just doesn't sit down at a Fender Rhodes (or the more sophisticated versions) and play it. He knows how those things are built from the ground up." [85]

Herbie is an expert in the use of rhythms of all kinds, but notably funk and African-derived pulses. Julian Joseph believes that you can quickly tell whether a musician is truly funky or not, but that funk simply oozes out of every pore of Herbie's body. [42]

Herbie is more wide-ranging in his use of different musical styles than almost any other jazz musician. He has never been constrained by musical boundaries, believing that anything is up for grabs. Thus it was fine for him to indulge in frothy popular music, even to the extent that he indecently exposed his own singing voice on albums of popular vocal crossover music, such as *Sunlight* (1978), *Feets Don't Fail Me Now* (1979) and *Lite Me Up* (1982). Few other serious jazz instrumentalists – only Stanley Clarke and Joe Zawinul spring to mind - have found the courage to indulge in such base behaviour, and he received an equally indecent amount of vitriol from the jazz world as a result. Fortunately, he is a big enough character not to care.

Herbie has always remained true to the legacy of Miles by only looking forward. Whilst being aware and appreciative of his heritage, Herbie has never wanted to reproduce the past. Bertrand Tavernier wrote about Herbie's ideas for the music to the film *Round Midnight* (1986) that Herbie was to score. "On my first meeting with Herbie, we immediately agreed on certain principles. We wouldn't try to duplicate exactly the music of the fifties. 'Otherwise', declared Herbie, 'we might just as well use the Blue Note records'. We wanted to avoid a rigid or scholarly approach to the style." [86] This principle permeates his style.

Herbie's career has mostly been played out in his own right, rather than as leader of one band or another. There has occasionally been a Herbie Hancock Quartet or a Trio. V.S.O.P., which consisted of existing stars who had made it big without Herbie, was *not* a Herbie Hancock quintet, despite the marketing that would have us believe otherwise. Obviously, there comes a point at which Herbie's name on the cover of an album results in more sales than would occur if it was replaced with an unknown band name. Mwandishi seems at first to have been a named band, but in fact it was simply Herbie's chosen name for himself.

I want at this point to make clear some of my observations about a band called the Headhunters, a term that has had an ambiguous existence. There are many references to Herbie as if he was actually leader and full member of the band. Wikipedia, for example, is (in 2010) confusing on this point, describing Headhunters as "a jazz fusion band founded by Herbie Hancock." Let's be clear about one thing: Head Hunters (two words) has been used for the name of the 1974 album, whilst Headhunters (one word) is the name of a band. Curiously, according to the discography, Herbie has not been a formal member of the Headhunters. The original *Head Hunters* album was under the name of Herbie Hancock. Other albums which have Herbie on all of the tracks and with Headhunter musicians present are marketed as Herbie Hancock albums, for example, *Thrust* (1974), *Man-Child* (1975), *Flood* (1975), *Secrets* (1976) and *Direct Step* (1978). (No doubt, his recording contract required this.) There have, however, been several albums by the band. Thus, when albums appeared under the name of the Headhunters band, for example, *Survival of the Fittest* (1975),

Straight from the Gate (1977) and *Evolution Revolution* (2003), Herbie was *not* present in the band. For the Headhunters' *Return of the Headhunters* (1998), Herbie was clearly appearing as a *guest*, rather than as a member of the band, and played on only four of the ten tracks. However, Herbie *did* tour with a band called Headhunters in 2005, which had *none* of the original band members present. What we do know is that the names Headhunters and Herbie Hancock are inextricably linked.

Strangely, although he has played consistently with the other Headhunters - Bill Summers, Bennie Maupin and Harvey Mason - these musicians have not gone on to big things in their own right. Many other musicians, if they were not famous when they joined him, remained notably anonymous after working with Hancock. Miles Davis was, of course, the most famous leader for mentoring his younger associates, and Chick Corea was also very successful at it, yet there are few musicians I can name that Herbie has, as it were, taken on as an apprentice. Bill Laswell who is now himself famous in hip-hop, not jazz, made it on the back of Herbie's fame, but the birth of the genre was very much of Laswell's making. Hence it is not appropriate to think of Herbie as a bandleader, in quite the same way as Davis or Corea.

One of Herbie's major successes has been in assisting the assimilation of jazz into the popular mainstream. Through his numerous albums in the late 70s and early 80s such as *Sunlight* (1978), *Feets Don't Fail Me Now* (1979), *Monster* (1980), *Magic Windows* (1981) and especially his album with the Michael Jackson team *Lite Me Up* (1982), Herbie promoted the jazz ethos in the world of popular music, demonstrating to a new generation of young people who did not incline towards rock and metal music, how popular music *could* sound. In case there is any doubt of that now, we only need to examine the awards of the music industry itself. Thus jazzers George Benson and Al Jarreau won a Grammy in 2007 for the 'Best Pop Instrumental Performance' with the track *Mornin'* from their album *Givin It Up* (2006). In the same category, Béla Fleck & The Flecktones were nominated for *Subterfuge*, a track from *The Hidden Land* (2006), an album that won the Grammy for 'Best Contemporary Jazz Album'. Meanwhile, the superb jazz saxophone player Gerald Albright was nominated for a Grammy for 'Best Pop Instrumental Album' for *New Beginnings* (2006), whilst cool jazz group Spyro Gyra was nominated for *Wrapped in a Dream* (2006) in the same category.

Herbie's own style is based mostly on having fun with the performance of music, rather than jazz composition as an academic pursuit. Even so, his credentials as a figure at the very heart of pure jazz are solid gold. He worked at the cutting edge of technology in jazz largely because it was the right thing to do at the time: he was interested in electronics, found them fun to work with and they allowed his creative juices to flow. He was also somewhat fortunate to be around at the time when the scene was right for the new methods adopted by hip hop. However, Herbie is not especially known for his compositions or his melodies, even though he has a large repertoire. *Watermelon Man* was his most successful early piece, but otherwise, during the Blue Note era, for every good composition there are five or ten that disappoint. When he played with Davis, the material emanated more from Shorter's pen or Davis's head than from Hancock. From his jazz-fusion work there isn't a lot that is truly memorable in terms of composition or melody; *Butterfly* is one of his more beautiful works, but it is hard to pinpoint many more. Great pieces such as *Maiden Voyage* are great more for the vibe of the feelings they convey than for their melodic lines. Tunes such as *Rockit* are certainly memorable, but hardly beautiful.

One of the good things about living in 2010 is that albums that disappeared from the radar many years ago have now reappeared as CDs on the shelves of the record shops, as well as on the internet, of course. As one of the major jazz musicians, Herbie has created an extensive catalogue of material that continues to be available. His Blue Note recordings are recognised as special, not just for the music and musicians, but because they were recorded by one of the great recording engineers, Rudy Van Gelder. As a result, this has become a focus for the re-design of the newly reissued 'RVG' albums. All three Warner Brothers albums *Fat Albert Rotunda* (1969), *Mwandishi* (1971) and *Crossings* (1972) were re-mastered in 2001 and republished in the new red card packs. The last four releases for Columbia, *Future Shock* (1983), *Sound-System* (1984), the soundtrack to *Round Midnight* (1986) and *Perfect Machine* (1988) were also recently re-mastered. So there has never been a better time than the present to revisit the works of a master musician.

Herbie Hancock is well educated and a deep thinker who nevertheless has a disarming sense of humour. He has contributed in many ways to the philosophy as well as the practice of jazz and having contributed to many genres is well qualified to comment upon them. "Jazz is purely about just the music, whereas any of the areas of rock n' roll, because it's a popular area, has in many cases show involved." This is a very significant point. When jazz was a purer genre in the 1950s and early 60s, its players would simply wear the dress-of-the-day – which was smart, according to the practice in those days when people were out in public – and play their music on an undecorated platform. However, when jazz became fused with rock, it took on showbiz characteristics, sometimes to the point where the showbiz – the entertainment process - became more important than the music. The volume went up by orders of magnitude, light shows became part of the act, and the psychedelia was sometimes even enhanced with pyrotechnics. The razzamatazz was often translated onto the covers of the albums as part of the process of commercialisation – i.e., in order to sell as many discs as possible. In so doing, jazz-fusion musicians made themselves unpopular with the purists, who simply continued to wear the dress-of-the-day and play on undecorated platforms. Herbie Hancock was one of the artists who took part in all parts of this spectrum of music-making, even to the extent that he was, at times, not performing in the jazz arena at all. Yet he has always been assessed as a jazz musician and the inclusion of albums from the world of popular music did not help the assessment of a career *in jazz*. However, if someone from the world of disco-dance music were to assess his contribution to that genre, he would come out as one of the all-time greats. It is, of course, all a matter of viewpoint.

Herbie: "Jazz has borrowed from other genres of music and also has lent itself to other genres of music. It's very different from classical music. In classical music, you are playing something that is written by someone else. In jazz, the song may be written by somebody else, but how you treat it is entirely with your notes and your expression. Jazz is a music that is open enough to borrow from any other form of music, and has the strength to influence any other form of music."

In a sense, this is one of Herbie's strongest arguments, for it sums up a lot of his career, in which he spent his time spread widely across the music scene instead of pursuing just one style. "Jazz is a music that translates the moment into a sense of inspiration for not only the musicians but for the listeners. Jazz is about being in the moment. Since time is a continuum, the moment is always different, so the music is always different."

A practising Buddhist for many years, Herbie considers himself a human being first and a musician second: "I'm a human being all the time, even when I sleep. But I'm not a musician when I sleep, and I'm not a musician when I eat, unless I'm paying attention to music or talking about music. I'm aiming that (what I do) towards people, towards humanity, not even just musicians, because this is about life, not about musicians. My approach to music doesn't come from me being a certain type of musician, or a musician at all. It comes from me being a human being."

Okay, but the flaw in his argument is that people buy the records for the music, not because he's a nice guy. It's because of this that Herbie has attracted more than his fair share of criticism over the years. There are many people – myself included - who have bought Hancock records with great expectation only to be disappointed when the disc is played. In the future, Herbie Hancock will always be compared with other musicians based on his recorded work rather than his philosophy, and there will always be judges who will view depth as making a greater, lasting contribution than breadth.

The mark of true greatness is not just the music a musician makes himself but the impact he has on others. We have to thank Herbie not only for his great music but for the indirect effect he has had on so many other great jazz musicians. Herbie's great friend Michael Brecker is probably the greatest exponent of the tenor saxophone since Coltrane. Of Herbie he says, "As a pianist, composer and innovator, Herbie has been an immense source of inspiration to me. I've been fortunate to tour and record with Herbie many times over the years and every time I play with him I'm reminded, quite simply, that he is a genius." [80]

References

1. http://www.artistwd.com/joyzine/music/hancock/hancock.php
2. John Harle, *The Guardian G2*, London, UK, Friday 29 Apr 2005.
3. Ken Trethewey, *Jazz-Fusion: Blue Notes and Purple Haze*, Jazz-Fusion Books (2009).
4. Phillip Ball, The Music Instinct, The Bodley Head, London (2010) p208.
5. Leonard Feather, sleeve notes to Donald Byrd, *Royal Flush*, RVG Edition, Blue Note Records (2006).
6. Donald Byrd, sleeve notes to *Free Form*, RVG Edition, Blue Note Records (2004).
7. Leonard Feather, sleeve notes to *Takin' Off*, Blue Note Records (1996).
8. Jamie Cullum *Rockit – Pt 1*, BBC Radio 2, 24 Jan 2007.
9. Herbie Hancock, sleeve notes to *Takin' Off*, Blue Note Records (1996).
10. Miles Davis, *Miles: The Autobiography*, Picador (1990) p100.
11. Miles Davis, p253.
12. Miles Davis, p265.
13. Ian Carr, *Miles Davis: The Definitive Biography*, Harper Collins (1999), p189-90.
14. Nat Hentoff, original liner notes, *Inventions and Dimensions*, RVG Edition, Blue Note Records (2005).
15. Steven Block: *Pitch-Class Transformation in Free Jazz*. In: *Music Theory Spectrum*, Vol. 12, No. 2, (Autumn, 1990), pp. 181-202.
16. Charles Mingus talking to Ira Gitler, *Down Beat*, 21 July 1960. Quoted in Brian Priestley's *Mingus – A Critical Biography*, da Capo Press (1983), p110.
17. Herbie Hancock, sleeve notes to Herbie Hancock, *Inventions and Dimensions*, RVG Edition, Blue Note Records (2005).
18. Bob Blumenthal, liner notes to Tony Williams, *Lifetime*, RVG Edition, Blue Note Records (1999).
19. Miles Davis, p258.
20. Miles Davis, p259.
21. Miles Davis, p263.
22. Lawrence Rutter, liner notes to Tony Williams, *Lifetime*, RVG Edition, Blue Note Records (1999).
23. Z. R Borman IMDB.com
24. Ken Trethewey, *Jazz-Fusion: Blue Notes and Purple Haze*, Jazz-Fusion Books (2009).
25. Wikipedia
26. Paul Tingen, *Miles Beyond: The Electric Explorations of Miles Davis, 1967-1991*, Billboard Books, New York (2001), p39.
27. Richard Cook, *It's About That Time*, Atlantic Books (2005), p190.
28. Richard Cook, p191.

29. Miles Davis, p283.
30. Ian Carr, p235-6.
31. Dave Holland in Paul Tingen, *Miles Beyond: The Electric Explorations of Miles Davis, 1967-1991*, Billboard Books, New York (2001) p52.
32. Miles Davis, p302-3.
33. Miles Davis, p284.
34. Herb Wong, sleeve notes to the original album, Herbie Hancock, *The Prisoner*, RVG Edition, Blue Note Records (1999).
35. Herbie Hancock to Herb Wong, sleeve notes to the original album, Herbie Hancock, *The Prisoner*, RVG Edition, Blue Note Records (1999).
36. Bob Blumenthal, sleeve notes to the original album, Herbie Hancock, *The Prisoner*, RVG Edition, Blue Note Records (1999).
37. Ira Girtler, sleeve notes to *The Space Book* (1964).
38. William Hogeland, sleeve notes to Herbie Hancock, *Baraka*, IMC Music (2005).
39. Bob Belden, sleeve notes to Herbie Hancock, Sextant, Columbia (1998).
40. Herbie Hancock, sleeve Notes (Dec 1996) to Herbie Hancock, *Head Hunters*, Columbia (1997).
41. Bob Belden and David Rubinson, sleeve notes to Herbie Hancock, *The Piano*, Columbia, (2004).
42. Jamie Cullum *in Rockit – Pt 2*, BBC Radio 2, 31 Jan 2007.
43. Herbie Hancock, sleeve notes to Herbie Hancock, *Mr. Hands*, Columbia (1992).
44. Herbie Hancock, sleeve notes to *V.S.O.P. – The Quintet*, Columbia (1988).
45. Conrad Silvert, sleeve notes to *V.S.O.P. – The Quintet*, Columbia (1988).
46. Herbie Hancock in *Rockit – Pt 2*.
47. Kevin Legendre, in *Rockit – Pt 2*.
48. David Rubinson, sleeve notes to CD edition of Herbie Hancock, *The Piano* (2003).
49. Bob Belden, sleeve notes to *V.S.O.P. – Live Under the Sky*, Columbia (2003).
50. Pat Metheny interviewed by Stuart Nicholson, *Jazzwise* (2004).
51. Bob Belden, sleeve notes to *V.S.O.P. – Live Under the Sky*, Columbia (2003).
52. anon: sleeve notes to Herbie Hancock, *Monster*, Columbia (1980).
53. Mark Gilbert, sleeve notes to Herbie Hancock, *Mr Hands*, Columbia (1992).
54. http://www.jazzoasis.com/jarrettonmarsalis.htm.
55. Jeffrey St. Clair (28 February 2001). "Now, That's Not Jazz" http://www.gerryhemingway.com/jazzburn.html.
56. David Ake, *Jazz Cultures*, University of California Press (2002) p164.
57. Miles Davis, p364.

58. Herbie Hancock talking to Steve Wright, BBC Radio 2, September 2005.
59. Bill Laswell, sleeve notes to Herbie Hancock, *Future Shock*, Columbia (1999).
60. Jamie Cullum in *Rockit – Pt 3*, BBC Radio 2, 7 Feb 2007.
61. Bill Laswell in *Rockit – Pt 3*.
62. Kevin Legendre in *Rockit – Pt 3*.
63. Herbie Hancock, sleeve notes to Herbie Hancock and Foday Musa Suso, *Village Life*, CBS Records (1985).
64. C. Michael Bailey, www.allaboutjazz.com, 5 Feb 2003.
65. Bill Laswell, sleeve notes to Herbie Hancock, *Perfect Machine*, Columbia (1999).
66. Anon, sleeve notes to Herbie Hancock and Wayne Shorter, *1+1*, Verve (1997).
67. Rodney Greenberg, *George Gershwin*, Phaidon Press Ltd (1998), p25.
68. Rodney Greenberg, p36.
69. Rodney Greenberg, p40.
70. Rodney Greenberg, p44.
71. Rouben Mamoulian in Rodney Greenberg, p47.
72. Rodney Greenberg, p72.
73. Rodney Greenberg, p55.
74. Herbie Hancock, sleeve notes to Herbie Hancock, *Gershwin's World* Verve, (1998).
75. Humphrey Lyttelton, *The Best of Jazz*, Portico (2008) p23.
76. Herbie Hancock, sleeve notes to Hancock, Hargrove, Brecker, *Directions in Music*, Verve (2002).
77. Wikipedia: Impressions (composition) by John Coltrane. en.wikipedia.org/wiki/Impressions_(instrumental)
78. wiki/Transition_(John_Coltrane_album)
79. Roy Hargrove, sleeve notes to Hancock, Hargrove, Brecker, *Directions in Music*, Verve (2002).
80. Michael Brecker, sleeve notes to Hancock, Hargrove, Brecker, *Directions in Music*, Verve (2002).
81. John L Walters, *The Guardian, London UK*, 14 November 2006
82. Karen O'Brien, *Joni Mitchell: Shadows and Light, The Definitive Biography* (2002) Virgin Books, p167.
83. http://www.theinsider.com/videos/1307729_The_50[th]_Grammy_Awards_Herbie_Hancock_and_Lang_Lang
84. http://www.langlang.com/mx/news/two-worlds-tune-lang-hancock-play-four-hand-mann
85. Gary Giddins *Rockit – Pt 2*
86. Bertrand Tavernier, sleeve notes to CD edition of *Round Midnight*, Columbia Legacy (2002).

Discography

AS LEADER

The following section contains details of all of Herbie Hancock's 'core' albums as a leader – a total of 52 as of July 2010, according to Herbie's official web site www.herbiehancock.com. It omits albums of previously recorded material.

Albums recorded in the studio:	41
Albums recorded in front of live audiences:	7
Soundtrack albums:	4
Total	52

The data has been prepared from my own collection of his music and any errors or omissions are entirely my own. In general, the albums are listed in the order in which they were recorded. This may not coincide with the order in which they were first commercially released. Publishers' details refer to the discs in my collection; other editions may have different IDs. The named musicians appear on the album; unfortunately, it has not been possible to identify every musician on every track. A number of the albums (annotated as Sony Japan) were made for release only in Japan. Some have been released only recently worldwide; others are available only as scarce imports.

Herbie Hancock
*** 1962 Takin' Off
CD Blue Note CDP 7243 8 37643 (1996)
Album Type: studio; Total Time: (57.24)
Musicians: Herbie Hancock (keyboard), Dexter Gordon (saxophone), Freddie Hubbard (trumpet), Butch Warren (bass), Billy Higgins (drums)
Tracks: 1 Watermelon Man (7.09), 2 Three Bags Full (5.27), 3 Empty Pockets (6.09), 4 The Maze (6.45), 5 Driftin' (6.58), 6 Alone and I (6.25), 7 Watermelon Man (Alt Take) (6.33), 8 Three Bags Full (Alt Take) (5.31), 9 Empty Pockets (Alt Take) (6.27)
Recorded: 1962/5/28

Herbie Hancock
*** 1963 My Point of View
CD Blue Note 7243 5 21226 2 2 (1999)
Album Series: RVG Edition
Album Type: studio; Total Time: (42.59)
Musicians: Herbie Hancock (keyboard), Donald Byrd (trumpet), Tony Williams (drums), Hank Mobley (saxophone), Grachan Moncur III (trumpet), Chuck Israels (bass), Grant Green (guitar)
Tracks: 1 Blind Man, Blind Man (8.15), 2 Tribute to Someone (8.40), 3 King Cobra (6.51), 4 The Pleasure is Mine (4.00), 5 And What If I Don't? (6.30), 6 Blind Man, Blind Man (Alt Take) (8.21)
Recorded: 1963/3/19

Herbie Hancock
*** 1963 Inventions and Dimensions
CD Blue Note 7243 5 63799 2 3 (2005)
Album Series: RVG Edition
Album Type: studio; Total Time: (49.44)
Musicians: Herbie Hancock (keyboard), Paul Chambers (bass), Willie 'Bobo' Corea (drums), Osvaldo (Chihuahua) Martinez (percussion)
Tracks: 1 Succotash (7.38), 2 Triangle (10.59), 3 Jack Rabbit (5.55), 4 Mimosa (8.35), 5 A Jump Ahead (6.31), 6 Mimosa (Alternate Take) (10.06)
Recorded: 1963/8/30

Herbie Hancock
*** 1964 Empyrean Isles
CD Blue Note 7243 4 98796 2 1 (1999)
Album Series: RVG Edition
Album Type: studio; Total Time: (53.29)
Musicians: Herbie Hancock (keyboard), Freddie Hubbard (trumpet), Tony Williams (drums), Ron Carter (bass)
Tracks: 1 One Finger Snap (7.17), 2 Ololoqui Valley (8.27), 3 Cantaloupe Island (5.30), 4 The Egg (13.57), 5 One Finger Snap (Alt Take) (7.33), 6 Ololoqui Valley (Alt Take) (10.45)
Recorded: 1964/6/17

Herbie Hancock
***** 1965 Maiden Voyage
CD Blue Note CDP 0777 7 46339 (1986)
Album Type: studio; Total Time: (42.17)
Musicians: Herbie Hancock (keyboard), George Coleman (saxophone), Freddie Hubbard (trumpet), Ron Carter (bass), Tony Williams (drums)
Tracks: 1 Maiden Voyage (7.58), 2 The Eye Of The Hurricane (6.02), 3 Little One (8.50), 4 Survival Of The Fittest (10.08), 5 Dolphin Dance (9.18)
Recorded: 1965/5/17
Notes: The album was inducted into the Grammy Hall of Fame in 1999.

Herbie Hancock
**** 1966 Blow-Up - The Original Soundtrack
CD Soundtracks 7243 8 52280 2 5 (1996)
Album Type: soundtrack; Total Time: (39.37)
Musicians: Herbie Hancock (keyboard), Freddie Hubbard (trumpet), Phil Woods (saxophone), Joe Henderson (saxophone), Jim Hall (guitar), Ron Carter (bass), Jack De Johnette (drums), Jimmy Smith (organ), Joe Newman (trumpet)
Tracks: 1 Main Title - Blow Up (1.41), 2 Verushka Pt 1 (2.47), 3 Verushka Pt 2 (2.15), 4 The Naked Camera (3.27), 5 Bring Down the Birds (1.55), 6 Jane's Theme (5.02), 7 Stroll On (2.49), 8 The Thief (3.17), 9 The Kiss (4.17), 10 Curiosity (1.35), 11 Thomas Studies Photos (1.17), 12 The Bed (2.39), 13 End Title - Blow Up (0.52), 14 Am I Glad to See You (4.28), 15 Blow Up (1.53)
Recorded: 1966
Notes: Hancock wrote all tracks except 7 (written and performed by the Yardbirds), 14 and 15 (performed and written by Tomorrow).

Herbie Hancock
*** 1968 Speak Like A Child
CD Blue Note 7243 8 75335 2 3 (2005)
Album Type: studio; Total Time: (52.32)
Musicians: Herbie Hancock (keyboard), Thad Jones (trumpet), Ron Carter (bass), Mickey Roker (drums), Peter Phillips (trombone), Jerry Dodgion (flute)
Tracks: 1 Riot (4.40), 2 Speak Like A Child (7.50), 3 First Trip (6.01), 4 Toys (5.52), 5 Goodbye to Childhood (7.06), 6 The Sorcerer (5.36), 7 Riot (First Alternate Take) (4.55), 8 Riot (Second Alternate Take) (4.40), 9 Goodbye to Childhood (First Alternate Take) (5.52)
Recorded: 1968/3/6,9
Notes: Tracks 1-6 are the originals released by Blue Note; tracks 7-9 are bonus tracks on the CD editions. The remastered version of track 2 won the 2004 Grammy for Best Jazz Instrumental Solo.

Herbie Hancock
*** 1969 The Prisoner
CD Blue Note 7243 5 25649 2 7 (1999)
Album Series: RVG Edition
Album Type: studio; Total Time: (55.22)
Musicians: Herbie Hancock (keyboard), Joe Henderson (saxophone), Garnett Brown (trombone), Charles (Buster) Williams (bass), Albert (Tootie) Heath (drums), Johnny Coles (trumpet), Hubert Laws (flute), Jerome Richardson (saxophone), Tony Studd (trombone), Romeo Penque (clarinet), Jack Jeffers (trombone)
Tracks: 1 I Have A Dream (10.56), 2 The Prisoner (7.54), 3 Firewater (7.30), 4 He Who Lives in Fear (6.49), 5 Promise of the Sun (7.50), 6 The Prisoner (Alternate Take) (5.45), 7 Firewater (Alternate Take) (8.38)
Recorded: 1969/4/18,21,23
Notes: Laws and Studd play on 1,2,4 and 6; Penque and Jeffers play on 3, 5 and 7. The other musicians play on all.

Herbie Hancock
** 2005 Baraka
CD Jazz World JWD 102.232 (2005)
Album Type: studio Total Time: (44.24)
Musicians: Herbie Hancock (keyboard), Don Cherry (trumpet), Jimmy Heath (saxophone), Albert (Tootie) Heath (drums), Charles (Buster) Williams (bass), Billy Bonner (flute), Ed Blackwell (percussion), James Mtume (percussion),
Tracks: 1 Baraka (9.53), 2 Maulana (13.20), 3 Kawaida (8.08), 4 Dunia (8.29), 5 Kamili (4.34)
Recorded: 1969/12/11
Notes: Not considered to be a 'core' album. Also released as The Very Best of Herbie Hancock. The CD also contains a bonus track of Pat Metheny and the Heath Brothers recorded in 1983 at Cannes, France. Hancock does not play on this track.

Herbie Hancock
*** 1969 Fat Albert Rotunda
CD Warner Bros 9362 47540 2 (1969)
Album Type: studio; Total Time: (33.41)
Musicians: Herbie Hancock (keyboard), Joe Henderson (saxophone), Garnett Brown

(trombone), Charles (Buster) Williams (bass), Albert (Tootie) Heath (drums), Johnny Coles (trumpet)
Tracks: 1 Wiggle-Waggle (5.48), 2 Fat Mama (3.45), 3 Tell Me A Bedtime Story (5.00), 4 Oh! Oh! Here He Comes (4.05), 5 Jessica (4.11), 6 Fat Albert Rotunda (6.27), 7 Lil' Brother (4.25)
Recorded: 1969

Herbie Hancock
* 1971 Mwandishi
CD Warner Bros Masters 9362 47541 2 (1971)
Album Type: studio; Total Time: (44.50)
Musicians: Herbie Hancock (keyboard), Bennie Maupin (saxophone), Eddie Henderson (trumpet), Julian Priester (trombone), Charles (Buster) Williams (bass), Billy Hart (drums), Ndugu Chancler (drums), Jose Cepito Areas (percussion), Ron Montrose (guitar)
Tracks: 1 Ostinato (Suite For Angela) (13.05), 2 You'll Know When You Get There (10.15), 3 Wandering Spirit Song (21.30)
Recorded: 1971

Herbie Hancock
* 1972 Crossings
CD Warner Bros Masters 9362 47542 2 (1972)
Album Type: studio; Total Time: (46.21)
Musicians: Herbie Hancock (keyboard), Bennie Maupin (saxophone), Eddie Henderson (trumpet), Julian Priester (trombone), Charles (Buster) Williams (bass), Billy Hart (drums), Patrick Gleeson (keyboard), Victor Pontoja (percussion)
Tracks: 1 Sleeping Giant (24.50), 2 Quasar (7.27), 3 Water Torture (14.04)
Recorded: 1972

Herbie Hancock
* 1973 Sextant
CD Columbia Legacy CK 64983 (1998)
Album Type: studio; Total Time: (39.02)
Musicians: Herbie Hancock (keyboard), Bennie Maupin (saxophone), Eddie Henderson (trumpet), Julian Priester (trombone), Charles (Buster) Williams (bass), Billy Hart (drums), Patrick Gleeson (keyboard), Buck Clarke (percussion)
Tracks: 1 Rain Dance (9.16), 2 Hidden Shadows (10.11), 3 Hornets (19.35)
Recorded: 1972
Notes: The third album for the Mwandishi band and the first for Columbia.

Herbie Hancock
**** 1973 Head Hunters
CD Columbia Legacy CK 65123 (1997)
Album Type: studio; Total Time: (41.34)
Musicians: Herbie Hancock (keyboard), Bennie Maupin (saxophone), Paul Jackson (bass), Harvey Mason (drums), Bill Summers (percussion)
Tracks: 1 Chameleon (15.41), 2 Watermelon Man (6.29), 3 Sly (10.15), 4 Vein Melter (9.09)
Recorded: 1972
Notes: In 2003 the album was ranked 498 in Rolling Stone magazine's 500 greatest albums of all time.

Herbie Hancock
* 1973 The Spook Who Sat By the Door
Vinyl United Artists Records UAR 7370 (1973)
Album Type: soundtrack; Total Time: (30.21)
Musicians: Herbie Hancock (keyboard)
Tracks: 1 Revolution (1.39), 2 The Spook Who Sat By The Door (Reprise) (4.10), 3 Revenge (1.43), 4 At the Lounge (1.28), 5 Training Day (2.30), 6 The Stick Up (1.56), 7 Main Theme (1.24), 8 Underground (2.03), 9 The Spook Who Sat By The Door (2.52), 10 The Big Rip Off (4.25), 11 Recruiting (0.50), 12 The Pick Up (2.04), 13 It Begins (0.36), 14 Dialog (2.27)
Recorded: 1973
Notes: Soundtrack to the movie with the same name, directed by Ivan Dixon.

Herbie Hancock
* 1974 Death Wish
CD Legend CD 25 (1996)
Album Type: soundtrack; Total Time: ()
Musicians: Herbie Hancock (keyboard) (no other musicians listed)
Tracks: 1 Death Wish (Main Title) (6.11), 2 Joanna's Theme (4.46), 3 Do A Thing (2.13), 4 Paint Her Mouth (2.16), 5 Rich Country (3.46), 6 Sweet Revenge (9.25), 7 Ochoa Knose (2.07), 8 Party People (3.32), 9 Fill Your Hand (6.15)
Recorded: 1974
Notes: The soundtrack for a film by Dino de Laurentiis starring Charles Bronson. It has the Italian name: "Il Giustiziere Della Notte".

Herbie Hancock
***** 1974 Thrust
CD Columbia Legacy CK 64984 (1998)
Album Type: studio; Total Time: (38.46)
Musicians: Herbie Hancock (keyboard), Bennie Maupin (saxophone), Paul Jackson (bass), Mike Clark (drums), Bill Summers (percussion)
Tracks: 1 Palm Grease (10.37), 2 Actual Proof (9.40), 3 Butterfly (11.17), 4 Spank-A-Lee (7.12)
Recorded: 1974

Herbie Hancock
*** 1974 Dedication
CD Sony Japan (2004)
Album Type: studio; Total Time: (40.38)
Musicians: Herbie Hancock (keyboard)
Tracks: 1 Maiden Voyage (7.42), 2 Dolphin Dance (11.14), 3 Nobu (7.34), 4 Cantaloupe Island (13.58)
Recorded: 1974/7/29
Notes: Recorded at the Koseinenkin Hall, Tokyo. This edition published in Japan only.

Herbie Hancock
*** 1975 Man-Child
CD Columbia Legacy COL 471235 2 (1992)
Album Type: studio; Total Time: (45.02)
Musicians: Herbie Hancock (keyboard), Mike Clark (drums), Harvey Mason (drums), James Gadson (drums), Paul Jackson (bass), Louis Johnson (bass), Henry Davis (bass), Wayne

Shorter (saxophone), Bennie Maupin (saxophone), Dewayne (Blackbird) McKnight (guitar), David T. Walker (guitar), Bill Summers (percussion), Bud Brisbois (trumpet), Jay DaVersa (trumpet), Ernie Watts (saxophone), Jim Horn (saxophone), Garnett Brown (trombone), Dick Hyde (tuba), Stevie Wonder (harmonica)
Tracks: 1 Hang Up Your Hang Ups (7.26), 2 Sun Touch (5.08), 3 The Trailor (9.35), 4 Bubbles (8.59), 5 Steppin' In It (8.38), 6 Heartbeat (5.16)
Recorded: 1974

Herbie Hancock
**** 1975 Flood
CD CBS/ Sony SICP 967 (1975)
Album Type: live; Total Time: (74.08)
Musicians: Herbie Hancock (keyboard), Bennie Maupin (saxophone), Paul Jackson (bass), Mike Clark (drums), Bill Summers (percussion), Dewayne (Blackbird) McKnight (guitar)
Tracks: 1 Introduction / Maiden Voyage (7.58), 2 Actual Proof (8.28), 3 Spank-A-Lee (8.47), 4 Watermelon Man (5.50), 5 Butterfly (12.44), 6 Chameleon (10.24), 7 Hang Up Your Hang Ups (19.54)
Recorded: 1975/6/28
Notes: Recorded live at Shibuya Koukaido 28/6/75 and Nakano Sun Plaza 1/7/75, Tokyo Japan. A Sony Music Japan International Edition.

Herbie Hancock
*** 1976 Secrets
CD Columbia CK 34280 (1976)
Album Type: studio; Total Time: (48.01)
Musicians: Herbie Hancock (keyboard), Bennie Maupin (saxophone), Melvin 'Wah Wah Watson' Ragin (guitar), Ray Parker Jr (voice), James Levi (drums), Paul Jackson (bass), Kenneth Nash (percussion)
Tracks: 1 Doin' It (8.02), 2 People Music (7.10), 3 Cantaloupe Island (7.06), 4 Spider (7.20), 5 Gentle Thoughts (7.04), 6 Swamp Rats (6.25), 7 Sansho Shima (4.50)
Recorded: 1975

Herbie Hancock
*** 1977 V.S.O.P.
2 CD Columbia COL 486569 2 (1977)
Album Series: Jazz Originals
Album Type: live; Total Time: (86.18)
Musicians: Herbie Hancock (keyboard), Ron Carter (bass), Wayne Shorter (saxophone), Tony Williams (drums), Freddie Hubbard (trumpet), Eddie Henderson (trumpet), Julian Priester (trombone), Bennie Maupin (saxophone), Charles (Buster) Williams (bass), Billy Hart (drums), Melvin 'Wah Wah Watson' Ragin (guitar), Ray Parker Jr (voice), Paul Jackson (bass), James Levi (drums), Kenneth Nash (percussion)
Tracks: 1 Piano Introduction (4.32), 2 Maiden Voyage (13.18), 3 Nefertiti (5.17), 4 Introduction of Players / Eye of the Hurricane (18.34), 5 Toys (13.45), 6 Introductions (1.47), 7 You'll Know When You Get There (7.00), 8 Hang Up Your Hang Ups (11.53), 9 Spider (10.17)
Recorded: 1976/6/29
Notes: Recorded at Newport Jazz Festival, Newport, Rhode Island.

Herbie Hancock
**** 1977 The Herbie Hancock Trio (1977)
CD Sony Japan SRCS 7051 (1977)
Album Type: studio; Total Time: (46.10)
Musicians: Herbie Hancock (keyboard), Ron Carter (bass), Tony Williams (drums)
Tracks: 1 Watch It (12.25), 2 Speak Like a Child (13.04), 3 Watcha Waitin' For (6.20), 4 Look (7.41), 5 Milestones (6.40)
Recorded: 1977/7/13
Notes: A rare recording released only in Japan. Recorded and mixed at the Automatt, San Francisco, 13 July 1977.

V.S.O.P.
*** 1977 The Quintet
CD Columbia CGK 34976 (1988)
Album Type: studio; Total Time: (71.41)
Musicians: Herbie Hancock (keyboard), Wayne Shorter (saxophone), Tony Williams (drums), Freddie Hubbard (trumpet), Ron Carter (bass)
Tracks: 1 One Of A Kind (9.16), 2 Third Plane (7.30), 3 Jessica (7.03), 4 Lawra (9.44), 5 Darts (8.45), 6 Dolores (11.41), 7 Little Waltz (9.34), 8 Byrdlike (8.04),
Recorded: 1977/7/16,18
Notes: Recorded live at the Greek Theatre, Berkeley, CA, 1977/7/16 and the San Diego Civic Theatre, 1977/7/18.

V.S.O.P. The Quintet
*** 1977 Tempest in the Colosseum
CD Sony Japan 23DP 5612 (1977)
Album Type: live; Total Time: (69.19)
Musicians: Herbie Hancock (keyboard), Wayne Shorter (saxophone), Ron Carter (bass), Tony Williams (drums), Freddie Hubbard (trumpet)
Tracks: 1 Eye of the Hurricane (16.16), 2 Diana (5.05), 3 Eighty One (12.56), 4 Maiden Voyage (12.18), 5 Lawra (8.15), 6 Red Clay (14.29)
Recorded: 1977/7/23
Notes: Recorded at the Denen Colosseum, Tokyo, Japan. This edition published in Japan only.

Herbie Hancock
*** 1978 Sunlight
CD Columbia COL 486570 2 (1978)
Album Series: Jazz Originals
Album Type: studio; Total Time: (39.15)
Musicians: Herbie Hancock (keyboard), Bennie Maupin (saxophone), Melvin 'Wah Wah Watson' Ragin (guitar), Ray Parker Jr (voice), Byron Miller (keyboard), Paul Jackson (bass), Jaco Pastorius (bass), Ndugu Chancler (drums), James Levi (drums), Harvey Mason (drums), Tony Williams (drums), Paul Rekow (percussion), Bill Summers (percussion)
Tracks: 1 I Thought It Was You (8.54), 2 Come Running to Me (8.23), 3 Sunlight (7.09), 4 No Means Yes (6.18), 5 Good Question (8.31)
Recorded: 1977

Herbie Hancock and Chick Corea
*** 1978 An Evening With Herbie Hancock and Chick Corea In Concert
2 CD Columbia Legacy C2K 65551 (1998)
Album Type: live; Total Time: (91.17)
Musicians: Chick Corea (keyboard), Herbie Hancock (keyboard)
Tracks: 1 Someday My Prince Will Come (12.39), 2 Liza (All the Clouds'll Roll Away) (9.00), 3 Button Up (17.37), 4 Introduction of Herbie Hancock by Chick Corea (0.41), 5 February Moment (15.47), 6 Maiden Voyage (13.31), 7 La Fiesta (22.02)
Recorded: 1978/2
Notes: Recorded February 1978, live at the Masonic Hall, San Francisco; Dorothy Chandler Pavilion, Los Angeles; Golden Hall, San Diego; and Hill Auditorium, Ann Arbor.

Chick Corea / Herbie Hancock
*** 1979 CoreaHancock: An Evening With Chick Corea and Herbie Hancock
CD Polydor 835 680-2 (1988)
Album Type: live Total Time: (71.41)
Musicians: Chick Corea (keyboard), Herbie Hancock (keyboard)
Tracks: 1 Homecoming (19.12), 2 Ostinato (from Mikrokosmos for Two Pianos, Four Hands) (3.02), 3 The Hook (13.30), 4 Bouquet (19.22), 5 Maiden Voyage (8.26), 6 La Fiesta (8.09)
Recorded: 1978/2
Notes: This is not a Herbie Hancock 'core' album but is considered to be a Chick Corea 'core' album. Recorded February 1978, live at the Masonic Hall, San Francisco; Dorothy Chandler Pavilion, Los Angeles; Golden Hall, San Diego; and Hill Auditorium, Ann Arbor.

Herbie Hancock
*** 1979 The Piano
CD Columbia Legacy CK 87083 (2004)
Album Type: studio; Total Time: (52.09)
Musicians: Herbie Hancock (keyboard)
Tracks: 1 My Funny Valentine (7.42), 2 On Green Dolphin Street (3.20), 3 Someday My Prince Will Come (4.35), 4 Harvest Time (4.49), 5 Sonrisa (3.44), 6 Manhattan Island (3.56), 7 Blue Otani (3.25), 8 My Funny Valentine (take 3 alternate) (6.08), 9 On Green Dolphin Street (take 2 alternate) (4.04), 10 Someday My Prince Will Come (take 3 alternate) (5.16), 11 Harvest Time (take 3 alternate) (5.10)
Recorded: 1978/10/25,26
Notes: The recording was made direct to disc in the CBS studios, Japan. Released in 1979 only in Japan as CRCS 7052.

Herbie Hancock
*** 1979 Direct Step
CD Sony Japan SRCS 7169 (1979)
Album Type: studio; Total Time: (30.38)
Musicians: Herbie Hancock (keyboard), Paul Jackson (bass), Alphonze Mouzon (drums), Ray Obiedo (guitar), Bennie Maupin (saxophone), Bill Summers (percussion), Webster Lewis (keyboard)
Tracks: 1 Butterfly (7.55), 2 Shiftless Shuffle (7.10), 3 I Thought It Was You (15.33)
Recorded: 1978/10/25,26
Notes: This edition published in Japan only.

Herbie Hancock
**** 1979 V.S.O.P. - Live Under the Sky
2 CD Columbia Legacy C2K 87165 (2004)
Album Type: live; Total Time: (154.17)
Musicians: Herbie Hancock (keyboard), Wayne Shorter (saxophone), Ron Carter (bass), Tony Williams (drums), Freddie Hubbard (trumpet)
Tracks: 1 Opening (0.47), 2 Eye Of The Hurricane (7.48), 3 Tear Drop (10.34), 4 Domo (12.35), 5 Para Oriente (7.28), 6 Pee Wee (8.13), 7 One of Another Kind (20.49), 8 Fragile (9.41), 9 Opening (0.23), 10 Eye Of The Hurricane (11.26), 11 Tear Drop (9.13), 12 Domo (11.42), 13 Para Oriente (6.51), 14 Pee Wee (6.27), 15 One of Another Kind (14.45), 16 Fragile (8.32), 17 Stella By Starlight (4.46), 18 On Green Dolphin Street (2.17)
Recorded: 1979/7/26,27
Notes: Recorded at the Denon Colosseum, Tokyo, Japan.

Herbie Hancock
*** 1979 Feets Don't Fail Me Now
CD Columbia 983 311 2 (1993)
Album Series: Collectors Choice
Album Type: studio; Total Time: (39.55)
Musicians: Herbie Hancock (keyboard), Bill Summers (percussion), James Gadson (drums), Ray Obiedo (guitar), Eddie Watkins (bass), Freddie Washington (bass), Sheila Escovedo aka Sheila E (percussion), Ray Parker Jr (voice)
Tracks: 1 You Bet Your Love (7.37), 2 Trust Me (5.48), 3 Ready or Not (6.43), 4 Tell Everybody (7.12), 5 Honey From the Jar (6.54), 6 Knee Deep (5.41)
Recorded: 1978

Herbie Hancock
*** 1980 Monster
CD Columbia COL 486571-2 (1980)
Album Series: Jazz Originals
Album Type: studio; Total Time: (41.57)
Musicians: Herbie Hancock (keyboard), Melvin 'Wah Wah Watson' Ragin (guitar), Ray Parker Jr (voice), Freddie Washington (bass), Alphonze Mouzon (drums), Sheila Escovedo aka Sheila E (percussion), Oren Waters (voice), Bill Champlin (voice), Greg Walker (voice), Gavin Christopher (voice), Julia Waters Tillman (voice), Luther Waters (voice), Maxine Waters Willard (voice), Randy Hansen (guitar)
Tracks: 1 Saturday Night (7.13), 2 Stars in Your Eyes (7.01), 3 Go For It (7.28), 4 Don't Hold It In (8.02), 5 Making Love (6.23), 6 It All Comes Around (5.50)
Recorded: 1979
Notes: Santana plays on 1; Hansen plays on 4, 6.

Herbie Hancock
**** 1980 Mr. Hands
CD Columbia COL 471240 2 (1992)
Album Series: Columbia Jazz
Album Type: studio; Total Time: (39.45)
Musicians: Herbie Hancock (keyboard), Harvey Mason (drums), Bill Summers (percussion), Paul Jackson (bass), Bennie Maupin (saxophone), Ndugu Chancler (drums), Byron Miller (keyboard), Jaco Pastorius (bass), Sheila Escovedo aka Sheila E (percussion), Tony Williams (drums), Ron Carter (bass), Alphonze Mouzon (drums), Freddie Washington (bass), Melvin

'Wah Wah Watson' Ragin (guitar)
Tracks: 1 Spiraling Prism (6.22), 2 Calypso (6.42), 3 Just Around The Corner (7.34), 4 4 AM (5.21), 5 Shiftless Shuffle (7.08), 6 Textures (6.38)
Recorded: 1979

Herbie Hancock
** 1981 Magic Windows
CD Columbia COL 486572 2 (1981)
Album Series: Jazz Originals
Album Type: studio; Total Time: (42.17)
Musicians: Herbie Hancock (keyboard), Michael Brecker (saxophone), Melvin 'Wah Wah Watson' Ragin (guitar), Adrian Belew (guitar), Ray Parker Jr (voice), George Johnson (guitar), Al McKay (guitar), Freddie Washington (bass), Louis Johnson (bass), Eddie Watkins (bass), John Robinson (drums), James Gadson (drums), Alphonze Mouzon (drums), Paulinho da Costa (percussion), Sheila Escovedo aka Sheila E (percussion), Pete Escovedo (percussion), Juan Escovedo (percussion), Moody Perry III (percussion), Kwawu Ladzekpo (percussion), Kwasi Dzidzornu (percussion), Sylvester (voice), Vicki Randle (voice), Gavin Christopher (voice)
Tracks: 1 Magic Number (7.21), 2 Tonight's the Night (6.28), 3 Everybody's Broke (7.05), 4 Help Yourself (6.40), 5 Satisfied With Love (6.28), 6 The Twilight Clone (8.15)
Recorded: 1980

Herbie Hancock Trio
**** 1981 Herbie Hancock Trio With Ron Carter and Tony Williams (1981)
CD Sony Japan SRCS 9172 (1981)
Album Type: studio; Total Time: (45.38)
Musicians: Herbie Hancock (keyboard), Ron Carter (bass), Tony Williams (drums)
Tracks: 1 Stablemates (11.04), 2 Dolphin Dance (10.17), 3 A Slight Smile (9.03), 4 That Old Black Magic (8.33), 5 La Maison Goree (6.41)
Recorded: 1981/7/27
Notes: This edition published in Japan only.

Herbie Hancock Quartet
*** 1982 Herbie Hancock Quartet
CD Sony Japan CGK 38275 (1982)
Album Type: studio; Total Time: (68.42)
Musicians: Herbie Hancock (keyboard), Ron Carter (bass), Tony Williams (drums), Wynton Marsalis (trumpet)
Tracks: 1 Well You Needn't (6.26), 2 'Round Midnight (6.38), 3 Clear Ways (5.01), 4 A Quick Sketch (16.24), 5 Eye Of The Hurricane (8.03), 6 Parade (7.56), 7 The Sorcerer (7.18), 8 Pee Wee (4.32), 9 I Fall In Love Too Easily (5.53),
Recorded: 1981
Notes: Digitally recorded at the CBS Sony Studios in Tokyo, Japan in 1981.

Herbie Hancock
*** 1982 Lite Me Up
CD CBS/Sony 35DP 31 (1982)
Album Type: studio; Total Time: (38.01)
Musicians: Herbie Hancock (keyboard), Rod Temperton (keyboard), Michael Boddicker (programming), Wayne Anthony (voice), Jeff Porcaro (drums), Abe Laboriel (bass), Jay

Graydon (guitar), David Foster (keyboard), Bill Champlin (voice), Richard Page (voice), Vennette Gloud (voice), Rick Kelly (programming), Narada Michael Walden (drums), Randy Jackson (bass), Carrado Rustici (guitar), Frank Martin (keyboard), Jim Gilstrap (voice), John Lehman (voice), Sheri Payne (voice), Linda Lawrence (voice), Patrice Rushen (keyboard), Louis Johnson (bass), Steve Lukather (guitar), David Williams (guitar), Chuck Findley (trumpet), Bill Reichenbach (trombone), Gary Herbig (saxophone), Larry Williams (saxophone)
Tracks: 1 Lite Me Up! (3.40), 2 The Bomb (3.58), 3 Gettin' to the Good Part (6.12), 4 Paradise (4.33), 5 Can't Hide Your Love (3.55), 6 The Fun Tracks (4.03), 7 Motor Mouth (3.58), 8 Give It All Your Heart (7.42)
Recorded: 1981
Notes: This edition CD published in Japan; Vinyl on Columbia: CBS 85650.

Herbie Hancock
*** 1983 Future Shock
CD Columbia Legacy CK 65962 (1999)
Album Type: studio; Total Time: (43.29)
Musicians: Herbie Hancock (keyboard), Bill Laswell (bass), Michael Beinhorn (keyboard), Sly Dunbar (percussion), Daniel Poncé (percussion), Roger Trilling (voice), Nicki Skopelitis (guitar), Bernard Fowler (voice), Grand Mixer DST (turntable)
Tracks: 1 Rockit (5.22), 2 Future Shock (8.02), 3 TFS (5.15), 4 Earth Beat (5.10), 5 Autodrive (6.25), 6 Rough (6.57), 7 Rockit (Mega mix) (6.18)
Recorded: 1982
Notes: Track 1 won Grammy for Best R&B Instrumental Performance

Herbie Hancock
*** 1984 Sound System
CD Columbia CK 39478 (1984)
Album Type: studio; Total Time: (33.42)
Musicians: Herbie Hancock (keyboard), Bill Laswell (bass), Grand Mixer DST (turntable), Nicky Skopelitis (guitar), Henry Kaiser (guitar), Daniel Ponce (percussion), Anton Fier (percussion), Rob Stevens (programming), Will Alexander (programming), Foday Musa Suso (kora), Wayne Shorter (saxophone), Toshinori Kondo (voice), Bernard Fowler (voice), Hamid Drake (percussion), Aiyb Dieng (percussion)
Tracks: 1 Hardrock (6.08), 2 Metal Beat (4.53), 3 Karabali (5.17), 4 Junku (5.30), 5 People Are Changing (6.03), 6 Sound System (5.51)
Recorded: 1984
Notes: Track 6 won Grammy for Best R&B Instrumental Performance.

Herbie Hancock, Foday Musa Suso
*** 1985 Village Life
CD Columbia CK39870 (1985)
Album Type: studio; Total Time: (40.41)
Musicians: Herbie Hancock (keyboard), Foday Musa Suso (kora)
Tracks: 1 Moon/Light (7.58), 2 Ndan Ndan Nyaria (9.51), 3 Early Warning (2.52), 4 Kanatente (20.00)
Recorded: 1984/8/7-9

Dexter Gordon / Herbie Hancock
*** 1986 Round Midnight
CD Columbia Legacy 507924-2 (2002)
Album Type: soundtrack; Total Time: (64.31)
Musicians: Dexter Gordon (saxophone), Herbie Hancock (keyboard), Chet Baker (trumpet), Ron Carter (bass), Billy Higgins (drums), Freddie Hubbard (trumpet), Bobby Hutcherson (vibraphone), Bobby McFerrin (voice), John McLaughlin (guitar), Pierre Michelot (bass), Wayne Shorter (saxophone), Cedar Walton (piano), Tony Williams (drums)
Tracks: 1 'Round Midnight (5.37), 2 Body and Soul (5.55), 3 Berangere's Nightmare (3.06), 4 Fair Weather (6.06), 5 Una Noce Con Francis (4.23), 6 The Peacocks (7.16), 7 How Long Has This Been Going On? (3.14), 8 Rhythm-A-Ning (4.12), 9 Still Time (3.51), 10 Minuit Aux Champs-Elysee (3.25), 11 Chan's Song (Never Said) (4.15), 12 'Round Midnight (13.11)
Recorded: 1985/7/1-12

Dexter Gordon
*** 1986 The Other Side of Round Midnight
CD Blue Note CDP 7 46397 2 (1986)
Album Type: soundtrack Total Time: (51.16)
Musicians: Dexter Gordon (saxophone), Herbie Hancock (keyboard), Billy Higgins (drums), Ron Carter (bass), Palle Mikkelborg (composer), Wayne Shorter (saxophone), Mads Vinding (bass), Cedar Walton (piano), Freddie Hubbard (trumpet), Tony Williams (drums), John McLaughlin (guitar), Pierre Michelot (bass),
Tracks: 1 'Round Midnight (6.36), 2 Berangere's Nightmare #2 (4.36), 3 Call Sheet Blues (6.26), 4 What Is This Thing Called Love (3.39), 5 Tivoli (4.15), 6 Society Red (5.39), 7 As Time Goes By (4.27), 8 It's Only a Paper Moon (7.46), 9 'Round Midnight (7.47),
Recorded: 1985/7/1-12
Notes: This is not considered to be a 'core' album. Track 3 won Grammy for Best Instrumental Composition.

Herbie Hancock, Foday Musa Suso
*** 1987 Jazz Africa
CD Verve 422-847145-2 (1987)
Album Series: Jazz Visions
Album Type: live; Total Time: (45.09)
Musicians: Herbie Hancock (keyboard), Foday Musa Suso (kora), Aiyb Dieng (percussion), Armando Peraza (percussion), Adam Rudolph (percussion), Joe Thomas (bass), Hamid Drake (percussion), Abdul Hakeem (guitar)
Tracks: 1 Kumbasora (6.15), 2 Debo (17.06), 3 Cigarette Lighter (13.05), 4 Jimbasing (7.51)
Recorded: 1986/12/2
Notes: Recorded live at the Haltern Theatre, Los Angeles. A Jack Lewis Production for Lorimar Telepictures.

Herbie Hancock
*** 1988 Perfect Machine
CD Columbia Legacy CK 65960 (1999)
Album Type: studio; Total Time: (50.29)
Musicians: Herbie Hancock (keyboard), Leon 'Sugarfoot' Bonner (voice), Nicki Skopelitis (guitar), William 'Bootsy' Collins (bass), Jeff Bova (programming), Grand Mixer DST (turntable), Micro Wave (keyboard)
Tracks: 1 Perfect Machine (6.35), 2 Obsession (5.20), 3 Vibe Alive (5.26), 4 Beat Wise

(5.52), 5 Maiden Voyage / B. Bop (6.34), 6 Chemical Residue (6.01),
7 Vibe Alive (Extended Dance Mix) (8.13), 8 Beat Wise (12-inch Edit) (6.28)
Recorded: 1988

Herbie Hancock / Wayne Shorter / Ron Carter / Wallace Roney / Tony Williams
**** 1992 A Tribute to Miles
CD Quest/Reprise 9362-45059-2 (1994)
Album Type: studio; Total Time: (58.37)
Musicians: Herbie Hancock (keyboard), Ron Carter (bass), Wayne Shorter (saxophone), Tony Williams (drums), Wallace Roney (trumpet)
Tracks: 1 So What (Live) (10.06), 2 RJ (4.05), 3 Little One (7.16), 4 Pinocchio (5.41), 5 Elegy (8.43), 6 Eighty-One (7.29), 7 All Blues (Live) (15.17)
Recorded: 1992
Notes: Tracks 1 and 7 recorded at Berkeley Community Theatre, 19/9/1992. Awarded a Grammy in February 1994 for Best Jazz Instrumental Performance, Individual or Group.

Herbie Hancock
**** 1994 Dis Is Da Drum
CD Polygram 528 185-2 (1994)
Album Type: studio; Total Time: (61.00)
Musicians: Herbie Hancock (keyboard), Bill Summers (percussion), Wallace Roney (trumpet), Bennie Maupin (saxophone), Melvin 'Wah Wah Watson' Ragin (guitar), Darryl 'Bob Dog' Robertson (guitar), Frank Thibeaux (bass), Ken Strong (drums), Will Kennedy (drums), Will 'Roc' Griffin (programming), Mars Lasar (keyboard), Darryl Smith (keyboard), Doug Scott (programming), Darryl Munyungo Jackson (percussion), Skip Bunny (percussion), Guy Eckstine (drums), Jay Shanklin (bass), Brady Speller (percussion)
Tracks: 1 Call It 95 (4.39), 2 Dis Is da Drum (4.49), 3 Shooz (1.17), 4 Melody (On the Deuce by 44) (4.05), 5 Mojuba (4.59), 6 Butterfly (6.08), 7 Ju Ju (5.03), 8 Hump (4.43), 9 Come and See Me (4.32), 10 Rubber Soul (6.40), 11 Bo Ba Be Da (8.04), 12 Butterfly (remix) (6.01)
Recorded: 1993

Herbie Hancock
**** 1996 The New Standard
CD Verve 314 529 584 2 (1996)
Album Type: studio; Total Time: (71.38)
Musicians: Herbie Hancock (keyboard), Michael Brecker (saxophone), John Scofield (guitar), Dave Holland (bass), Jack De Johnette (drums), Don Alias (percussion)
Tracks: 1 New York Minute (8.33), 2 Mercy Street (8.36), 3 Norweigan Wood (8.04), 4 When Can I See You (6.15), 5 You've Got It Bad Girl (7.13), 6 Love Is Stronger Than Pride (7.57), 7 Scarborough Fair (8.21), 8 Thieves In The Temple (7.30), 9 All Apologies (5.04), 10 Manhattan (Island of Lights And Love) (4.05)
Recorded: 1996
Notes: Herbie Hancock and Jean Hancock won Grammy for track 10: Best Instrumental Composition.

Herbie Hancock and Wayne Shorter
*** 1997 1 + 1
CD Verve 314 537 564-2 (1997)
Album Type: studio; Total Time: (61.35)
Musicians: Herbie Hancock (keyboard), Wayne Shorter (saxophone)

Tracks: 1 Meridianne - A Wood Sylph (6.09), 2 Aung San Suu Kyi (5.45), 3 Sonrisa (6.26), 4 Memory Of Enchantment (6.20), 5 Visitor From Nowhere (7.44), 6 Joanna's Theme (5.22), 7 Diana (5.32), 8 Visitor From Somewhere (9.04), 9 Manhattan Lorelei (7.22), 10 Hale Bopp, Hip-Hop (1.51)
Recorded: 1996

Herbie Hancock
***** 1998 Gershwin's World
CD Verve 314 557 797-2 (1998)
Album Type: studio; Total Time: (67.08)
Musicians: Herbie Hancock (keyboard), Madou Dembelle (percussion), Massamba Diop (percussion), Cyro Baptista (percussion), Bireyma Guiye (percussion), Cheik Mbaye (percussion), Eddie Henderson (trumpet), Kenny Garrett (saxophone), James Carter (saxophone), Ira Coleman (bass), Terri Lynne Carrington (drums), Wayne Shorter (saxophone), Marlon Graves (guitar), Robert Sadin (programming), Stevie Wonder (keyboard), Alex Al (bass), Orpheus Chamber Orchestra (orchestra), Chick Corea (keyboard), Joni Mitchell (voice), Bakithi Kumalo (bass), Charles Curtis (cello)
Tracks: 1 Overture (Fascinatin' Rhythm) (0.55), 2 It Ain't Necessarily So (4.46), 3 The Man I Love (5.56), 4 Here Come De Honey Man (3.58), 5 St. Louis Blues (5.49), 6 Lullaby (11.03), 7 Blueberry Rhyme (3.29), 8 It Ain't Necessarily So (Interlude) (1.24), 9 Cotton Tail (4.43), 10 Summertime (4.38), 11 My Man's Gone Now (1.56), 12 Prelude In C# Minor (4.42), 13 Concerto For Piano And Orchestra In G, 2nd Movement (9.11), 14 Embraceable You (4.38),
Recorded: 1998
Notes: Album won Grammy for Best Jazz Instrumental Performance, Individual Or Group. St Louis Blues won Grammy for Best Instrumental Arrangement Accompanying Vocal.

Herbie Hancock
**** 2001 Future 2 Future
2 CD Transparent Music Herbie CD1 (2001)
Album Type: studio; Total Time: (109.10)
Musicians: Herbie Hancock (keyboard), Bill Laswell (bass), Jack De Johnette (drums), Charnett Moffett (bass), Wayne Shorter (saxophone), Karsh Kale (drums), Carl Craig (programming), Elenni Davis-Knight (voice), Chaka Khan (voice), Grand Mixer DST (turntable), Gerald Simpson (programming), Dana Bryant (voice), Tony Williams (drums), Imani Uzuri (voice), Gigi Hancock (voice), Rob Swift (turntable)
Tracks: 1 Hebero Pt 1 (3.10), 2 Wisdom (0.33), 3 The Essence (4.54), 4 This is Rob Swift (6.55), 5 Black Gravity (5.29), 6 Tony Williams (6.08), 7 Be Still (5.11), 8 Ionosphere (3.59), 9 Hebero Pt 2 (4.47), 10 Alphabeta (5.29), 11 Virtual Hornets (8.50), 12 The Essence (Album Edit) (3.33), 13 The Essence (DJ Krush Main Mix) (5.47), 14 The Essence (Bukem's DJ Mix) (9.08), 15 The Essence (Extra 90 Dub Mix) (6.21), 16 The Essence (Future 2 Future Album Mix) (4.48), 17 The Essence (Joe Clausell Cosmic Ritual Interlude) (1.20), 18 The Essence (Joe Clausell Sacred Opus Mix) (13.45), 19 The Essence (Joe Clausell Bonita) (6.07), 20 The Essence (Joe Clausell Drumming) (2.56)
Recorded: 2001
Notes: This edition contains a bonus CD entitled The Essence Mixes (tracks 12-20).

Herbie Hancock
***** 2002 Directions in Music
CD Verve 589 654 2 (2002)
Album Type: live; Total Time: (78.19)
Musicians: Herbie Hancock (keyboard), Roy Hargrove (trumpet), Michael Brecker (saxophone), John Patitucci (bass), Brian Blade (drums)
Tracks: 1 The Sorcerer (8.53), 2 The Poet (6.35), 3 So What/ Impressions (12.51), 4 Misstery (8.16), 5 Naima (7.29), 6 Transition (10.26), 7 My Ship (8.40), 8 D Trane (15.09)
Recorded: 2001/10/25
Notes: Recorded live at the Massey Hall, Toronto, Canada on 25 Oct 2001. Album won Grammy for Best Jazz Instrumental Album, Individual or Group; Track 7 won Grammy for Best Jazz Instrumental Solo.

Herbie Hancock
**** 2005 Possibilities
CD Hear Music, Hancock Music 50-51011-0111-2- (2005)
Album Type: studio; Total Time: (58.27)
Musicians: Herbie Hancock (keyboard), Trey Anastasio (voice), John Mayer (voice), Carlos Santana (guitar), Angilique Kidjo (voice), Christina Aguilera (voice), Paul Simon (voice), Raul Midon (guitar), Stevie Wonder (keyboard), Damien Rice (guitar), Lisa Hannigan (voice), Jonny Lang (guitar), Joss Stone (voice), Sting (bass), Annie Lennox (voice)
Tracks: 1 Stitched Up (5.28), 2 Safiatou (5.25), 3 A Song For You (7.05), 4 I Do It For Your Love (5.58), 5 Hush, Hush, Hush (4.46), 6 Sister Moon (6.54), 7 When Love Comes To Town (8.41), 8 Don't Explain (4.53), 9 I Just Called To Say I Love You (5.27), 10 Gelo No Montana (3.50)
Recorded: 2005

Herbie Hancock
2005 Live Detroit / Chicago
CD Hudson Street HD 1101-2 (2005)
Album Type: live Total Time: (41.33)
Musicians: Clifford Carter (keyboard), Freddie Hubbard (trumpet), Jack De Johnette (drums), Eric Gale (guitar), Stanley Turrentine (saxophone), Herbie Hancock (keyboard)
Tracks: 1 Hornets (9.35), 2 Interlude (1.16), 3 Hornets (9.41), 4 Gibraltar (20.58)
Recorded: not known
Notes: This is not a 'core' album.

Herbie Hancock
***** 2007 River: The Joni Letters
CD Verve 1744826 (2007)
Album Type: studio; Total Time: (67.38)
Musicians: Herbie Hancock (keyboard), Wayne Shorter (saxophone), Dave Holland (bass), Vinnie Colaiuta (drums), Lionel Louecke (guitar), Norah Jones (voice), Tina Turner (voice), Corinne Bailey Rae (voice), Joni Mitchell (voice), Luciana Souza (voice), Leonard Cohen (voice)
Tracks: 1 Court And Spark (featuring Norah Jones) (7.35), 2 Edith And The Kingpin (featuring Tina Turner) (6.32), 3 Both Sides Now (7.38), 4 River (featuring Corinne Bailey Rae) (5.25), 5 Sweet Bird (8.15), 6 Tea Leaf Prophecy (featuring Joni Mitchell) (6.34), 7 Solitude (5.42), 8 Amelia (featuring Luciana Souza) (7.26), 9 Nefertiti (7.30), 10 The Jungle Line (featuring Leonard Cohen) (5.01)

Recorded: 2007
Notes: Won Grammys for the Album of the Year and Best Contemporary Jazz Album.

Herbie Hancock
***** 2010 The Imagine Project
CD Sony Music 88697718992 (2010)
Album Type: studio; Total Time: (66.16)
Musicians: Herbie Hancock (keyboard), Alecia Beth Moore (Pink) (voice), Seal Samuel (voice), Alex Acuna (percussion), Jeff Beck (guitar), Vinnie Colaiuta (drums), Larry Klein (bass), India.Arie (voice), Fatoumata Diawara (voice), Larry Goldings (organ), Lionel Louecke (guitar), Marcus Miller (bass), Oumou Sangare (voice), Augustin Makuntima Mawangu (likembe), Menga Waku (likembe), Makonda Mbuta (likembe), Visi Vincent (drums), Mbiyavanga Ndofusu (percussion), John Legend (voice), Dean Parks (guitar), George Whitty (keyboard), Tal Wilkenfeld (bass), Maria do Céu Whitaker Poças (Céu) (voice), Rodrigo Campos (percussion), Curumin (drums), Lucas Martins (bass), Kofi Burbridge (organ), Oteil Burbridge (bass), Mike Mattison (voice), Susan Tedeschi (voice), Derek Trucks (guitar), Paddy Maloney (pipes), Sean Keane (fiddle), Kevin Conneff (bodhran), Matt Molloy (flute), Toumani Diabete (kora), Lisa Hannigan (voice), Manu Katche (percussion), Rhani Krija (percussion), Richard Bravo (percussion), Juanes Esteban Aristizabal (voice), Fernando Tobon (guitar), Pete Wallace (keyboard), Jessica Hancock (voice), Alan Mintz (voice), Maria Ruvalcaba (voice), Keinan Abdi Warsame (K'naan) (voice), David Hidalgo (voice), Conrad Lozano (voice), Louie Perez (voice), Ibrahim Ag Alhabib (voice), Abdallah Ag Alhousseyni (guitar), Elaga Ag Hamid (guitar), Abdallah Ag Lamida (guitar), Eyadou Ag Leche (bass), Alhassane Ag Touhami (guitar), Said Ag Ayad (percussion), Danny Barnes (bass), Matt Chamberlain (drums), Michael Chaves (guitar), Dave Matthews (voice), James Morrison (voice), Paulinho da Costa (percussion), K. S. Chithra (voice), Bhawai Shankar Kathak (percussion), Chaka Khan (voice), Sridhar Parthasarthy (percussion), Anoushka Shankar (sitar), Wayne Shorter (saxophone), Satyajit Talwalkar (percussion)
Tracks: 1 Imagine (7.20), 2 Don't Give Up (7.27), 3 Tempo De Amor (4.44), 4 Space Captain (6.54), 5 The Times, They Are A' Changin' (8.05), 6 La Tierra (4.50), 7 Tamatant Tilay / Exodus (4.45), 8 Tomorrow Never Knows (5.22), 9 A Change Is Gonna Come (8.46), 10 The Song Goes On (7.49)
Recorded: 2009/10

ALBUMS COMPRISED OF PREVIOUSLY RELEASED MATERIAL

Because of Herbie Hancock's high profile in the jazz world, there are a very large number of collections of his music that could be described as being 'comprised of previously released material'. In some cases, there is an unfortunate duplication of titles, which can add to the confusion of collecting Herbie's repertoire. It is also the case that many of these discs contain the same material so record collectors should be aware that duplication of recordings is inevitable. This is particularly true of some of the very early recordings during Herbie's time with the Donald Byrd / Pepper Adams bands. Collectors should also beware that the artwork on many CDs is misleading: photos of Herbie used on the covers may give the impression that the material on the disc is much more recent than it actually is. The following is an inevitably incomplete list of available CDs.

(In alphabetical order of title)

Herbie Hancock: A Jazz Collection
Columbia (1990) CD
Album Series: Columbia Jazz
Tracks: 1 Lisa 2 I Fall In Love Too Easily 3 Nefertiti 4 Someday My Prince Will Come 5 'Round Midnight 6 Well You Needn't 7 Parade 8 Eye Of The Hurricane 9 Maiden Voyage

Herbie Hancock: Anthology
Deju Vu (2006) 2 CD
Album Series: Dejavu Retro Jazz
Tracks: 1 Bird House / Herbie's Blues 2 Rock Your Soul (Mr Lucky Theme) 3 Jammin' With Herbie / Curro's 4 Hot and Heavy 5 Day Dream (Soul Power) / Night Walkers 6 Hot Piano 7 8 Scoochie 9 Witch Fire 10 Afro Boogie 11 You Will Know When You Get There 12 Toys 13 Be What
Notes: The content of Anthology, Rock Your Soul (2007), Voyager (2000), Day Dreams (2002) and Out of This World (2000) is similar.

Quincy Jones / Herbie Hancock: Backtracks
Renaissance / Backtrax CRANCH 12 (1999) CD
Tracks: 1 Watermelon Man 2 Take Five 3 Cast Your Fate To The Wind 4 Bossa Nova 5 Gravy Waltz 6 Exodus 7 Back At The Chicken Shack 8 Walk On The Wild Side 9 Mannlana 10 Rock Your Soul (Mr Lucky Theme) 11 Kamili 12 Bunia 13 Hot Piano 14 Live and Awake / One and Awake 15 Jammin' With Herbie / Curro's
Notes: Tracks 1-8 by Qunicy Jones; Tracks 9-15 by Herbie Hancock.

Herbie Hancock: Cantaloupe Island
Blue Note RVG Edition CDP 7243 8 29331 (1966) CD
Tracks: 1 Cantaloupe Island 2 Watermelon Man 3 Driftin' 4 Blind Man, Blind Man 5 And What If I Don't 6 Maiden Voyage

Corea / Hancock / Jarrett / Tyner: Corea/Hancock/Jarrett/Tyner
Atlantic 7567-81402-2 (1976) CD

Tracks: 1 Margot 2 Love No. 1 3 Tones For Joan's Bones 4 This is New 5 Lazy Bird 6 In Your Own Sweet Way 7 Einbahnstrasse 8 Doom
Notes: Originally released as SD 1696.

Herbie Hancock: Dancin' Grooves
CBS (2008) CD
Tracks: 1 Chameleon 2 Watermelon Man 3 Sly 4 Butterfly 5 Spank-a-Lee 6 Actual Proof 7 Doin' It 8 Hang Up Your Hang Ups 9 Spider 10 I Thought It Was You 11 Sunlight 12 Tell Everybody 13 You Bet Your Love 14 Chameleon (1983 UK Remix)

Herbie Hancock: Day Dreams
Prism PLATCD 753 (2002) CD
Tracks: 1 Day Dream (Soul Power) / Night Walkers 2 Kamili 3 Jammin' With Herbie / Curro's 4 Bird House / Herbie's Blues 5 It's A Beautiful Evening 6 Rock Your Soul (Mr Lucky Theme) 7 Live and Awake / One and Awake 8 Hot Piano 9 Jammin' With Herbie / Curro's 10 Witch Fire 11 Day Dream (Soul Power) / Night Walkers
Notes: A recent compilation of early Hancock recordings with Donald Byrd and Pepper Adams. Track 2 is incorrectly labelled Kamli. Track 1 is incorrectly called Day Dreams. The content of Rock Your Soul (2007), Voyager (2000), Late Night Jazz Favourites (2008), De Luxe (2005), Day Dreams (2002) and Out of This World (2000) is similar.

Herbie Hancock: De Luxe
Phantom (2005) CD
Tracks: 1 Afro Boogie 2 Far Out 3 Herbie's Blues 4 Hot Piano 5 Jammin' With Herbie / Curro's 6 Kamili 7 Live and Awake / One and Awake 8 Night Awake 9 Rock Your Soul (Mr Lucky Theme) 10 Scoochie 11 Witch Fire

Herbie Hancock: Dr Jazz
Blue Note (1999) CD

Herbie Hancock: Great Sessions
Blue Note (2006) 3 CD
Album Series: Great Sessions
Tracks: 1 One Finger Snap 2 Oliloqui Valley 3 Cantaloupe Island 4 Egg 5 One Finger Snap 6 Oliloqui Valley 7 Maiden Voyage 8 Eye Of The Hurricane 9 Little One 10 Survival of the Fittest 11 Dolphin Dance 12 Riot 13 Speak Like A Child 14 Toys 15 Goodbye To Childhood 16 The Sorcerer 17 Riot 18 Riot 19 Goodbye To Childhood

Herbie Hancock: Herbie Hancock Box
Sony Jazz (2004) 4 CD
Tracks: 1 Introduction to Maiden Voyage 2 Maiden Voyage (live) 3 Para Oriente 4 Harvest Time 5 The Sorcerer 6 Diana (live) 7 Finger Painting 8 'Round Midnight 9 The Eye of the Hurricane 10 Domo 11 Dolphin Dance 12 Liza (All the Clouds'll Roll Away (live) 13 Eighty-One (live) 14 Milestones 15 Stella By Starlight / On Green Dolphin Street (live) 16 Red Clay 17 Rain Dance 18 Watermelon Man 19 Butterfly 20 Death Wish (Main Title) 21 Actual Proof 22 Sun Touch 23 4 A.M. 24 Come Running To Me 25 People Music 26 Chameleon 27 Stars in Your Eyes 28 Rockit 29 Calypso 30 Satisfied With Love 31 Karabali 32 Spider 33 Nobu 34 Maiden Voyage / B. Bop

Herbie Hancock: Herbie Hancock: The Collection
Brilliant (2008) CD

Herbie Hancock: Hot And Heavy
Galaxy Music (2006) CD
Album Series: Jazz Café Presents

Herbie Hancock: Jammin' With Herbie
Warwick (1995) CD
Tracks: 1 Jammin' With Herbie / Curro's 2 Bird House / Herbie's Blues 3 Rock Your Soul (Mr Lucky Theme) 4 T.C.B. With Herbie / Out of This World / Live and Awake / One and Awake 5 Day Dream (Soul Power) / Night Walkers 6 Cat Call

Herbie Hancock: Jammin' With Herbie Hancock
Collectables Jazz Classics (2000) CD
Tracks: 1 Jammin' With Herbie / Curro's 2 Bird House / Herbie's Blues 3 Rock Your Soul (Mr Lucky Theme) 4 Out Of This World 5 Day Dream (Soul Power) / Night Walkers 6 I'm An Old Cowhand

Herbie Hancock: Jazz Biography
United (2007) CD
Tracks: 1 Day Dream (Soul Power) / Night Walkers 2 Hot Piano 3 Live and Awake / One and Awake 4 Scoochie 5 Witch Fire 6 Afro Boogie 7 Far Out 8 Jammin' With Herbie / Curro's 9 Bird House / Herbie's Blues 10 Rock Your Soul (Mr Lucky Theme) 11 T.C.B. With Herbie / Out of This World / Live and Awake / One and Awake 12 Day Dream (Soul Power) / Night Walkers 13 Cat Call

Herbie Hancock: Jazz Moods: Round Midnight
Columbia Legacy 516427-2 (2004) CD
Album Series: Jazz Moods
Tracks: 1 On Green Dolphin Street 2 'Round Midnight 3 Minuit Aux Champs-Elysees 4 Look 5 Circle 6 Harvest Time 7 Pee Wee 8 Someday My Prince Will Come 9 Little One 10 Chan's Song (Never Said) 11 My Funny Valentine

Herbie Hancock: Jazz Profile
Blue Note (2002) CD
Tracks: 1 Empty Pockets 2 Jack Rabbit 3 Yams 4 Eye Of The Hurricane 5 Cantaloupe Island 6 Sorcerer 7 I Have A Dream

Herbie Hancock: Jazz to Funk
Aim (2007) 2 CD

Herbie Hancock: Late Night Jazz Favourites
Cleopatra (2008) CD
Tracks: 1 Live and Awake / One and Awake 2 Witch Fire 3 Cat Call 4 Scoochie 5 Hot Piano 6 Rock Your Soul (Mr Lucky Theme) 7 Bird House / Herbie's Blues 8 Jammin' With Herbie / Curro's 9 Day Dream (Soul Power) / Night Walkers 10 Afro Boogie 11 Far Out (From Blow Up) 12 Hot and Heavy
Notes: Originally released under the label Donald Byrd / Pepper Adams Quintet: Out of This World. The content of Rock Your Soul (2007), Voyager (2000), Day Dreams (2002), Late

Night Jazz Favourites (2008) and Out of This World (2000) is similar.

Herbie Hancock: Mr Funk
Columbia (1999) CD
Tracks: 1 Watermelon Man 2 Actual Proof 3 Hang Up Your Hang Ups 4 Heartbeat 5 Kuru/Speak Like a Child 6 Cantaloupe Island 7 Swamp Rat 8 Come Running To Me 9 4 A.M. 10 Everybody's Broke 11 Rockit

Herbie Hancock: Mwandishi: The Complete Warner Bros. Recordings
Warner Bros. (1994) CD
Notes: Box set for collectors.

Herbie Hancock: Night Walker
(2000) CD
Tracks: 1 Day Dream (Soul Power) / Night Walkers 2 Live and Awake / One and Awake 3 Scoochie 4 Witch Fire 5 Afro Boogie 6 Far Out 7 Hot and Heavy 8 Bird House / Herbie's Blues 9 T.C.B. With Herbie / Out of This World / Live and Awake / One and Awake 10 Day Dream (Soul Power) / Night Walkers

Herbie Hancock / Chick Corea: Piano Fiesta
JHR (2006) CD
Album Series: A Jazz Hour With
Tracks: 1 Hornets 2 Interlude 3 Hornets 4 Gibraltar 5 Sea Breeze 6 Moment's Notice 7 Come Rain or Come Shine 8 Fiesta (Piano Solo)
Notes: One of the Series "A Jazz Hour With". Tracks 1-4 also appear as Herbie Hancock CD, Live Detroit / Chicago.

Herbie Hancock: Portrait
Sony (2000) CD
Tracks: 1 Sorcerer 2 Gentle Thoughts 3 Actual Proof 4 Peacocks 5 Calypso 6 Maiden Voyage

Herbie Hancock: Riot: The Newly Discovered Takes from Blue Note Sixties Sessions
Import (1999) CD
Tracks: 1 Riot (First Alt Take) 2 Riot (Second Alt Take) 3 Blind Man, Blind Man 4 Mimosa 5 Goodbye To Childhood 6 Prisoner 7 Firewater
Notes: A Japanese edition.

Herbie Hancock: Rockit
Delta (2004) CD
Tracks: 1 Rockit 2 Autodrive 3 Hardrock 4 Chameleon 5 I Thought It Was You 6 You Bet Your Love 7 Watermelon Man 8 Go for It 9 Karabali 10 Stars in Your Eyes 11 Motor Mouth 12 Ready Or Not 13 Doin' It 14 Vibe Alive

Herbie Hancock: The Best of Herbie Hancock
Sony BMG (1999) CD
Tracks: 1 Doin' It 2 I Thought It Was You 3 Chameleon 4 Hang Up Your Hang Ups 5 Ready Or Not 6 Tell Everybody

Herbie Hancock: The Best of Herbie Hancock
EMI France (2009) 3 CD
Notes: Box set for collectors.

Herbie Hancock: The Best of Herbie Hancock - The Blue Note Years
Blue Note (1988) CD
Tracks: 1 Watermelon Man 2 Driftin' 3 Maiden Voyage 4 Dolphin Dance 5 One Finger Snap
6 Cantaloupe Island 7 Riot 8 Speak Like A Child 9 King Cobra (1963 Digital Remaster)

Herbie Hancock: The Best of Herbie Hancock - The Hits
Sony Jazz (1999) CD

Herbie Hancock: The Best of Herbie Hancock Vol. 2
Euro Parrot (1992) CD
Tracks: 1 Watermelon Man 2 Future Shock (Edited Version) 3 Go For It (Edited Version) 4
Can't Hide Your Love (Edited Version) 5 Vibe Alive (Edited Version) 6 Textures 7 Doin' It 8
Chameleon 9 Early Warning 10 Paradise 11 People Are Changing 12 Tell Everybody (Edited
Version) 13 Hardrock (Edited Version) 14 Mega Mix

Herbie Hancock: The Collection
Brilliant (2008) CD
Tracks: 1 Far Out 2 Scoochie 3 Witchfire 4 Rock Your Soul (Mr Lucky Theme) 5 Day Dream
(Soul Power) / Night Walkers 6 Afro Boogie 7 Live and Awake / One and Awake 8 Soul
Power 9 Herbie's Blues 10 Cat Call 11 TCB With Herbie 12 Hot & Heavy 13 Hot Piano 14
Jammin' With Herbie / Curro's

Herbie Hancock: The Collection: A Selection of Tracks From the Blue Note Years
EMI Gold 094635 6085 2 6 (2006) CD
Tracks: 1 Empty Pockets 2 Jack Rabbit (1988 Digital remaster) 3 Yams 4 The Eye of the
Hurricane 5 Cantaloupe Island 6 The Sorcerer 7 I Have A Dream

Herbie Hancock: The Columbia Years: '72 - '86
Columbia (2002) CD
Notes: Box set for collectors.

Herbie Hancock: The Complete Blue Note Sixties Sessions
Blue Note (1998) 6 CD

Herbie Hancock: The Definitive Herbie Hancock
Columbia Legacy 501036-2 (2000) CD
Album Series: Ken Burns Jazz
Tracks: 1 Watermelon Man 2 Cantaloupe Island 3 Maiden Voyage 4 Speak Like A Child 5
Tell Me A Bedtime Story 6 Chameleon 7 Actual Proof 8 Rockit 9 You've Got It Bad Girl

Herbie Hancock: The Essential Herbie Hancock
Mastercuts / Apace Music MCUTAC021 (2007) CD
Album Series: Mastercuts
Tracks: 1 Afro Boogie 2 Bunia 3 Out of This World 4 Kamili 5 Far Out 6 Kawaida 7
Scoochie 8 Rock Your Soul (Mr Lucky Theme) 9 Baraka 10 Witch Fire 11 Hot and Heavy 12
Jammin' With Herbie / Curro's 13 Day Dream (Soul Power) / Night Walkers 14 Bird House /

Herbie's Blues 15 Hot Piano

Herbie Hancock: The Essential Herbie Hancock
Columbia Legacy 82796 94593 2 (2006) CD
Tracks: 1 Watermelon Man 2 'Round Midnight 3 Cantaloupe Island 4 Maiden Voyage 5 Circle 6 The Sorcerer 7 Tell Me a Bedtime Story 8 Hidden Shadows 9 Chameleon 10 Joanna's Theme 11 Butterfly 12 People Music 13 Milestones 14 4 A.M. 15 Come Running to Me 16 Finger Painting 17 Stars in Your Eyes 18 Rockit 19 St. Louis Blues 20 Manhattan (Island Of Lights And Love)

Herbie Hancock: The Finest in Jazz
Blue Note 0946 3 94897 2 5 (2007) CD
Tracks: 1 Watermelon Man 2 Blind Man, Blind Man 3 First Trip 4 Cantaloupe Island 5 Maiden Voyage 6 Firewater

Herbie Hancock: The Very Best of Herbie Hancock
Columbia COL 467974 2 (1991) CD
Tracks: 1 Rockit 2 You Bet Your Love 3 I Thought It Was You 4 The Bomb 5 Ready Or Not 6 Stars In Your Eyes 7 Motor Mouth 8 Makin' Love 9 Lite Me Up! 10 People Music 11 'Round Midnight 12 Sound System 13 Sun Touch 14 Karabali 15 Autodrive

Herbie Hancock: The Very Best of Herbie Hancock
Music Brokers (2006) CD
Album Series: Jazz Collectors
Tracks: 1 Baraka 2 Maulana 3 Kawaida 4 Dunia 5 Kamili
Notes: Previously released as Baraka. (See main discography)

Herbie Hancock: The Very Best of Herbie Hancock
Columbia Legacy 88697 38353 2 (2008) CD
Album Series: Playlist
Tracks: 1 Maiden Voyage (live) 2 Chan's Song (Never Said) 3 Dolphin Dance 4 Calypso 5 Watermelon Man 6 Chameleon (Single version) 7 Butterfly 8 Hang Up Your Hang Ups (Single version) 9 Rockit

Herbie Hancock: Then and Now - The Definitive Herbie Hancock
Verve 0602517809666 (2008) CD
Tracks: 1 Maiden Voyage 2 Cantaloupe Island 3 Wiggle Waggle 4 Chameleon (Edit) 5 St. Louis Blues 6 Chan's Song (Never Said) 7 River 8 Don't Explain 9 All Apologies 10 Watermelon Man 11 Rockit (live) 12 River (live)
Notes: Stevie Wonder plays on 5. Corinne Bailey Rae sings on 7. Damien Rice and Lisa Hannigan appear on 8. Joni Mitchell appears on 12.

Herbie Hancock: This is Jazz
Columbia Legacy CK 65051 (1998) CD
Tracks: 1 The Sorcerer 2 Gentle Thoughts 3 Actual Proof 4 The Peacocks 5 Calypso 6 Maiden Voyage
Notes: Track 1 recorded Tokyo (1980), originally on Quartet (1982). Track 2 recorded San Francisco (1975 or 76), originally on Secrets (1976). Track 3 recorded San Francisco (1973 or 74), originally on Thrust (1974). Track 4 recorded France (1986), originally on Round Midnight (1986). Track 5 recorded San Francisco (1979 or 80), originally on Mr Hands

(1980), Track 6 originally on An Evening with Herbie Hancock and Chick Corea in Concert

Donald Byrd, Pepper Adams: Touchstone
Starburst (2000) CD
Tracks: 1 Bird House / Herbie's Blues 2 Rock Your Soul (Mr Lucky Theme) 3 Day Dream (Soul Power) / Night Walkers 4 I'm An Old Cowhand 5 Jammin' With Herbie / Curro's 6 It's A Beautiful Evening 7 Out Of This World 8 Scoochie

Herbie Hancock: Voyager
New Sound 2000 NST 032 (2000) CD
Tracks: 1 Jammin' With Herbie / Curro's 2 Bird House / Herbie's Blues 3 Rock Your Soul (Mr Lucky Theme) 4 Out of This World 5 Day Dream (Soul Power) / Night Walkers 6 Cat Call
Notes: Track 3 is actually labelled Mr Lucky (Rock Your Soul). The content of Rock Your Soul (2007), Voyager (2000), Day Dreams (2002) and Out of This World (2000) is similar.

CONTRIBUTIONS TO OTHER ALBUMS

Herbie Hancock has been in great demand as a 'sideman' for musicians across a wide spectrum of genres and the following list is but a sample of albums to which he has contributed. In each case, it may range from just one brief appearance to a presence on all selections of an album.

1961 Day Dreams, Herbie Hancock
1961 Chant, Donald Byrd
1961 Royal Flush, Donald Byrd
1961 Free Form, Donald Byrd
1962 Gaslight 1962, Eric Dolphy
1963 Vertigo, Jackie McLean
1963 A New Perspective, Donald Byrd
1963 Hub-Tones, Freddie Hubbard
1963 Straight No Filter, Hank Mobley
1963 Illinois Concert, Eric Dolphy
1963 Step Lightly, Blue Mitchell
1963 Seven Steps to Heaven, Miles Davis
1963 Miles in Antibes, Miles Davis
1964 Miles in Tokyo, Miles Davis
1964 The Complete Concert 1964, Miles Davis
1964 Four And More, Miles Davis
1964 My Funny Valentine, Miles Davis
1964 Miles Davis in Europe, Miles Davis
1964 Lifetime, Tony Williams
1964 Search For The New Land, Lee Morgan
1964 It's Time!, Jackie McLean
1964 Some Other Stuff, Grachan Moncur III
1964 In Memory Of, Stanley Turrentine
1965 E.S.P., Miles Davis
1965 Spring, Tony Williams
1965 SpeakNo Evil, Wayne Shorter
1965 Et Cetera, Wayne Shorter
1965 Miles in Berlin, Miles Davis
1965 Freedom, Kenny Burrell
1965 Components, Bobby Hutcherson
1965 I'm Tryin' To Get Home, Donald Byrd
1965 Cornbread, Lee Morgan
1966 Happenings, Bobby Hutcherson
1966 The All Seeing Eye, Wayne Shorter
1966 Adam's Apple, Wayne Shorter
1967 Schizophrenia, Wayne Shorter
1967 Nefertiti, Miles Davis
1967 Sorcerer, Miles Davis
1967 The Procrastinator, Lee Morgan
1967 Oblique, Bobby Hutcherson
1967 Standards, Lee Morgan
1967 Miles Smiles, Miles Davis

1968 Miles in the Sky, Miles Davis
1968 Filles de Kilimanjaro, Miles Davis
1969 In A Silent Way, Miles Davis
1969 Uptown Conversation, Ron Carter
1971 A Tribute To Jack Johnson, Miles Davis
1971 Zawinul, Joe Zawinul
1971 He Who Lives in Many Places, Terry Plumeri
1972 On The Corner, Miles Davis
1972 Moon Germs, Joe Farrell
1974 Get Up With It, Miles Davis
1974 Big Fun, Miles Davis
1975 Native Dancer, Wayne Shorter
1976 Milton, Milton Nascimento
1976 Identity, Airto Moreira
1976 Jaco Pastorius, Jaco Pastorius
1976 Water Babies, Miles Davis
1979 The Swing of Delight, Carlos Santana
1979 Circle in the Round, Miles Davis
1979 Mingus, Joni Mitchell
1981 Word of Mouth, Jaco Pastorius
1981 The Dude, Quincy Jones
1982 Conrad Silvert Presents Jazz at the Opera House, Various Artists
1984 Live in Lugano - Supertrio in Concert, Herbie Hancock / Ron Carter / Billy Cobham
1987 Yauraete, Milton Nascimento
1987 Joy Ryder, Wayne Shorter
1988 Don't Try This at Home, Michael Brecker
1989 Something More, Buster Williams
1989 Back on the Block, Quincy Jones
1990 Live In Concert, De Johnette / Hancock / Holland / Metheny
1990 Parallel Realities Live, De Johnette, Metheny, Hancock, Holland
1994 Vinnie Colaiuta, Vinnie Colaiuta
1995 Q's Jook Joint, Quincy Jones
1995 Highlights from the Plugged Nickel, Miles Davis
1995 Antonio Carlos Jobim: An All Star Tribute, Various Artists
1997 Wilderness, Tony Williams
1998 Return of the Headhunters, Headhunters
2001 M2, Marcus Miller
2001 Nearness of You: The Ballad Book, Michael Brecker
2003 Miles Davis Quintet 1965-68: The Complete Columbia, Miles Davis Studio Recordings
2003 Left Alone, Eric Dolphy
2005 In Tokyo, Herbie Hancock / Wayne Shorter / Dave Holland / Brian Blade
2006 Piano Fiesta, Herbie Hancock / Chick Corea
2006 Virgin Forest, Lionel Louecke
2007 The Jewel in the Lotus, Benny Maupin
2007 Pilgrimage, Michael Brecker
2008 Awake Live, Josh Groban
2008 32 Festival de Jazz de Vitoria-Gasteiz, Various Artists
2009 One Night in Japan, Herbie Hancock & The New Standard All Stars
2009 Shape of My Heart, Katia Labeque

HERBIE HANCOCK DVDs

Herbie Hancock / Ron Carter / Billy Cobham
1984 Live in Lugano - Supertrio in Concert
DVD Jazz Door (1984)
Album Type: live
Musicians: Herbie Hancock (keyboard), Ron Carter (bass), Billy Cobham (drums)
Tracks: 1 Toys, 2 First Trip, 3 Speak Like A Child, 4 Little Waltz, 5 Willow Weep For Me, 6 Dolphin Dance, 7 Ili's Treasure, 8 Princess, 9 Eye Of The Hurricane, 10 Walkin'
Recorded: 1984

Dexter Gordon / Herbie Hancock
1986 Round Midnight
DVD Warner Brothers 1-4198-6800-4 (2008)
Album Type: soundtrack
Musicians: Herbie Hancock (keyboard)
Recorded: 1985

De Johnette / Hancock / Holland / Metheny
1990 Live In Concert
DVD Arthaus 4006680101842 (1990)
Album Type: live Total Time: (99.00)
Musicians: Jack De Johnette (drums), Herbie Hancock (keyboard), Dave Holland (bass), Pat Metheny (guitar)
Tracks: 8 Eye Of The Hurricane (15.09), 9 The Bat (8.02), 1 Shadow Dance (15.12), 2 Indigo Dreamscapes (6.51), 3 Nine Over Reggae (7.33), 10 Cantaloupe Island (9.03), 4 Solar (12.40), 5 Silver Hollow (8.19), 6 The Good Life (6.01), 7 Blue (6.57),
Recorded: 1990/6/23
Notes: Recorded at the Mellon Jazz Festival, Academy of Music, Philadelphia.

Herbie Hancock
2002 Future 2 Future Live
DVD Columbia Legacy 5 099720 181293 (2002)
Album Type: live Total Time: (103.49)
Musicians: Herbie Hancock (keyboard), Wallace Roney (trumpet), Darrell Diaz (keyboard), Terri Lynne Carrington (drums), Matthew Garrison (bass), DJ Disk (turntable)
Tracks: 1 Wisdom, 2 Kebero, 3 This Is DJ Disk, 4 Dolphin Dance, 5 Virtual Hornets, 6 The Essence, 7 Butterfly, 8 Tony Williams, 9 Rockit, 10 Chameleon
Recorded: 2002
Notes: Recorded at the Knitting Factory, Hollywood, Los Angeles, CA. This edition contains the original video of Rockit.

Herbie Hancock
2003 Herbie Hancock Trio (DVD)
DVD TDK (2003)
Album Type: live
Musicians: Herbie Hancock (keyboard), Charles (Buster) Williams (bass), Al Foster (drums)
Tracks: 1 Dolphin Dance, 2 Air Dancing, 3 Just One of Those Things
Recorded:
Notes: Recorded live at the Munich Philharmonie.

Herbie Hancock
2004 Herbie Hancock Special with Bobby McFerrin and Michael Brecker
DVD TDK / Loft 5 450270 008131 (2004)
Album Type: live
Musicians: Herbie Hancock (keyboard), Bobby McFerrin (voice), Michael Brecker (saxophone)
Tracks: 1 Air Dancing (8.30), 2 Oleo (18.41), 3 Improvisation (2 hands) (8.42), 4 Improvisation (4 hands) (8.49), 5 Cantaloupe Island (2 hands) (5.01), 6 Cantaloupe Island (4 hands) (4.29)
Recorded: 1988/7/15
Notes: Recorded live at the Munich Philharmonie.

Herbie Hancock / Wayne Shorter / Dave Holland / Brian Blade
2005 In Tokyo
DVD Jazz Door (2005)
Album Type: live
Musicians: Herbie Hancock (keyboard), Wayne Shorter (saxophone), Dave Holland (bass), Brian Blade (drums), Lionel Louecke (guitar)
Tracks: 1 Sonrisa, 2 Pathways, 3 Footprints, 4 Aung San Suu Kyi, 5 Prometheus Unbound
Recorded: 2004/9/18
Notes: Live at the Tokyo Big Sight.

Herbie Hancock
2006 World of Rhythm
DVD TDK (2006)
Album Type: live
Musicians: Herbie Hancock (keyboard), Ron Carter (bass), Billy Cobham (drums)

Herbie Hancock
2007 Herbie Hancock Trio In Concert (DVD)
DVD Delta Home Entertainment (2007)
Album Type: live Total Time: (60.00)
Musicians: Herbie Hancock (keyboard), Ron Carter (bass), Billy Cobham (drums)

Herbie Hancock's Headhunters
2008 Watermelon Man
DVD Jazz Door JD11042 (2008)
Album Type: live Total Time: (70.49)
Musicians: Herbie Hancock (keyboard), Marcus Miller (bass), Terri Lynne Carrington (drums), Roy Hargrove (trumpet), Darryl Munyungo Jackson (percussion), Lionel Louecke (guitar), Melvin 'Wah Wah Watson' Ragin (guitar)
Tracks: 1 Watermelon Man (3.49), 2 Spider (16.55), 3 Safiatou (8.54), 4 Actual Proof (13.34), 5 Hang Up Your Hang Ups (14.31), 6 Butterfly (12.48)
Recorded: 2005/8/20
Notes: Recorded live in Japan.

Herbie Hancock & The New Standard All Stars
2009 One Night in Japan
DVD Immortal (2009)

Album Type: live Total Time: (74.00)
Musicians: Herbie Hancock (keyboard), John Scofield (guitar), Michael Brecker (saxophone), Dave Holland (bass), Jack De Johnette (drums), Don Alias (percussion)
Tracks: 1 New York Minute (13.31), 2 Norwegian Wood (9.05), 3 Mercy Street (12.52), 4 You've Got It Bad Girl (15.39), 5 Love is Stronger Than Pride (14.42)
Recorded: 1996/8/3
Notes: Recorded at Lake Stella Theater, Kawaguchi, Japan.

Index

1 + 1, 163
245, 23
32 Festival de Jazz de Vitoria-Gasteiz, 175
4 A.M., 160, 168, 170, 172
A Change Is Gonna Come, 138, 140, 166
A Jazz Collection, 167
A Jump Ahead, 29, 152
A New Perspective, 174
A Quick Sketch, 160
A Slight Smile, 89, 160
A Song For You, 165
A Tribute To Jack Johnson, 175
A Tribute to Miles, 105, 124, 163
AC Cobra, 21, 24
Actual Proof, 54, 59, 64, 136, 155, 156, 168, 170, 171, 172, 177
Acuna, Alex, 166
Adams, Park 'Pepper', 14, 15, 167, 168, 169, 173
Adderley, Julian Edwin, 39
Adler, Larry, 118
Aeolin Hall (performance venue), 116
Africa, 53, 64, 96, 98, 102, 109, 162
Afro Boogie, 167, 168, 169, 170, 171
Ag Alhabib, Ibrahim, 166
Ag Alhousseyni, Abdallah, 166
Ag Ayad, Said, 166
Ag Hamid, Elaga, 166
Ag Lamida, Abdallah, 166
Ag Leche, Eyadou, 166
Ag Touhami, Alhassane, 166
Aguilera, Christina, 128, 165
Air Dancing, 106, 176, 177
Ake, David, 91, 149
Al, Alex, 164
Albright, Gerald, 144
Alexander, William, 161
Alias, Don, 111, 163, 178
Alive, 103, 104, 162, 163, 170, 171
All Apologies, 112, 163, 172
All Blues, 105, 163
Alone and I, 20, 151
Alpert, Herb, 66
Alphabeta, 122, 164
Always and Forever, 92
Am I Glad to See You, 152
Amelia, 134, 165
An Evening With Herbie Hancock and Chick Corea In Concert, 7, 80, 158
Anastasio, Trey, 165
And What If I Don't, 151, 167
Anthology, 167
Anthony, Wayne, 93, 160
Antonio Carlos Jobim
    An All Star Tribute, 175
Areas, Jose, 154
Armageddon, 137

Armour, Eddie, 22
Armstrong, Louis, 13
ARP (instrument manufacturer), 53, 61, 77
ARP 2600 (instrument), 53, 61, 77
ARP 3604 (instrument), 61
ARP Odyssey (instrument), 53, 61, 77
ARP PE-IV (instrument), 61
ARP Pro-Soloist (instrument), 53
Art Blakey's Jazz Messengers, 13, 16, 23, 90
As Time Goes By, 102, 162
At the Lounge, 155
Aung San Suu Kyi, 114, 115, 164, 177
Autodrive, 95, 161, 170, 172
Autumn, 148
avant-garde, 22, 27, 28, 29, 30, 32, 35, 44, 49, 77, 83
Awake Live, 175
Ayler, Albert, 28
Baby Be Mine, 92
Babyface, aka Kenneth Edmonds, 111
Back At The Chicken Shack, 167
Back on the Block, 175
Backtracks, 15, 167
Bailey Rae, Corinne, 134, 165, 172
Baker, Chet, 14, 15, 101, 162
Baptista, Cyro, 164
Baraka, 7, 47, 48, 149, 153, 171, 172
Barnes, Danny, 166
Basie, William Allen, 40
Bat, 176
Bateman, Edgar, 22
Be Still, 121, 164
Be What, 167
Beat Wise, 103, 104, 162, 163
Beatles (band), 35, 110, 111, 137, 138, 140
Beck, Jeff, 36, 138, 166
Beck, Joe, 38, 39
Beijing, 135
Beinhorn, Michael, 94, 161
Belew, Adrian, 160
Benson, George, 39, 144
Berkeley CA, 71, 157, 163
Berklee College of Music, 107
Between Nothingness and Eternity, 99
Beyond, 4, 148, 149
Big Fun, 175
Bill Evans, 11, 58
Billboard (magazine), 31, 111, 138, 148, 149
Bird House / Herbie's Blues, 167, 168, 169, 170, 172, 173
Birdland, 21
Birds of Fire, 99
Bitches Brew, 40, 50, 52, 126
Black Gravity, 121, 164
Blackbird, 13, 64, 156
Blackwell, Ed, 47, 153
Blade, Brian, 123, 165, 175, 177

179

Blakey, Arthur, 13, 16, 18, 23, 32, 90, 91
Blind Man, Blind Man, 24, 25, 35, 151, 167, 170, 172
Blow Up, 35, 54, 152, 169
Blue Otani, 82, 158
Blueberry Rhyme, 117, 164
Bluementhal, Bob, 29, 32, 44, 148, 149
Bo Ba Be Da, 110, 163
Boddicker, Michael, 92, 160
Body and Soul, 11, 101, 162
Bonner, Billy, 47, 153
Bonner, Leon, 162
Bono, 128
Bossa Nova, 139, 167
Both Sides Now, 132, 133, 134, 165
Bouquet, 80, 158
Bova, Jeff, 103, 162
Bravo, Richard, 166
Braxton, Anthony, 49
Brazil, 40, 45, 139
Brecker, Michael, 8, 43, 88, 106, 111, 112, 122, 124, 147, 150, 160, 163, 165, 175, 177, 178
Bring Down the Birds, 36, 152
Brisbois, Bud, 156
Broadway, 21, 25, 115
Brooklyn, 48
Brooks, Harvey, 40
Brown, Garnett, 42, 46, 153, 156
Brown, James, 38, 55
Bruford, Bill, 59
Bryant, Dana, 164
Bubbles, 63, 156
Bud Powell, 18, 58, 100, 101
Buddhism, 55, 59, 66
Bunia, 167, 171
Bunny, Skip, 163
Burbridge, Kofi, 166
Burbridge, Oteil, 166
Burrell, Kenneth Earl, 45, 174
Bush, Kate, 88, 138
Butterfly, 60, 64, 82, 109, 110, 145, 155, 156, 158, 163, 168, 172, 176, 177
Button Up, 80, 158
Bye Bye Blackbird, 13
Byrd, Donald, 13, 14, 18, 19, 21, 24, 25, 45, 72, 148, 151, 167, 168, 169, 173, 174
Byrdlike, 72, 157
California, 19, 42, 71, 149
Call It 95, 163
Call Sheet Blues, 102, 162
Calypso, 84, 160, 168, 170, 172
Campos, Rodrigo, 166
Cannonball, 39
Cantaloupe Island, 30, 31, 35, 55, 57, 62, 65, 107, 131, 152, 155, 156, 167, 168, 169, 170, 171, 172, 176, 177
Carlos, Wendy, 75
Carpenter, Dave, 126
Carpenter, Karen, 128

Carpenters (band), 128
Carr, Ian, 27, 40, 148, 149
Carrington, Terri Lynne, 107, 164, 176, 177
Carter, Clifford, 165
Carter, James, 164
Carter, Ron, 7, 8, 26, 27, 29, 33, 36, 37, 40, 67, 68, 70, 71, 72, 84, 89, 99, 101, 102, 104, 152, 153, 156, 157, 159, 160, 162, 163, 175, 176, 177
Cast Your Fate To The Wind, 167
Cat Call, 14, 169, 171, 173
Chamberlain, Matt, 166
Chambers, Dennis, 59
Chambers, Paul, 28, 29, 152
Chameleon, 56, 57, 63, 64, 127, 131, 154, 156, 168, 170, 171, 172, 176
Champlin, Bill, 87, 159, 161
Chancler, Ndugu Leon, 154, 157, 159
Chant, 15, 174
Charles, Teddy, 15
Chaves, Michael, 166
Chemical Residue, 103, 104, 163
Cher, 75
Cherry, Don, 23, 47, 153
Chicago Symphony Orchestra, 11
Chieftains, The (band), 140
Childs, Billy, 119
Chithra, K. S., 141, 166
Christopher, Gavin, 86, 88, 159, 160
Cigarette Lighter, 102, 162
Circle in the Round, 38, 41, 175
Clapton, Eric, 58
Clark, Michael, 59, 64, 119, 155, 156
Clarke, Buck, 154
Clarke, Stanley, 50, 57, 58, 63, 75, 143
Clear Ways, 160
Clouds, 132, 158, 168
Cobain, Kurt, 112
Cobb, Jimmy, 14
Cobham, Billy, 58, 99, 175, 176, 177
Cobra, 21, 24, 25, 151, 171
Cocker, Joe, 139
Cohen, Leonard, 134, 165
Colaiuta, Vincent, 59, 130, 141, 165, 166, 175
Coleman, George, 31, 34, 152
Coleman, Ira, 164
Coleman, Ornette, 17, 22, 23, 28, 32, 47
Coles, John, 42, 46, 153, 154
Collection, 167, 171
Collins, William, 162
Coltrane, John, 13, 23, 38, 122, 123, 150
Columbia Records, 38, 39, 45, 48, 52, 80, 81, 82, 83, 95, 102, 103, 145, 149, 150, 154, 155, 156, 157, 158, 159, 160, 161, 162, 167, 169, 170, 171, 172, 175, 176
Come and See Me, 110, 163
Come Rain or Come Shine, 170
Come Running to Me, 76, 157, 172
Concerto, 11, 118, 136, 164
Concerto For Piano And Orchestra In G, 2nd

180

Movement, 164
Conneff, Kevin, 166
Cook, Richard, 148
Cooke, Sam, 140
Corea, Chick, 7, 40, 45, 49, 66, 80, 108, 144, 158, 164, 170, 173, 175
Corea, William, 152
Corea/Hancock/Jarrett/Tyner, 167
Cornbread, 174
Coryell, Larry, 106
Cosey, Peter, 94
Cotton Tail, 117, 164
Court and Spark, 134, 165
Craig, Carl, 62, 120, 164
Crisol (band), 123
Crossings, 7, 51, 145, 154
Curiosity, 36, 152
Curtis, Charles, 164
Curumin, 166
Cuscuna, Michael, 102
D Trane, 124, 125, 165
da Costa, Paulinho, 141, 160, 166
Daniel, 161
Darts, 72, 157
DaVersa, Jay, 156
Davis, Henry, 155
Davis, Miles, 7, 9, 10, 11, 13, 18, 19, 20, 25, 27, 29, 31, 41, 45, 50, 52, 57, 58, 62, 64, 66, 67, 69, 80, 91, 95, 99, 104, 106, 115, 117, 122, 123, 124, 126, 134, 144, 148, 149, 174, 175
Davis, Richard, 22
Davis-Knight, Elenni, 120, 164
Day Dream (Soul Power) / Night Walkers, 167, 168, 169, 170, 171, 173
De Johnette, Jack, 152, 163, 164, 165, 176, 178
De Luxe, 168
Death Wish, 7, 43, 54, 155, 168
Debo, 102, 162
Dedication, 7, 61, 82, 155
Dembelle, Madou, 164
Denen Colosseum (performance venue), 72, 83, 157, 159
Diabete, Toumani, 166
Diana, 73, 114, 157, 164, 168
Diawara, Fatoumata, 166
Diaz, Darrell, 176
Dieng, Aiyb, 102, 161, 162
Diop, Massamba, 164
Direct Step, 8, 82, 143, 158
Directions in Music, 8, 122, 123, 150, 165
direct-to-disc recording, 81, 82, 83
Dis Is Da Drum, 8, 97, 108, 109, 163
Disk, DJ, 176
DMX (instrument0, 97, 98
Dodgion, Jerry, 37, 153
Dog Eat Dog, 133
Doi, Toshi, 81
Dolores, 72, 90, 157
Dolphin Dance, 35, 61, 69, 89, 99, 152, 155, 160, 168, 171, 172, 176
Dolphy, Eric Allan, 7, 21, 22, 28, 32, 68, 174, 175
Domo, 159, 168
Doom, 168
Dorham, Kenny, 101
Down Beat magazine, 28, 148
Dr Jazz, 168
Drake, Hamid, 97, 98, 102, 161, 162
DST, Grandmixer, 94, 161, 162, 164
Dunbar, Sly, 161
Dunia, 48, 153, 172
Dylan, Bob, 139, 141
Dzidzornu, Kwasi, 160
E.S.P., 27, 34, 73, 105, 174
Eagles (band), 111
Early Warning, 100, 161, 171
Earth Beat, 94, 95, 161
East, Nathan, 130, 131
Eckstine, Guy, 163
Edith and the Kingpin, 134, 165
Edmonds, Kenneth 'Babyface', 111
Egg, 30, 152, 168
Eighty-One, 73, 105, 163, 168
Einbahnstrasse, 168
Einstein, Albert, 135
electric keyboard, 39, 55, 136
Electric Light Orchestra (band), 75
electric piano, 39, 41, 43, 44, 45, 46, 49, 51, 53, 56, 57, 60, 61, 76, 78, 119, 121, 126
Elegy, 105, 163
Ellington, Duke, 19, 117, 134
Ellis, Don, 68
Embraceable You, 116, 117, 164
Empty Pockets, 20, 151, 169, 171
Empyrean Isles, 7, 29, 30, 31, 33, 107, 152
Enchantment, 114, 164
Escovedo, Juan, 160
Escovedo, Peter, 160
Escovedo, Sheila, 159, 160
Estival Lugano Switzerland, 99
Et Cetera, 174
Eubanks, Robin, 107
Europe, 19, 27, 29, 38, 77, 97, 136, 174
Evans, Gil, 38, 39, 42, 43, 110, 111
Evolution Revolution, 144
Exodus, 138, 140, 166, 167
Eye Of The Hurricane, 152, 159, 160, 167, 168, 169, 176
Fair Weather, 101, 162
Fairlight CMI (instrument), 88, 103
Faithless (band), 138
Far Out, 168, 169, 170, 171
Farmer, Arthur, 13
Farrell, Joe, 175
Fast, 72, 133
Fat Albert Rotunda, 7, 45, 46, 47, 48, 55, 71, 79, 145, 153, 154
Fat Mama, 46, 154
February Moment, 80, 158

Feets Don't Fail Me Now, 159
Feldman, Victor, 25
Fender Rhodes (keyboard), 39, 53, 61, 76, 142
Festival, 29, 66, 90, 92, 104, 118, 156, 175, 176
Fier, Anton, 98, 161
Fiesta (Piano Solo), 170
Fill Your Hand, 155
Filles de Kilimanjaro, 27, 39, 41, 175
Fillmore, West (performance venue), 48, 74
Findley, Charles B, 161
Finger Painting, 168, 172
Firewater, 43, 153, 170, 172
First Trip, 37, 99, 153, 172, 176
Fitzgerald, Ella, 117, 128
Fleck, Béla, 144
Flood, 7, 63, 97, 143, 156
Foday Musa Suso, 96, 97, 98, 99, 102, 150, 161, 162
Footprints, 177
Forman, James, 48
Foster, Al, 106, 176
Foster, David, 92, 93, 161
Four, 31, 158, 174
Four And More, 174
Fowler, Bernard, 98, 161
Fragile, 159
France, 29, 153, 171, 172
Frankie and Kevin, 119
Free Form, 16, 17, 148, 174
Free Jazz, 17, 22, 23, 148
Frelon Brun, 41
Frère Jacques, 98
Funk Hunter, 119
Furse, Tony, 88
Future 2 Future, 8, 54, 120, 122, 164, 176
Future Shock, 8, 87, 93, 94, 97, 99, 103, 122, 145, 150, 161, 171
G.W., 22
Gabriel, Peter, 77, 111, 138
Gadson, James, 78, 155, 159, 160
Gale, Eric, 165
Gambia Africa, 96
Garrett, Kenny, 164
Garrison, Matthew, 176
Gaslight 1962, 174
Gelo No Montana, 165
Genesis, 16
Genres, classical, 9, 11, 22, 70, 73, 80, 90, 91, 108, 116, 118, 135, 136, 146
Genres, disco, 9, 76, 77, 78, 79, 85, 86, 87, 88
Genres, folk, 112, 116, 132, 139, 140
Genres, fusion, 11, 19, 35, 39, 41, 45, 47, 55, 58, 64, 66, 69, 73, 78, 80, 89, 90, 93, 94, 97, 117, 118, 120, 122, 126, 132, 135, 140, 141, 143
Genres, jazz-fusion, 10, 11, 21, 32, 35, 36, 37, 40, 41, 46, 47, 53, 55, 57, 58, 59, 64, 66, 68, 72, 74, 77, 79, 80, 84, 87, 100, 102, 109, 110, 119, 121, 122, 130, 131, 137, 138, 141, 142, 145, 146

Genres, mainstream, 9, 10, 11, 18, 23, 33, 45, 55, 58, 69, 70, 72, 83, 89, 90, 91, 100, 101, 110, 112, 123, 129, 141, 144
Genres, R&B, 79, 93, 111, 138, 161
Genres, rock, 13, 35, 36, 39, 41, 44, 47, 48, 55, 57, 58, 60, 79, 87, 95, 110, 112, 114, 116, 122, 130, 131, 144, 145
Genres, soul, 11, 21, 47, 53, 138, 139, 140
Genres, world music, 103, 137, 138
Gentle Thoughts, 65, 156, 170, 172
Germany, 18, 77
Gershwin, George, 8, 9, 20, 101, 115, 116, 117, 118, 132, 135, 136, 150, 164
Get Up With It, 175
Getz, Stan, 135
Gibraltar, 165, 170
Giddins, Gary, 142, 150
Gilberto, Joao, 135
Gilstrap, Jim, 161
Girtler, Ira, 44, 149
Give It All Your Heart, 93, 161
Gleeson, Patrick, 154
Gloud, Vennette, 161
Go For It, 86, 159, 171
Goldings, Larry, 166
Golson, Benny, 89
Good Question, 76, 157
Goodbye To Childhood, 168, 170
Gordon, Dexter, 8, 16, 18, 19, 20, 100, 101, 102, 151, 162, 176
Gorelick, Kenneth, 164
Graham, Bill, 48, 102
Grammy (award), 35, 37, 93, 96, 97, 98, 102, 105, 111, 113, 115, 119, 123, 125, 132, 135, 144, 150, 152, 153, 161, 162, 163, 164, 165, 166
Grandmixer DXT, 95, 120
Graves, Marlon, 164
Gravy Waltz, 167
Graydon, Jay, 93, 161
Great Sessions, 168
Greatest Hits, 125
Greek Theater, 71, 157
Green Dolphin Street, 82, 158, 159, 169
Green, Grant, 24, 25, 151
Greenberg, Rodney, 115, 150
Grey, Al, 22
Griffin, Will 'Roc', 163
Grinnell College Iowa, 12
Griot, 97, 98
Groban, Joshua, 175
Guiye, Bireyma, 164
Hackensack, 16
Hakeem, Abdul, 102, 162
Hale Bopp, Hip-Hop, 164
Hall, Jim, 36, 152
Hammer, Jan, 88
Hampton, Lionel, 19
Hancock, Gigi, 164
Hancock, Jessica, 166
Handy, W. C., 117

182

Hang Up Your Hang Ups, 62, 64, 67, 137, 156, 168, 170, 172, 177
Hannigan, Lisa, 139, 165, 166, 172
Hansen, Randy, 87, 159
Happenings, 174
Hardrock, 97, 161, 170, 171
Hargrove, Roy, 8, 122, 136, 137, 150, 165, 177
Harle, John, 126, 148
Hart, William, 49, 67, 154, 156
Harvest Time, 82, 158, 168, 169
Hawkins, Coleman, 14
He Who Lives in Fear, 43, 153
He Who Lives in Many Places, 175
Head Hunters, 7, 21, 54, 55, 57, 58, 59, 61, 74, 126, 129, 136, 143, 149, 154
Headhunters (band), 8, 61, 66, 78, 82, 87, 119, 136, 143, 144, 175, 177
Heartbeat, 63, 156, 170
Heath, Albert, 153, 154
Heath, Jimmy, 47, 153
Hebero Pt 1, 164
Hebero Pt 2, 164
Help Yourself, 88, 160
Henderson, Eddie, 49, 67, 154, 156, 164
Henderson, Joseph, 36, 42, 43, 46, 152, 153
Hendrix, Jimi, 38
Henley, Don, 111
Hentoff, Nat, 28, 29, 148
Herbie Hancock
 The Collection, 169, 171
Herbie Hancock Box, 168
Herbie Hancock Quartet, 8, 90, 105, 125, 143, 160
Herbie Hancock Special with Bobby McFerrin and Michael Brecker, 177
Herbie Hancock Trio (DVD), 176
Herbie Hancock Trio In Concert (DVD), 177
Herbie Hancock Trio With Ron Carter and Tony Williams (1981), 160
Herbig, Gary, 161
Here Come De Honey Man, 164
Hey, Jerry, 92
Hidalgo, David, 166
Hidden Shadows, 52, 53, 154, 172
Higgins, William, 15, 17, 18, 19, 20, 101, 102, 151, 162
Highlights from the Plugged Nickel, 175
Hiseman, Jon, 59
Hohner D6 (instrument), 77
Hold It, 159
Holiday, Billy, 22
Holland, Dave, 40, 50, 111, 133, 149, 163, 165, 175, 176, 177, 178
Hollywood, 176
Homecoming, 80, 158
Honey From the Jar, 79, 159
Hooker, John Lee, 11
Horn, Jim, 156
Hornets, 52, 54, 122, 154, 164, 165, 170, 176
Hot and Heavy, 167, 169, 170, 171

Hot Piano, 15, 167, 168, 169, 171, 172
How Long Has This Been Going On?, 162
Hubbard, Frederick Dewayne, 7, 18, 19, 23, 27, 30, 32, 45, 67, 101, 133, 151, 152, 156, 157, 159, 162, 165, 174
Hub-Tones, 7, 23, 174
Hump, 110, 163
Hush, Hush, Hush, 165
Hutcherson, Bobby, 33, 101, 162, 174
Hyde, Dick, 156
I Do It For Your Love, 165
I Fall in Love Too Easily, 92
I Have A Dream, 42, 153, 169, 171
I Just Called To Say I Love You, 165
I Love You, 107, 128, 131, 165
I Thought It Was You, 82, 157, 158, 168, 170, 172
If I Were A Bell, 13
Illinois, 11, 174
Imagine, 111, 137, 138, 139, 142, 166
Impressions, 123, 150, 165
In A Silent Way, 41, 175
In Concert, 8, 80, 99, 158, 175, 176, 177
In Tokyo, 175, 177
In Your Eyes, 172
In Your Own Sweet Way, 168
India, 138, 166
Indigo Dreamscapes, 176
Inventions and Dimensions, 7, 28, 148, 152
Ionosphere, 121, 164
Islands, 33
Israels, Chuck, 25, 151
It Ain't Necessarily So, 164
It All Comes Around, 159
It Begins, 155
Itoh, Yasohachi, 81
Jack Rabbit, 29, 152, 169, 171
Jackson Jr, Dwight, 94
Jackson Jr, Paul M., 56, 63, 64, 67, 76, 85, 119, 154, 155, 156, 157, 158, 159
Jackson, Darryl Munyungo, 163, 177
Jackson, Gene, 107
Jackson, Laymon, 14
Jackson, Michael, 92, 144
Jackson, Randy, 93, 161
Jaco Pastorius, 46, 50, 58, 76, 84, 106, 157, 159, 175
Jamal, Ahmad, 123
James, Robert (Bob) McElhiney, 66, 79
Japan, 52, 61, 64, 68, 69, 72, 80, 81, 82, 83, 90, 99, 136, 142, 151, 155, 156, 157, 158, 159, 160, 161, 175, 177, 178
Jarre, Jean-Michel, 77, 88
Jarreau, Al, 93, 144
Jarrett, Keith, 10, 91
Jarvis, Clifford, 23
Jazz Africa, 8, 102, 162
Jazz Biography, 169
Jazz club, Gaslight Café, 7, 21, 22, 28, 174
Jazz club, Village Vanguard, 100

183

Jazz club, White Whale, 15
Jazz Crusaders, The (band), 42
Jazz Door, 105, 176, 177
Jazz Moods
   Round Midnight, 169
Jazz Profile, 169
Jazz to Funk, 169
Jazzvisions, 102
Jeffers, Jack, 42, 153
Jessica, 46, 47, 71, 154, 157, 166
Jimbasing, 102, 162
Jobim, Antonio Carlos, 175
John Coltrane, 13, 23, 32, 38, 122, 123, 124, 125, 150, 165
John McLaughlin, 4, 41, 97, 101, 162
John Patitucci, 123, 165
John Scofield, 111, 112, 163, 178
Johnson, Alphonso, 63
Johnson, George, 160
Johnson, James P, 115, 117
Johnson, Louis, 155, 160, 161
Jolson, Al, 116
Jones, Norah, 134, 165
Jones, Philly Joe, 58
Jones, Quincy, 92, 105, 167, 175
Jones, Quincy Delight, 167
Jones, Thad, 37, 153
Jones, Thaddeus Joseph, 37, 153
Joni, 8, 113, 132, 133, 134, 135, 150, 164, 165, 172, 175
Joplin, Scott, 115
Joseph, Julian, 142
Joshua, 26, 27
Joy Ryder, 175
Juju, 110
Julliard School of Music, 118
Junku, 98, 161
Just Around The Corner, 84, 160
Just One of Those Things, 106, 107, 108, 176
Kaiser, Henry, 98, 161
Kale, Karsh, 121, 164
Kamili, 48, 153, 167, 168, 171, 172
Kanatente, 100, 161
Kansas, 96
Karabali, 97, 161, 168, 170, 172
Katche, Manu, 166
Kathak, Bhawai Shankar, 166
Katia, 175
Kawaida, 48, 153, 171, 172
Keane, Sean, 166
Kebero, 176
Kelly, Rick, 161
Kelly, Wynton, 11
Kennedy, Robert, 42
Kennedy, William, 163
Kern, Jerome, 116
Khan, Chaka, 120, 141, 164, 166
Kidjo, Angilique, 165
Kilenyi, Edward, 118
Kilimanjaro, 27, 40, 41, 175

Kind of Blue, 30, 33, 105
King Cobra, 24, 25, 151, 171
King, Martin Luther, 42
Klein, Larry, 133, 135, 138, 141, 166
Knee Deep, 78, 79, 159
Kondo, Toshinori, 98, 161
Konono No 1 (band), 138
kora (instrument), 96, 97, 98, 99, 102, 140, 161, 162, 166
Korg, 75
Koseinenkin Hall (performance venue), 61, 155
Kraftwerk (band), 75
Krija, Rhani, 166
Kumalo, Bakithi, 164
Kumbasora, 102, 162
Kuru/Speak Like a Child, 170
Kwanzaa, 119
La Fiesta, 80, 158
La Maison Goree, 89, 160
La Tierra, 140, 166
La Villette, 104
Labeque, Katia, 175
Laboriel, Abe, 93, 160
Ladzekpo, Kwawu, 160
Lament for Booker, 24
Lang Lang, 9, 135
Lang, Jonny, 165
Lasar, Mars, 163
Laswell, Bill, 94, 96, 97, 99, 120, 121, 144, 150, 161, 164
Late Night Jazz Favourites, 168, 169, 170
Latin, 35, 36, 37, 70, 86, 102, 111, 128, 136, 140
Lawra, 69, 72, 74, 157
Lawrence, Linda, 161
Laws, Hubert, 42, 110, 153
Lazy Bird, 168
Left Alone, 22, 175
Legend, John, 138, 166
Legendre, Kevin, 77, 87, 96, 129, 149, 150
Lehman, John, 161
Lennon, John, 137
Lennox, Annie, 128, 165
Levi, James, 67, 76, 156, 157
Lewis, Jack, 102, 162
Lewis, Webster, 82, 158
Lifetime, 7, 31, 32, 148, 174
Lincoln Center, 31
Lion, Alfred, 18
Lisa, 139, 165, 166, 167, 172
Lite Me Up, 8, 92, 93, 143, 144, 160, 161, 172
Little One, 34, 105, 152, 163, 168, 169
Little Waltz, 72, 157, 176
Littleton, Jeff, 107
Live and Awake / One and Awake, 167, 168, 169, 170, 171
Live Detroit / Chicago, 165, 170
Live Evil, 52
Live In Concert, 175, 176

Live in Lugano - Supertrio in Concert, 175, 176
Live in New York, 105
Liza (All the Clouds'll Roll Away (live), 158, 168
Los Angeles, 13, 18, 25, 80, 96, 102, 107, 113, 158, 162, 176
Louecke, Lionel, 129, 133, 136, 137, 140, 165, 166, 175, 177
Love is Stronger Than Pride, 112, 178
Love No. 1, 168
Lozano, Conrad, 166
Lukather, Steve, 93, 161
Lullaby, 118, 164
Lyttelton, Humphrey, 150
Mademoiselle Mabry, 41
Madonna, 75
Magic Number, 88, 160
Magic Windows, 8, 87, 106, 144, 160
Mahavishnu Orchestra (band), 58, 87, 99
Maiden Voyage, 7, 33, 34, 35, 48, 61, 64, 67, 73, 80, 103, 104, 105, 108, 127, 145, 152, 155, 156, 157, 158, 163, 167, 168, 170, 171, 172
Maloney, Paddy, 166
Mamoulian, Rouben, 117, 150
Man-Child, 7, 62, 143, 155
Mandinga, 96
Manhattan (Island Of Lights And Love), 113, 172
Manhattan Island, 82, 158
Manhattan Lorelei, 114, 164
Manhattan School of Music, 18, 68
Mannlana, 167
Marcus Miller, 136, 137, 166, 175, 177
Marsalis, Branford, 107
Marsalis, Wynton, 90, 160
Martin, Frank, 161
Martinez, Osvaldo, 152
Martins, Lucas, 166
Mason, Harvey, 56, 57, 59, 76, 85, 144, 154, 155, 157, 159
Matthews, Dave, 138, 140, 166
Mattison, Mike, 166
Maulana, 48, 153, 172
Maupin, Bennie, 49, 51, 56, 62, 67, 76, 144, 154, 155, 156, 157, 158, 159, 163
Mawangu, Augustin Makuntima, 166
Mayer, John, 128, 165
Mbaye, Cheil, 164
Mbuta, Makonda, 166
McFerrin, Bobby, 101, 106, 162, 177
McKay, Al, 160
McKnight, Dewayne, 156
McLaughlin, John, 4, 41, 97, 101, 162
McLean, Jackie, 16, 22, 45, 174
Mellotron (instrument), 53
Memory Of Enchantment, 164
Mercy Street, 111, 163, 178
Meridianne - A Wood Sylph, 164
Metal Beat, 98, 161
Metallica, 19
Metheny, Pat, 4, 59, 79, 83, 149, 153, 176

Miami, 88, 140
Miami Vice (TV Series), 88
Michael Brecker, 8, 43, 88, 106, 111, 112, 122, 124, 147, 150, 160, 163, 165, 175, 177, 178
Michelot, Pierre, 101, 162
Midon, Raul, 165
Mikkelborg, Palle, 162
Miles, 7, 8, 9, 10, 11, 13, 18, 19, 20, 21, 23, 25, 26, 27, 29, 30, 31, 32, 33, 34, 38, 39, 40, 41, 43, 45, 48, 50, 52, 55, 57, 58, 62, 64, 66, 67, 68, 69, 72, 73, 80, 91, 94, 95, 99, 104, 105, 106, 115, 117, 122, 123, 124, 126, 131, 134, 143, 144, 148, 149, 163, 174, 175
Miles Ahead, 20, 124
Miles Beyond, 148, 149
Miles Davis, 7, 9, 10, 11, 13, 18, 19, 20, 25, 27, 29, 31, 41, 45, 50, 52, 57, 58, 62, 64, 66, 67, 69, 80, 91, 95, 99, 104, 106, 115, 117, 122, 123, 124, 126, 134, 144, 148, 149, 174, 175
Miles Davis in Europe, 27, 174
Miles in Antibes, 174
Miles in Berlin, 32, 174
Miles in the Sky, 27, 39, 175
Miles in Tokyo, 32, 174
Miles Smiles, 27, 72, 174
Milestones, 69, 70, 157, 168, 172
Miller, Byron, 84, 157, 159
Miller, Marcus, 136, 137, 166, 175, 177
Milton, 175
Mimosa, 29, 152, 170
Mingus, 28, 132, 148, 175
Mingus, Charles, 28, 148
Minimoog (instrument), 53
Mintz, Alan, 166
Minuit Aux Champs-Elysees, 169
Miss Ann, 22
Misstery, 124, 165
Mitchell, Joni, 113, 132, 135, 150, 164, 165, 172, 175
Mitchell, Richard 'Blue', 45, 174
Mobley, Hank, 13, 22, 24, 45, 151, 174
Modern Jazz Quartet, 13
Moffett, Charnett, 120, 164
Mojuba, 109, 163
Molloy, Matt, 166
Moncur, Grachan, 24, 151, 174
Monk, Thelonius, 18, 113
Monster, 8, 85, 86, 87, 144, 149, 159
Montana, 165
Montgomery, Monk, 23
Montreal Jazz Festival, 92
Montrose, Ron, 154
Moon Germs, 175
Moon/Light, 161
Moore, Alecia Beth, 166
Moore, Demie, 142
Moore, Matthew, 139
Moose the Mooch, 106
More, 31, 39, 75, 98, 117, 174, 175

Moreira, Airto, 73, 109, 175
Morgan, Lee, 45, 174
Morrison, James, 141, 166
Morton, Jelly Roll, 13
Motor Mouth, 93, 161, 170, 172
Mouzon, Alphonze, 84, 86, 158, 159, 160
Mozart, Wolfgang, 11
Mr Funk, 170
Mr Lucky, 15, 167, 168, 169, 171, 173
Mr. Hands, 82, 149, 159
Mtume, James, 48, 153
MTV, 93, 96
Mulligan, Gerry, 14, 15
Mwandishi, 7, 48, 49, 52, 54, 55, 60, 67, 78, 143, 145, 154, 170
   The Complete Warner Bros. Recordings, 170
Mwandishi (band), 7, 48, 49, 52, 54, 55, 60, 67, 78, 143, 145, 154, 170
My Favourite Things, 13, 112
My Funny Valentine, 31, 82, 158, 169, 174
My Man's Gone Now, 164
My Point of View, 7, 24, 25, 151
My Ship, 20, 124, 125, 165
Naima, 124, 165
Nascimento, Milton, 175
Nash, Kenneth, 67, 156
Native Dancer, 175
Ndan Ndan Nyaria, 161
Ndofusu, Mbiyavanga, 166
Nearness of You
   The Ballad Book, 175
Nefertiti, 27, 67, 105, 134, 156, 165, 167, 174
New Jersey, 15, 44, 45
New Orleans, 13, 90
New Orleans Philharmonic Orchestra, 90
New York, 8, 9, 13, 14, 15, 16, 19, 21, 23, 25, 38, 40, 48, 66, 90, 94, 95, 100, 105, 107, 111, 115, 116, 129, 148, 149, 163, 178
New York Minute, 111, 163, 178
Newman, Joseph, 36, 152
Newport Jazz Festival, 66, 90, 156
Night Awake, 168
Night Flower, 16
Night Walker, 167, 168, 169, 170, 171, 173
Nine Over Reggae, 176
Nirvana (band), 111, 112
No Means Yes, 76, 157
Nobu, 62, 155, 168
Norwegian Wood, 111, 178
Obiedo, Ray, 78, 82, 158, 159
Obsession, 103, 162
Ochoa Knose, 155
Odyssey, 53, 61, 77
Oh! Oh! Here He Comes, 46, 154
Oleo, 177
Oliloqui Valley, 31, 34, 168
Oliver, Joseph, 13
Oliver, King, 13
Ololoqui Valley, 152

Olympic Games, 96, 97, 98
On Green Dolphin Street, 82, 158, 159, 168, 169
On the Corner, 27, 41, 175
One Finger Snap, 30, 31, 107, 152, 168, 171
One Night in Japan, 175, 177
One Of A Kind, 71, 157
One of Another Kind, 159
Opening, 16, 159
Orchestra, Orpheus Chamber, 118, 164
Oriente, 159, 168
Osby, Greg, 105
Ostinato (from Mikrokosmos for Two Pianos, Four Hands), 158
Ostinato (Suite For Angela), 49, 154
Out of This World, 167, 168, 169, 170, 171, 173
Overture (Fascinatin' Rhythm), 164
Page, Richard, 161
Paint Her Mouth, 155
Palm Grease, 58, 155
Para Oriente, 159, 168
Parade, 160, 167
Paradise, 93, 161, 171
Parallel Realities Live, 175
Paraphernalia, 39
Paris, 57, 100, 104
Parker Jr, Ray, 78, 156, 157, 159, 160
Parker, Charlie, 14, 15, 22, 28, 58, 106, 134, 165, 167, 168, 169, 170, 171, 173
Parks, Dean, 139, 141, 166
Parthasarthy, Sridhar, 166
Party People, 155
Pastorius, Jaco, 46, 50, 58, 76, 84, 106, 157, 159, 175
Pathways, 177
Patitucci, John, 123, 165
Payne, Sheri, 161
PBS TV (USA), 91
Peacocks, 101, 162, 170, 172
Pearson, Columbus Calvin, 14, 15, 44
Pee Wee, 92, 159, 160, 169
Penque, Romeo, 42, 153
People Are Changing, 98, 161, 171
People Music, 65, 156, 168, 172
Peraza, 103, 162
Peraza, Armando, 102, 162
Perez, Louie, 166
Perfect Machine, 8, 103, 145, 150, 162
Perry III, Moody, 160
Peterson, Oscar, 11
Philharmonic Hall, 31
Phillips, Peter, 37, 153
Piano Fiesta, 170, 175
Pilgrimage, 175
Pinocchio, 105, 163
Plumeri, Terry, 175
Polydor Records, 80, 158
Poncé, Daniel, 161
Pontoja, Victor, 154

186

Porcaro, Jeff, 92, 93, 160
Porter, Cole, 9, 107
Portrait, 170
Possibilities, 8, 128, 129, 131, 133, 136, 141, 165
Powell, Bud, 18, 58, 100, 101
Prelude In C# Minor, 164
Premonition, 119
Priester, Julian, 49, 67, 154, 156
Prince, 80, 82, 111, 112, 124, 158, 167, 169
Prism, 84, 160, 168
Prisoner, 41, 42, 43, 47, 149, 153, 170
Prometheus Unbound, 177
Promise of the Sun, 43, 153
Prophet Jennings, 24
Purim, Flora, 73
Purple Haze, 1
Quasar, 52, 154
Quiet Times, 68
Ragin, Melvin ('Wah Wah Watson'), 64, 65, 67, 75, 78, 84, 86, 136, 137, 156, 157, 159, 160, 163, 177
Rain Dance, 52, 53, 154, 168
Randle, Vicki, 88, 160
Rattle, Simon, 116
Ravel, Maurice, 118, 136
Ready Or Not, 78, 170, 172
Record label, Blue Note, 1, 4, 7, 14, 15, 16, 18, 19, 23, 30, 31, 32, 44, 45, 46, 100, 102, 143, 145, 148, 149, 151, 152, 153, 162, 167, 168, 169, 170, 171, 172
Record label, Capitol Records, 48
Record label, CBS, 121, 150, 156, 158, 160, 161, 168
Record label, Columbia, 38, 39, 45, 48, 52, 80, 81, 82, 83, 95, 102, 103, 145, 149, 150, 154, 155, 156, 157, 158, 159, 160, 161, 162, 167, 169, 170, 171, 172, 175, 176
Record label, EMI, 44, 171
Record label, Jazz Door, 105, 176, 177
Record label, Liberty Records, 44
Record label, Mapleshade Records, 91
Record label, Polydor, 80, 158
Record label, United Artists, 44, 155
Record label, Verve, 108, 150, 162, 163, 164, 165, 172
Record label, Warner Bros., 45, 48, 52, 105, 145, 153, 154, 170, 176
Record label, Warwick, 14, 169
Recording Studio, Automatt, 48, 68, 69, 71, 157
Red Clay, 74, 157, 168
Red Sea, 140
Redford, Robert, 142
Reichenbach, Bill, 92, 161
Rekow, Paul, 76, 157
Return of the Headhunters, 8, 61, 119, 144, 175
Rhythm-A-Ning, 101, 162
Rice, Damien, 165, 172
Rich, Buddy, 58

Richardson, Jerome, 42, 153
Riddle, Nelson (orchestra), 117
Riot, 37, 153, 168, 170, 171
The Newly Discovered Takes from Blue Note Sixties Sessions, 170
River, 8, 132, 134, 135, 165, 172
The Joni Letters, 165
Rivers, Sam, 32
Robertson, Darryl 'Bob Dog', 163
Robinson, John, 160
Rock Your Soul, 14, 167, 168, 169, 171, 173
Rockit, 93, 94, 95, 96, 97, 103, 129, 145, 148, 149, 150, 161, 168, 170, 171, 172, 176
Roker, Mickey, 37, 153
Roland, 131
Rollins, Sonny, 13
Roney, Wallace, 104, 109, 110, 163, 176
Roosevelt University, 14
Round About Midnight, 11
Round Midnight, 8, 11, 92, 100, 101, 102, 143, 145, 150, 160, 162, 167, 168, 169, 172, 176
Round Midnight (movie), 8, 11, 92, 100, 101, 102, 143, 145, 150, 160, 162, 167, 168, 169, 172, 176
Roundhouse Camden London (performance venue), 5, 8, 129
Royal Flush, 15, 16, 148, 174
Rubber Soul, 110, 163
Rubinson, David, 48, 59, 61, 63, 68, 71, 74, 80, 81, 83, 86, 87, 149
Rudolph, Adam, 97, 102, 162
Rushen, Patrice, 93, 161
Rustici, Carrado, 93, 161
Ruvalcaba, Maria, 166
Ryrie, Kim, 88
Sadin, Robert, 117, 119, 164
Safiatou, 128, 136, 165, 177
Samuel, Seal, 166
San Diego Civic Theater, 71
San Francisco, 48, 68, 71, 74, 80, 157, 158, 172
Sangare, Oumou, 138, 166
Sansho Shima, 66, 156
Santamaria, Mongo, 21
Santana, Carlos, 86, 128, 136, 165, 175
Satisfied With Love, 160, 168
Saturday Night, 86, 159
Scarborough Fair, 112, 163
Schizophrenia, 174
Scofield, John, 111, 112, 163, 178
Scoochie, 15, 167, 168, 169, 170, 171, 173
Scott, Doug, 163
Scott, Tom, 59
Sea Breeze, 170
Search For The New Land, 174
Second Genesis, 16
Secrets, 7, 64, 65, 84, 136, 143, 156, 172
Sennheiser vocoder, 75
Sequential Circuits Prophet Synthesiser, 24, 77

Seven Steps to Heaven, 25, 26, 27, 174
Sextant, 7, 52, 122, 149, 154
Sexton, Anne, 111
Shadow Dance, 176
Shadows and Light, 150
Shankar, Anoushka, 166
Shanklin, Jay, 163
Shape of My Heart, 175
Shearing, George, 11
Shepp, Archie, 32
Shiftless Shuffle, 82, 85, 158, 160
Shooz, 109, 163
Shorter, Wayne, 8, 16, 19, 23, 32, 45, 63, 67, 97, 100, 101, 104, 113, 120, 121, 122, 123, 133, 141, 150, 156, 157, 159, 161, 162, 163, 164, 165, 166, 174, 175, 177
Silver Hollow, 176
Silver, Horace, 13, 18, 23, 68
Simmons (drums), 97, 98
Simon and Garfunkel (band), 111, 112
Simon, Paul, 128, 165
Simpson, Gerald, 121, 164
Simpson, India Arie, 138, 166
Sister Moon, 129, 165
Skank It, 119
Skopelitis, Nicky, 98, 103, 161, 162
Sleeping Giant, 51, 154
Sly, 55, 57, 154, 161, 168
Smile, 89, 160
Smith, Darryl, 163
Smith, Jimmy, 36, 152
So Near, So Far, 26
So What, 33, 105, 123, 163, 165
Solitude, 134, 165
Some Other Stuff, 174
Someday My Prince Will Come, 80, 82, 124, 158, 167, 169
Something More, 175
Somewhere, 53, 164
Sonrisa, 82, 114, 158, 164, 177
Sony Music Corporation, 52, 61, 81, 82, 83, 90, 151, 155, 156, 157, 158, 160, 166, 168, 170, 171
Sorcerer, 27, 38, 92, 105, 106, 123, 153, 160, 165, 168, 169, 170, 171, 172, 174
Soul Power, 14, 167, 168, 169, 170, 171, 173
Sound System, 8, 96, 97, 99, 161, 172
Souza, Luciana, 165
Space Captain, 138, 139, 166
Spank-A-Lee, 60, 155, 156
Spaulding, James, 23
Speak Like A Child, 70, 153, 168, 171, 176
Speller, Brady, 163
Spider, 65, 67, 136, 156, 168, 177
Spiraling Prism, 84, 160
Sprey, Pierre, 91
Spyro Gyra (band), 144
St. Louis Blues, 164, 172
Stablemates, 160
Stanley Clarke, 50, 57, 58, 63, 75, 143

Stars in Your Eyes, 86, 159, 168, 170, 172
Starsky and Hutch (TV series), 59
Stella By Starlight, 69, 159, 168
Stevens, Rob, 161
Sting, 128, 165
Stitched Up, 128, 131, 165
Stone, Joss, 128, 165
Stone, Sly, 55, 57
Straight No Filter, 174
Stroll On, 36, 152
Strong, Ken, 163
Studd, Anthony, 42, 153
Subterfuge, 144
Succotash, 29, 152
Summers, Bill, 56, 57, 64, 76, 78, 84, 85, 109, 144, 154, 155, 156, 157, 158, 159, 163
Sun Touch, 62, 156, 168, 172
Sunlight, 7, 74, 75, 76, 82, 87, 143, 144, 157, 168
Survival Of The Fittest, 152
Suso, Foday Musa, 8, 96, 97, 99, 102, 150, 161, 162
Swamp Rat, 66, 156, 170
Sweet Bird, 134, 165
Sweet Revenge, 155
Swift, Rob, 120, 164
Switzerland, 99, 129
synthesiser, 9, 51, 52, 56, 59, 61, 78, 86, 88, 99, 109, 131
T.C.B. With Herbie / Out of This World / Live and Awake / One and Awake, 169, 170
Take Five, 167
Talking Book, 112
Talwalkar, Satyajit, 166
Tamatant Tilay / Exodus, 138, 140, 166
Taumbu International Ensemble (band)+B278, 107
Tavernier, Bertrand, 100, 143, 150
Taylor, Cecil, 10, 28, 42
TCB With Herbie, 171
Tea Leaf Prophecy (featuring Joni Mitchell), 165
Tear Drop, 159
Tedeschi, Susan, 139, 166
Tell Everybody, 79, 159, 168, 170, 171
Tell Me A Bedtime Story, 46, 154, 171
Temperton, Rod, 92, 160
Tempest in the Colosseum, 7, 72, 157
Tempo De Amor, 139, 166
TFS, 94, 95, 161
That Old Black Magic, 89, 160
The All Seeing Eye, 174
The Bat, 176
The Best of Herbie Hancock, 170, 171
The Best of Herbie Hancock - The Blue Note Years, 171
The Best of Herbie Hancock - The Hits, 171
The Best of Herbie Hancock Vol. 2, 171
The Big Rip Off, 155
The Bomb, 93, 161, 172

188

The Cat Walk, 15
The Chase, 19
The Chicken, 167
The Chief, 139
The Collection, 169, 171
   A Selection of Tracks From the Blue Note
      Years, 171
The Columbia Years
   '72 - '86, 171
The Complete Blue Note Sixties Sessions, 171
The Complete Concert 1964, 174
The Definitive Herbie Hancock, 171, 172
The Dude, 175
The Egg, 30, 152
The Essence, 120, 164, 176
The Essential Herbie Hancock, 171, 172
The Eye Of The Hurricane, 152
The Finest in Jazz, 172
The Fun Tracks, 93, 161
The Good Life, 176
The Herbie Hancock Quartet Live, 8, 105
The Herbie Hancock Trio (1977), 90, 157
The Hidden Land, 144
The Hook, 80, 158
The Imagine Project, 8, 111, 137, 138, 139, 142, 166
The Inner Mounting Flame, 99
The Jewel in the Lotus, 175
The Jungle Line (featuring Leonard Cohen), 165
The Lady in My Life, 92
The Man I Love, 164
The Maze, 20, 151
The Naked Camera, 36, 152
The New Standard, 8, 110, 111, 128, 163, 175, 177
The Other Side of Round Midnight, 8, 102, 162
The Peacocks, 101, 162, 172
The Piano, 8, 80, 82, 149, 158
The Pick Up, 155
The Pleasure is Mine, 25, 151
The Poet, 124, 125, 165
The Prisoner, 7, 41, 42, 43, 47, 149, 153
The Procrastinator, 174
The Quintet, 7, 68, 71, 72, 149, 157
The Song Goes On, 141, 166
The Sorcerer, 38, 123, 153, 160, 165, 168, 171, 172
The Spook Who Sat By the Door, 7, 54, 155
The Stick Up, 155
The Swing of Delight, 175
The Thief, 36, 152
The Times, They Are A' Changin', 166
The Trailor, 62, 156
The Twilight Clone, 88, 160
The Very Best of, 47, 153, 172
Thelonius Monk Institute of Jazz (Los Angeles), 113
Then and Now - The Definitive Herbie Hancock, 172

Thibeaux, Frank, 163
Thieves In The Temple, 163
Third Plane, 7, 68, 69, 71, 157
This Is DJ Disk, 176
This is Jazz, 172
This is New, 168
This is Rob Swift, 120, 164
Thomas Studies Photos, 36, 152
Thomas, Joe, 102, 162
Three Bags Full, 20, 151
Three Wishes, 16
Thriller, 92, 93
Thrust, 7, 54, 58, 61, 110, 136, 143, 155, 172
Tingen, Paul, 148, 149
Tip Toe, 119
Tivoli, 102, 162
Tobon, Fernando, 166
Together, 14, 115
Tokyo Japan, 32, 61, 63, 72, 81, 90, 99, 136, 155, 156, 157, 159, 160, 172, 174, 175, 177
Tomorrow Never Knows, 138, 140, 166
Tones For Joan's Bones, 168
Tony Williams, 7, 8, 25, 26, 27, 29, 31, 32, 40, 43, 45, 58, 67, 68, 69, 70, 71, 76, 84, 89, 101, 104, 118, 121, 148, 151, 152, 156, 157, 159, 160, 162, 163, 164, 174, 175, 176
Too Hot, 92
Touch Me, 131
Touchstone, 173
Tout de Suite, 40
Toys, 38, 67, 153, 156, 167, 168, 176
Training Day, 155
Transition, 123, 124, 150, 165
Triangle, 29, 152
Trilling, Roger, 161
Trucks, Derek, 139, 166
Trust Me, 79, 159
Turbulent Indigo, 132
Turner, Tina, 134, 165
Turrentine, Stanley, 45, 165, 174
Two But Not Two, 119
Tyner, McCoy, 11, 68
Ulrich, Lars, 19
Una Noce Con Francis, 162
United Blues, 69
Universe, 23, 64, 137, 140
Uptown Conversation, 68, 175
Uzuri, Imani, 121, 164
V.S.O.P., 7, 8, 66, 67, 68, 71, 72, 82, 83, 143, 149, 156, 157, 159
V.S.O.P. - Live Under the Sky, 159
V.S.O.P. (band), 7, 8, 66, 67, 68, 71, 72, 82, 83, 143, 149, 156, 157, 159
Van Gelder, Rudy, 44, 145
Vein Melter, 57, 154
Vertigo, 174
Verushka Pt 1, 152
Verushka Pt 2, 152
Vibe Alive, 103, 104, 162, 163, 170, 171
Village Life, 8, 99, 150, 161

189

Village Vanguard, 100
Vincent, Visi, 166
Vinding, Mads, 162
Vinnie Colaiuta, 59, 130, 141, 165, 166, 175
Virgin Forest, 175
Virtual Hornets, 122, 164, 176
Visitor From Nowhere, 114, 164
Visitor From Somewhere, 164
Vitous, Miroslav, 40
vocoder (instrument), 75, 76, 77, 78, 79, 92, 93, 103, 129, 131
Vogel, Peter, 88
Voyager, 167, 168, 169, 173
Waku, Menga, 166
Walden, Narada Michael, 92, 161
Walk On The Wild Side, 167
Walker, David T., 156
Walker, Greg, 86, 159
Wallace, Pete, 166
Walton, Cedar, 101, 162
Wandering Spirit Song, 51, 154
Warren, Butch, 15, 18, 19, 151
Warsame, Keinan Abdi, 166
Washington, Freddie, 78, 84, 86, 159, 160
Watch It, 70, 157
Watch Your Back, 119
Watcha Waitin' For, 157
Water Babies, 41, 175
Water on the Pond, 39
Watermelon Man, 8, 18, 19, 20, 21, 24, 31, 35, 55, 57, 64, 101, 104, 112, 130, 136, 145, 151, 154, 156, 167, 168, 170, 171, 172, 177
Waters Tillman, Julia, 159
Waters Willard, Maxine, 159
Waters, Luther, 159
Waters, Muddy, 11, 38
Waters, Oren, 86, 159
Watkins, Doug, 15
Watkins, Eddie, 78, 159, 160
Watson, Wah Wah (aka Melvin Ragin), 65, 67, 75, 84, 86, 136, 137, 156, 157, 159, 160, 163, 177
Watts, Ernie, 156
Wave, Micro, 103, 162
We Come 1, 138

Weather Report (band), 30, 40, 49, 131
Weckl, Dave, 58
Weill, Kurt, 20
Wein, George, 66
Well You Needn't, 160, 167
When Can I See You, 111, 163
When Love Comes To Town, 165
Whitaker Poças, Maria do Céu, 139, 166
Whitty, George, 139, 166
Wiggle-Waggle, 46, 154, 172
Wild Things Run Fast, 133
Wilkenfeld, Tal, 139, 141, 166
Williams, Anthony, 7, 8, 25, 26, 27, 29, 31, 32, 40, 43, 45, 58, 67, 68, 69, 70, 71, 76, 84, 89, 101, 104, 118, 121, 148, 151, 152, 156, 157, 159, 160, 162, 163, 164, 174, 175, 176
Williams, Charles Anthony, 153, 154, 156, 176
Williams, David, 161
Williams, Larry, 92, 161
Willow Weep For Me, 99, 176
Winner, Michael, 54
Wisdom, 120, 121, 164, 176
Witch Fire, 167, 168, 169, 170, 171
Withers, Bill, 65
Wolff, Francis, 18
Wonder, Stevie, 63, 111, 112, 119, 128, 131, 138, 156, 164, 165, 172
Wong, Herb, 42, 149
Woods, Phil, 36, 152
Word of Mouth, 85, 175
Workman, Reggie, 23
Wrapped in a Dream, 144
Wright, Steve, 94, 150
Yamaha CP-30 (instrument), 77
Yamaha DX-1 (instrument), 99
Yams, 169, 171
Yauraete, 175
Yogi, Maharishi Mahesh, 140
You Bet Your Love, 78, 159, 168, 170, 172
You Will Know When You Get There, 167
Young, Lester, 100
Your Eyes, 86, 159, 168, 170, 172
Zawinul, Josef, 39, 41, 58, 75, 143, 175